THE POEMS OF ALEXANDER POPE

VOLUME III ii

EPISTLES TO SEVERAL PERSONS
(MORAL ESSAYS)

The Twickenham Edition of the Poems of Alexander Pope

★

GENERAL EDITOR: JOHN BUTT

★

VOLUME I

PASTORAL POETRY and AN ESSAY ON CRITICISM. E. Audra, formerly Professor of English, Lille University, and Aubrey Williams, Professor of English, The Rice Institute, Houston, Texas.

VOLUME II

THE RAPE OF THE LOCK and other poems. Geoffrey Tillotson, Professor of English, Birkbeck College, University of London.

VOLUME III i

AN ESSAY ON MAN. Maynard Mack, Professor of English and Fellow of Davenport College, Yale University.

VOLUME III ii

EPISTLES TO SEVERAL PERSONS (MORAL ESSAYS). F. W. Bateson, University Lecturer in English, Corpus Christi College, Oxford.

VOLUME IV

IMITATIONS OF HORACE and AN EPISTLE TO DR ARBUTHNOT and THE EPILOGUE TO THE SATIRES. John Butt, Regius Professor of Rhetoric and English, Literature, University of Edinburgh.

VOLUME V

THE DUNCIAD. James Sutherland, Lord Northcliffe Professor of English, University College, University of London.

VOLUME VI

MINOR POEMS. Norman Ault and John Butt.

A. Pr a Plasterer white washing & Bespattering
B. any Body that comes in his way
C. not a Dukes Coach as appears by if Crescent at one Corner

D. Taste
E. a standing Proof
F. a Labourer.

Price 6ᵈ

HOGARTH'S COMMENT ON EPISTLE IV
(*See Note on the Illustrations*)

ALEXANDER POPE

EPISTLES TO SEVERAL PERSONS

(MORAL ESSAYS)

★

Edited by
F. W. BATESON

LONDON: METHUEN & CO. LTD
NEW HAVEN: YALE UNIVERSITY PRESS

PRINTED IN ENGLAND AT
THE BROADWATER PRESS
WELWYN GARDEN CITY
HERTFORDSHIRE . FIRST
PUBLISHED IN THIS EDITION
1951
SECOND EDITION 1961

2.1

CATALOGUE NO. 2/4774/10 (METHUEN)

PREFACE

"I SCARCE meet with anybody that understands delicacy." Pope's *cri de cœur* to Spence—made apparently in 1742, shortly after the publication of the fourth book of the *Dunciad*—remains a standing challenge to his editors. It is our job, as I see it, to provide the modern reader with the information that Pope generally took for granted in his original readers (though, as his disillusionment about their "delicacy" increased, he himself added more and more notes of all kinds to his poems). In the *Epistles to Several Persons*—which Warburton, the official editor, impudently renamed *Moral Essays* after Pope's death—the "delicacy" resolves itself to a large extent into the nature and degree of personal allusion that is intended. The problem is not simply "Who is Pope getting at here?" It is rather "How far in fact does the purely personal satire go?" Often the immediate intention seems to be an impersonal ethical generalization, to which a dash of contemporary insult has only been added to make it more piquant. On the other hand, there are, of course, the passages of brilliant invective, in which the abstract moral framework does not provide much more than a polite pretence of objectivity. And in between the two extremes a series of double, two-facing attitudes can sometimes be discerned, even within a single passage or in relation to a single satiric butt. An editor, like Pope's own contemporaries, is often compelled to fumble in the dark, but at least the attempt at definitions has to be made. If some measure of certainty proves to be recoverable a note can be written.

The determination of Pope's text is also a "delicate" matter. Other things being equal, it is no doubt a sound editorial rule—at any rate if the poet is an English Augustan—to prefer a later to an earlier reading. But in textual criticism other things are rarely equal, and as Pope revised and re-revised his poems—each of the Epistles in this volume underwent five or six separate revisions after it had been printed—the alternatives are often both later readings. Moreover, as I have argued in the General Note on the Text, many of the final readings cannot be considered specific rejections of earlier variants, since Pope did not normally have all his versions of

v

a passage in front of him when revising it. Sometimes indeed we can be fairly sure that he had temporarily forgotten one or more of his earlier attempts to improve it. In such instances the onus of selecting the reading to incorporate into the text necessarily reverts to the editor. It is not the policy of this edition to record manuscript variants, but I have tried to list in the textual footnotes all the readings—other than obvious misprints or vagaries of spelling and punctuation—of the printed versions of the four poems up to and including Warburton's first collected edition of 1751. Justification of the more controversial departures from Warburton's texts will generally be found in the Note on the Text preceding each Epistle. Others are discussed in the respective textual notes.

The first edition of this volume was prepared under conditions of special difficulty in the spring of 1940. I had the privilege then, however, of being able to call on the learning and good sense of three distinguished Pope scholars—George Sherburn, John Butt, and Norman Ault—who generously came to my help in passage after passage. But much remained undone, or only half done, and the exhaustion of the edition has enabled me to re-check texts and variant readings by the original editions, and to consult the autograph manuscripts of *To Bathurst* and *To Burlington* in the Huntington and Pierpont Morgan Libraries. Several corrections have been made. The notes have been revised in the light of Mr Sherburn's definitive edition of the letters (5 vols., 1956) and of the more recent companion volumes to this in the "Twickenham" series. I have also consulted most of the current books and articles about Pope, deriving particular benefit from *The Major Satires of Alexander Pope* (1955) by Robert W. Rogers—whose review of my first edition in the *Philological Quarterly* (July 1952) had been a model of tactful correction—and from an article by Vinton A. Dearing in the *Harvard Library Bulletin* (1950). Professor Earl R. Wasserman, Mr G. K. Hunter, and Mr J. C. Maxwell have contributed a number of useful suggestions and corrections, and the Earl of Pembroke has kindly provided the photograph of his ancestress that is reproduced opposite page 48.

F. W. B.

1959

CONTENTS

PLATES

vii

INTRODUCTION

I

THE last months of Pope's life were spent in preparing a definitive edition of his poems. "I *must* make a perfect edition of my works," he told his friend, and would-be biographer, the Rev. Joseph Spence, early in 1744, "and then shall have nothing to do but to die."[1] In the end, dropsy complicated by asthma won the race against time, and of the great edition—which was to include not only Pope's final revision of his text and notes, but also an elaborate running commentary on each poem by his new friend Warburton ("the greatest general critic I ever knew"[2])—only the *Dunciad*, the *Essay on Man*, and the *Essay on Criticism* had been published when he died on 30 May 1744. The four poems in this volume that have come to be known as Pope's "Moral Essays", though Pope himself always called them his "Epistles",[3] were due to have been published next, and Pope's letters to Warburton show the special importance that both poet and commentator attached to them. "I know it is there I shall be seen most to advantage."[4]

Warburton had made a start on the commentary to the four Epistles in the autumn of 1743, and instalments were apparently sent to Pope throughout the winter. "I go on softly," Pope wrote to him on 12 January, "to prepare the Great Edition of my things with your Notes, and as fast as I receive any from you, I add others in order."[5] Warburton had completed the commentaries on *To*

---

1. Spence, pp. 295–6. Malone's edition (1820) supplies the date.

2. Spence, p. 337.

3. All Pope's references to the four poems in his letters are to his "Epistles". The expanded alteration "Ethic Epistles", used by some modern scholars—though preferable to "Moral Essays" (a title invented by Warburton after Pope's death)—would not have been acceptable to Pope himself, who only uses it as a general title for *E. on Man* and the four Epistles *considered as a single entity*. See, for example, his letter to Warburton of 18 January 1742/3 (Sherburn, IV 439). The running title to *Epistles to Several Persons* (1744) is simply "Epistles". See also pp. xii and xxxvii below.

4. Pope to Warburton, 24 March 1742/3 (Sherburn, IV 448).

5. Sherburn, IV 491.

Cobham (i.e. Epistle I) and *To Bathurst* (Epistle III) by the end of January, and it was then decided to have shorter notes for *To a Lady* (Epistle II) and *To Burlington* (Epistle IV).[1] By this time Pope was a very sick man, but he kept doggedly at the work, and on 21 February he was able to write to Warburton to say that he had finished revising the commentary on *To Bathurst*.[2] By March the proofs were starting to come in. On 3 March Pope wrote to William Bowyer, the printer:

> On Second thoughts, let the Proof of the Epistle to Lord Cobham, I, be done in the *Quarto*, not the *Octavo*, size: contrive the Capitals and evry thing exactly to correspond with that Edition. The first proof send me, the Number of the whole but *1000*, and the Royal *over* and above.[3]

Quarto (instead of octavo), because that was the format in which the earlier volumes of the definitive edition had been appearing, including the *Essay on Man* and the *Essay on Criticism* with Warburton's commentaries which Bowyer had just finished printing.[4] The next stage in the book's evolution is recorded by the faithful Spence. Apparently the first complete copies of the book were not in Pope's hands until early in May, and Spence, who was seeing Pope regularly at this time, found him one day ("about three weeks before we lost him") busy sorting out presentation copies for his friends. "Here am I," Pope said, "like Socrates, distributing my morality among my friends, just as I am dying."[5]

At this point the drama passes into melodrama. By Pope's will Warburton was left "the Property of all such of my Works already Printed, as he hath written, or shall write Commentaries or Notes upon, and which I have not otherwise disposed of or alienated; and all the Profits which shall arise after my Death from such Editions

---

1. Sherburn, IV 495.   2. Sherburn, IV 500.

3. Sherburn, IV 504. See also p. lv below.

4. See Pope's letter to Bowyer, 23 February [1743/4], Sherburn, IV 502, where he specifies the friends who are to be sent complimentary copies of the two poems. They were Chesterfield, Bathurst, Carteret, and Murray, but *not* Bolingbroke (who might not have liked to read Warburton's commentary on the poem he had inspired).

5. Spence, p. 318. An earlier version of Spence's note, from Huntington Library MS. 1271, is in Sherburn, IV 525.

as he shall publish without future Alterations".[1] Pope's unpublished MSS., on the other hand, were left to Bolingbroke, the rival guide, philosopher, and friend. Shortly before Pope's death, Lord Marchmont, one of the executors, was approached by the Dowager Duchess of Marlborough (the great Sarah), who at eighty-three was still the zealous and formidable defender of Marlborough's good name. The Duchess had reason to believe that among the unpublished MSS. there were satires on both the Duke and herself.[2] Would Marchmont please ask Bolingbroke to hand these satires over to her? Bolingbroke's answer, written on 30 May (the day on which Pope died), was that he would not surrender any of the MSS., but if there *were* satires on the Marlboroughs he would destroy them in Marchmont's presence.[3] A few days later he made, or thought he had made, a discovery. And in an undated letter he wrote and told Marchmont about it:

> Our friend Pope, it seems, corrected and prepared for the press just before his death an edition of the four Epistles, that follow the Essay on Man. They were then printed off, and are now ready for publication. I am sorry for it, because, if he could be excused for writing the character of Atossa formerly, there is no excuse for his design of publishing it, after he had received the favour you and I know; and the character of Atossa is inserted. I have a copy of the book. Warburton has the propriety of it, as you know. Alter it he cannot, by the terms of the will. Is it worth while to suppress the edition? or should her Grace's friends say,

1. The will is printed in *The Gentleman's Magazine*, June 1744, XIV, 313–14.

2. She was right in thinking Pope had satirized Marlborough (see vol. VI of this edition, pp. 358–9) and almost right, apparently, about herself. Arbuthnot's daughter Anne, a close friend of Pope's, told Spence in August 1744 (p. 364) that *To a Lady* had once included "a character of the old Duchess of Marlborough under the name of Orsini (written before Mr. Pope was so familiar with her and very severe)". This has not survived, though some of the "Orsini" lines may have been worked into the portrait of "Atossa" (who was probably the Dowager Duchess of Buckinghamshire). According to Warburton, Pope himself read the Atossa lines to the Duchess of Marlborough as describing the Duchess of Buckinghamshire, "but she spoke of it afterwards, and said she knew very well whom he meant" (Spence, p. 364). See also Appendix A, pp. 159–70 below.

3. *A Selection from the Papers of the Earls of Marchmont* (1831), II 332–3.

as they may from several strokes of it, that it was not intended to be her character? and should she despise it?[1]

It is almost certain that Bolingbroke was wrong in thinking that the character of "Atossa" (*To a Lady*, ll. 115–50) was intended to represent the Duchess of Marlborough. The probability is that in it Pope was satirizing another Duchess, the Duchess of Buckinghamshire, who was an old enemy of his. The way in which Bolingbroke came to make the mistake is discussed below in Appendix A (Who was Atossa?). Here it will be sufficient to trace the repercussion of this mistake on the "death-bed edition", as it has been called, of Pope's four Epistles. The person most directly affected by Bolingbroke's "discovery" was Warburton. If the edition was suppressed his commentary would be suppressed with it, and the income that he might have anticipated from an edition of one thousand copies would not be forthcoming. In any case he can have felt no enthusiasm for obliging Bolingbroke, with whom he was on the worst of terms. On 20 June he wrote to Bowyer:

> If the executors inquire of you, and when they do, about the state of Mr. Pope's Works in your hands yet unfinished (that is to say, of the Epistles), I then desire you would let Mr. Murray have a copy of all those Epistles; and you may tell him I desired you would do so: but say nothing till then. Pray preserve all the Press Copy to the least scrap.—I have looked over the corrected proof of the half-sheet, title, &c. and of the leaf that was ordered to be cancelled, and find them right: so desire they may be printed off, and one sent me by the first opportunity.[2]

Warburton, it is evident, was being hard pressed. It is perhaps significant that, if the worst came to the worst, Bowyer was to supply a copy of the book to William Murray (the future Lord Mansfield) but not apparently to Lord Marchmont, the co-executor. To Warburton at this juncture Marchmont must have been primarily the much too zealous agent of the Duchess of Marlborough. The refer-

---

1. *Ibid.*, II 334–5. It is curious that Bolingbroke had not seen the book before. Had he not had a presentation copy of this work either? See note 4 on p. x. The favour Pope had received from the Duchess had apparently been a gift of money for the use of Martha Blount.

2. Nichols, II 165.

ence to the "leaf" that "was ordered to be cancelled" suggests that
Warburton was taking some precautionary measures himself. And
if, as is probable, the new "leaf" that Warburton alludes to is the
same as the "insert" pasted into surviving copies of the edition,
his reasons for ordering the cancel become plain. For the original
page almost certainly included four lines satirizing Marlborough's
avariciousness that the Duchess would not have liked at all, though
they had in fact appeared—unknown presumably to her—in all
the earlier collected editions of the Epistles.[1] Unfortunately no
more letters on the matter survive from this period, and all that we
can say for certain is that the edition *was* suppressed. Possibly, as in
the parallel case of Bolingbroke's *The Idea of a Patriot King* (which
Pope had also had printed, but not published, without Boling-
broke's knowledge), the edition was burnt.[2] If so, a number of
copies escaped the bonfire. Bowyer may have been able to secrete
some. At any rate in 1748 the Knaptons, the publishers of the great
edition with Warburton's commentaries, brought out a small edi-
tion of *Four Ethic Epistles by Alexander Pope, Esq; with the Commentary
and Notes of Mr. Warburton*, which proves to be the "death-bed
edition" with a new title-page prefixed to it.[3] A copy with what
looks like a provisional pre-publication title-page[4] is in the British
Museum and has been used as the basis for this edition.[5] In several

---

1. They will be found in the textual note *To Cobham*, 145. The cancelled leaf
is A4 and the insert includes ll. 120–47 of the present edition. The presence of the
insert and the identity of format, type, and paper with the *E. on Man* and *E. on
Criticism* editions of 1743/4 make it morally certain that the British Museum copy
of *Epistles to Several Persons* (1744) (shelfmark C.59.e.1(2)) belongs to the "death-
bed" edition.

2. The *Patriot King* was burnt at Marchmont's house in October 1744. See
Marchmont Papers, II 338.

3. Professor George Sherburn has a copy. He has seen letters from Murray to
Martha Blount, which show that about 1748 all the unsold copies of Pope's poems
were sold by the executors to Warburton, and he thinks that the Knaptons' edi-
tion may be connected with this transaction. See also Sherburn, IV 504.

4. The fact that the *Epistles* is bound between copies of Warburton's editions of
the *E. on Man* and the *E. on Criticism* (both 1743/4) suggests that it was not one of
the copies distributed by Pope shortly before his death, but it is almost certainly
textually and bibliographically identical with the "death-bed" presentation
copies.

5. Mr Sherburn's and the B.M. copies are probably not the only extant copies;

important respects it differs from the text that Warburton printed in 1751 (*The Works of Alexander Pope, Esq. Volume III, containing his Moral Essays*), which has been the *fons et origo* of all later editions. For one thing, a different title is given to the four poems. Instead of "Moral Essays" (a term only applied in Pope's lifetime, apparently, to the *Essay on Man*[1]) the "death-bed edition's" title is "Epistles to Several Persons", which was the heading Pope had used for a section in the 1739, 1740, and 1743 editions of the second volume of his *Works*, in which he had collected all his letters in verse (i.e. the four poems reprinted here *plus* seven other "Epistles" including the *Epistle to Arbuthnot*).

There can be no doubt that Warburton was responsible for this change.[2] A certain officious "tidiness" was one of Warburton's most pronounced intellectual characteristics; the emendations in his edition of Shakespeare often seem prompted by a desire to clarify what no one has found obscure. During the period when the commentaries were being prepared Warburton frequently suggested "improvements" of this kind to Pope,[3] and it was perhaps with a view to curbing this tendency that Pope inserted the special clause in his will assigning his copyright to Warburton provided he made no "future Alterations". Warburton apparently interpreted

---

in *Notes and Queries*, 4 June 1881, W. T. Brooke stated that he had a copy identical with the B.M. copy (which had been described in *The Athenaeum*, 16 April 1881).

1. By Bolingbroke (Sherburn, III 414).

2. It was apparently a last-minute decision. In the notes and the "Advertisement" of the 1751 edition Warburton consistently refers to the poems as Pope's "Epistles"; it is only in page-headings and on the title-page that they appear as "Moral Essays". In a letter to Hurd of 6 August 1749 Warburton calls these poems "Mr. Pope's Moral Epistles" (*Letters from a Late Eminent Prelate to One of his Friends*, 1809, p. 7). This may have been a slip for "Ethic Epistles", the term Pope used in all the collected editions of 1735 and 1736 for both the *E. on Man* and the four poems. The Warburton edition of the *E. on Man* (1743) retains the general title of the earlier collections (*An Essay on Man. Being the First Book of Ethic Epistles*). The complementary formula (*Ethic Epistles, the Second Book. To Several Persons*), which is used in the 1735/6 collections on which the text of the "death-bed" edition appears to be based, would presumably have been its full title if publication had been reached before Pope died.

3. See the Textual Introductions to *To Cobham* and *To Bathurst* in this edition.

this clause to mean that he was to make no *verbal* changes in the poems.[1] Short of this he seems to have felt himself at liberty to do anything he liked. The change in the title from "Epistles" to "Essays" reflects one of his most ingenious efforts. In the 1751 edition *To Bathurst* becomes an imaginary conversation between Pope and Lord Bathurst, a transformation effected without changing a word, simply by prefixing "P." (= Pope) to most of the poem, with "B." (= Bathurst) occasionally interjecting a few lines.[2] As in the case of the *Epistle to Arbuthnot*, where Warburton made a similar change, the dramatic and colloquial nature of Pope's verse made the transformation from the letter-form into a dialogue easy and plausible. But, of course, there is really no excuse for it. Indeed for Warburton the editor there is almost nothing to be said. The irrelevance and the verbosity of most of his commentaries must be read to be believed.[3]

Towards the end of Pope's life Lord Marchmont is said to have told him that "he was convinced he was one of the vainest men living":

"How so?" says Pope. "Because, you little rogue," replied

---

1. The author of *A Criticism on the Elegy written in a Country Church Yard* (1783), a friend of Pope's printer Bowyer, had apparently seen some of Warburton's attempts to improve Pope's text. "In the private corrections of Warburton," he comments, "I find little that can create regret for that precaution of the Poet, which prevented them from being made publick" (p. 9). *A Criticism* was edited by John Young of Glasgow, but its author has not been identified.

2. The real Lord Bathurst was most indignant at the change. See p. 79 below.

3. The commentaries and notes in vol. III of Warburton's 1751 edition derive for the most part from the "death-bed edition" of 1744. In spite of the fact that those in the 1744 edition must have been sanctioned by Pope it seems unnecessary to add to the sum of human tedium by reprinting them here. But owing to the rarity of *Epistles to Several Persons* it may be useful to indicate briefly the principal differences between Warburton's contributions to the two editions:

COMMENTARIES. Identical, except that *1744* is without the first sections of *To Cobham* and *To Bathurst*.

NOTES. *1751* adds as follows:

   To Cobham, ll. 5, 56, 81, 93, 152, 174, 189, 213, 227.

   To a Lady, ll. 1, 20, 23, 52, 57, 89, 203, 206, 216, 253, 269, 285.

   To Bathurst, ll. 3, 9, 12, 20, 33, 34, 47, 102, 105, 173, 402.

   To Burlington, ll. 29, 104, 146, 156, 173. (*1751* omits *1744*'s note on l. 33.)

VARIATIONS. These extracts from rejected drafts are not in *1744*.

Lord Marchmont, "it is manifest from your close connection with your new commentator you want to show posterity what an exquisite poet you are, and what a quantity of dullness you can carry down on your back without sinking under the load."[1]

The four Epistles are not in any case among Pope's very best work, and it is unfortunate that hitherto they have carried down more than their fair share of the commentator's dullness. In this edition I have tried, with the help of the "death-bed" text, to relieve the poems as far as possible from the load of Warburtonian incrustation.

II

The "death-bed" *Epistles to Several Persons* contains an elaborate "Advertisement", which is worth reprinting because it is the most detailed exposition that either Pope or Warburton ever made of the philosophical "*Opus Magnum*",[2] the "system of Ethics in the Horatian way",[3] that occupied so much of Pope's time between 1729[4] and 1734:[5]

---

1. The anecdote was recorded by Edmond Malone. See Sir James Prior, *Life of Malone* (1860), p. 386.

2. Pope to Swift, 6 January 1733/4 (Sherburn, III 401).

3. Pope to Swift, 28 November 1729 (Sherburn, III 81).

4. The first that is heard of Pope's Horatian ambitions is in a letter that Fenton wrote to Broome in June 1729 (Sherburn, III 37): "I saw our friend Pope twice when I was at London. . . He told me that for the future he intended to write nothing but epistles in Horace's manner, in which I question not but he will succeed very well."

5. Pope never explicitly abandoned the project, but the new qualification "If I have health and leisure to make any progress", which follows the promise to supply still more exemplary epistles in "The Design" prefixed to the *E. on Man* in the later 1735 collections has an ominous ring. And it is clear from a letter to Swift of 25 March 1736 that he had lost interest in it by then: "If ever I write more Epistles in Verse, one of them shall be address'd to you. I have long concerted it, and begun it, but I would make what bears your name as finished as my last work ought to be" (Sherburn, IV 5). It is perhaps also significant that in the 1739 reprint of the *Works*, vol. II, the four epistles no longer form a section of their own headed "Ethic Epistles, the Second Book" (with the *E. on Man* constituting the first book), as in the octavo editions of 1735 and 1736, but are grouped with the other letters in verse as "Epistles to Several Persons". On the other hand the

THE ESSAY ON MAN was intended to have been comprised in Four Books:

The *First* of which, the Author has given us under that title, in four Epistles.

The *Second* was to have consisted of the same number: 1. Of the extent and limits of human Reason. 2. Of those Arts and Sciences, and of the parts of them, which are useful, and therefore attainable, together with those which are unuseful, and therefore unattainable. 3. Of the Nature, Ends, Use, and Application of the different Capacities of Men. 4. Of the Use of Learning, of the Science of the World, and of Wit: concluding with a Satyr against the Misapplication of them, illustrated by Pictures, Characters, and Examples.

The *Third* Book regarded Civil Regimen, or the Science of Politics, in which the several forms of a Republic were to have been examined and explained; together with the several Modes of Religious Worship, as far forth as they affect Society; between which, the Author always supposed there was the most interesting relation and closest connection; so that this part would have treated of Civil and Religious Society in their full extent.

The *Fourth* and last Book concerned private Ethics or practical Morality, considered in all the Circumstances, Orders, Professions, and Stations of human Life.

The Scheme of all this had been maturely digested, and communicated to the L. Bolingbroke, Dr Swift, and one or two more, and was intended for the only work of his riper Years: But was, partly thro' ill health, partly thro' discouragements from the depravity of the times, and partly on prudential and other con-

---

"great scheme" was one of the first things that Pope talked to Warburton about when they met in 1740. On his return from a fortnight's stay with Pope about June 1740 Warburton told a Cambridge friend of his that "the great scheme which he has in view is the continuation of the Essay. The first you know was only a general map of man, wherein the extent and limits of his faculties were marked out. The second is to treat of false science at large, and the third is to inquire into the use and abuse of civil society" (Charles to Philip Yorke, *c.* June 1740, in G. Harris, *The Life of Lord Chancellor Hardwicke*, 1847, I 475–6). The second stage of this programme also appears in a 1739 addition to *E. on. Man*, I 207*n*: "The Extent, Limits and Use of *Human Reason* and *Science*, the Author design'd as the subject of his next Book of Ethic Epistles."

B

siderations, interrupted, postponed, and, lastly, in a manner
laid aside.

But as this was the Author's favourite Work, which more ex-
actly reflected the Image of his strong capacious Mind, and as we
can have but a very imperfect idea of it from the *disjecta membra
Poetae* that now remain, it may not be amiss to be a little more
particular concerning each of these projected books.

The FIRST, as it treats of Man in the abstract, and considers
him in general under every of his relations, becomes the founda-
tion, and furnishes out the subjects, of the *three* following; so that

The SECOND Book takes up again the *First* and *Second*
Epistles of the *First* Book, and treats of man in his intellectual
Capacity at large, as has been explained above. Of this, only a
small part of the conclusion (which, as we said, was to have con-
tained a Satyr against the misapplication of Wit and Learning)
may be found in the *Fourth* Book of the *Dunciad*, and up and
down, occasionally, in the other *three*.

The *Third* Book, in like manner, reassumes the subject of the
Third Epistle of the *First*, which treats of Man in his Social,
Political, and Religious Capacity. But this part the Poet after-
wards conceived might be best executed in an EPIC POEM; as
the Action would make it more animated, and the Fable less
invidious; in which all the great Principles of true and false
Governments and Religions should be chiefly delivered in
feigned Examples.

In pursuance of this design, he plan'd out a Poem on the sub-
ject of the fabulous BRUTUS, the great Grandson of Æneas:
whose first and predominant principle he makes to be Benevo-
lence; from this Ruling Passion arises a strong desire to redeem
the remains of his countrymen, then captives amongst the
Greeks, from slavery and misery, and to establish their freedom
and felicity on a just form of Civil Government. He had seen how
false Policy, and Superstitions and Vices proceeding from it, had
caused the ruin of Troy; and he was enabled to avoid the *one* by
the lights his countrymen, whom he had now gathered from
their dispersion, could afford him from their observations on the
various policies of the Grecian Cities; and to reform the *other*
by the Wisdom he himself had gained in Italy, where Evander,

as we are told by Virgil, had reformed the reigning Superstitions:

> *Rex Evandrus ait: non hæc sollemnia nobis*
> *Vana superstitio veterumque ignara Deorum*
> *Imposuit—*

Thus qualified for the office of Legislation, he puts to sea with a number of brave followers; enters the Atlantic Ocean; and after various traverses (each of which produces some new lesson of Politics) he arrives in Britain, where having surmounted many successive difficulties, which bring him still nearer and nearer to the point the poet aims at, he at length establishes for his Trojans that perfect form of Civil Government which it was our author's purpose to recommend. The poem opens (of which very few lines of the introduction only were written) with Brutus at the Straits of Calpé, in sight of the *ne plus ultra* on Hercules's Pillars, debating in councel whether he should enter the great ocean.[1]

The FOURTH and last Book pursues the subject of the *Fourth* Epistle of the *First*, and treats of *Ethics*, or practical Morality; and would have consisted of many members; of which the four following Epistles were detached Portions: the *two first*, on the *Characters of Men and Women* being the *introductory* part of this concluding Book.[2]

Here in the final paragraph is the explanation of the order in which the four Epistles have always been printed, since they were first collected by Pope himself in the second volume of his *Works*

---

1. The fullest account of Pope's projected epic is in Owen Ruffhead's *The Life of Alexander Pope* (1769), pp. 409–23. Ruffhead summarizes the plot of the poem on the basis of Pope's notes which had been passed on to him by Warburton and are now in the British Museum. Warburton had previously lent the notes to John Brown, the author of the famous *Estimate*, who began to write them up into an epic (*Letters from a Late Eminent Prelate*, 1809, p. 36). See also Spence, pp. 288–9, and vol. vi of this edition, pp. 404–5, where a fragment is printed.

2. Warburton reprinted part of this "Advertisement" in his 1751 edition. How much of it Pope himself is responsible for is not clear, but the first paragraph is almost identical with an account Pope gave Swift of the "*Opus Magnum*" on 25 March 1736 (Sherburn, iv 5). Pope's other summaries of the projected scheme are given by Spence, pp. 137, 289, 315. See also the Introduction to the *E. on Man* in vol. iii i of this edition, pp. xi, xii.

(1735). It is not, of course, by any means the order of composition or publication (which is *To Burlington, To Bathurst, To Cobham, To a Lady*, i.e., IV, III, I, II). It is certainly not that of merit (which I should say is *To a Lady, To Burlington, To Bathurst, To Cobham*, i.e., II, IV, III, I). No, the order in which these poems are printed—that in which most of us still tend, perhaps wrongly, to read them—was entirely determined by the requirements of the almost non-existent "*Opus Magnum*". The fact is a striking example of the way the *Essay on Man* has cast its distracting shadow over what are essentially four Horatian satires.

By the side of the "Advertisement" of 1744, which represents Pope's last words on the abandoned "*Opus Magnum*", it will perhaps be instructive to set another document that was not available to earlier editors, which throws a flood of light on the early stages of the project and in particular on the relationship of the four Epistles to the *Essay on Man*. Here then is a transcript *verbatim et literatim* of the rough notes that Spence took of Pope's table-talk during the period 1 to 7 May 1730:[1]

[*To Cobham, 51 ff.*]

May 1–7, 1730   Mr. Pope

How wrong yᵉ Greatest men have been in judging of the Cause of Human Actions. Instance frō Machiavel, of concluding in yᵉ general frō particulars (wʳ Besiegd Forces ought to sally or not?) Instance frō—of judgˢ of a particular frō yᵉ General: (a person fights too soon: *bec*: he is of a Vindicative temper.) Montaigne hence concludes Pyrrhonically, That nothing can be known of the Workings of men's minds: 1 Essay, lib. 2? (The best in his whole book. There? yᵉ Instance of Tiberius' growing an open man all at once. That Openness really

---

1. The importance of the summer of 1730 as the gestatory period *par excellence* for the whole scheme is indicated by a question Atterbury put to Pope in his letter of 23 November 1731: "Do you pursue the moral plan you marked out, and seemed sixteen months ago so intent upon?" (Sherburn, III 247).

ye highest piece of Dissimulation.)—
New Hypothesis, That a prevailing
passion in ye mind is brought wth it
into ye world, & continues till death
(illustrated, by ye Seeds of ye Illness
y^t is at last to destroy us, being planted
in ye body at our births.)

We s^d not speak agst one large Vice,
without speaking agst its contrary.—
As to ye General Design of Providence
ye two Extremes of a Vice, serve like
two opposite biasses to keep up ye Bal-
lance of things. Avarice, lays up (w^t
w^d be hurtful;) Prodigality, scatters
abroad (w^t may be useful in other
hands:) The middle ye point for Vir-
tue: M^r P has very large (prose) col-
lections on ye Happiness of Content-
ment. Prodigality (in his piece) flings
away all in wrong tastes. (Tis there
in particular y^t some of ye Gardening
Poem will be of Service.) (Ld Boling-
broke has sent M^r P a long letter on
these heads; & has by him w^t w^d make
6 or 7 sheets in print toward a Second;
& does not know how far it may grow;
Mr Sav:)[1]

The first Epistle? is to be to y^e
Whole work, w^t a Scale is to a book of
Maps: in this lies ye greatest difficulty:
not only in settling all ye parts, but in
making them agreeable enough to be
read with pleasure. Sr Balaam: The
man of Ross: The Standing jest of
Heaven. And sure ye Gods & We are
of a mind. The Man possesd of Debts

[*To Cobham*, 174 *ff.*]

[*E. on Man*, II 133 *ff.*]

[*E. on Man*, II 195–6.]
[*To Burlington*, 169 *ff.*]
[*To Bathurst*, 163–4.]
[*E. on Man*, II 205–6.]

[*To Burlington*, 1–4.]

[*To Bathurst*, 246.]

[*To Burlington*, 15 *ff.*]

[*E. on Man*, The Design,
final paragraph.]

[*To Bathurst*, 339 *ff*, 250 *ff*, 4, 8.]

[*To Bathurst*, 279–80.]

---

1. "Mr Sav:" is Richard Savage, who presumably gave Spence the informa-
tion he has recorded in the final parenthesis at some later date.

[*To Bathurst*, 264 *ff.*]

[*To Bathurst*, 81–2.]

& Taxes clear, Children & Wife—
Five hundred pound a year (Publ:
Buildings Alms Houses, Walks,
Road;) The man of Ross divides yᵉ
weekly bread: Public Table twice a
week for Strangers &c.—Will give wᵗ
we desire; Fire, Meat, & Drink—
What more? Meat, Drink, & fire. No
judging of a piece frō yᵉ Scatter'd
parts: yᵉ 3 dots, & Hieroglyphic: (not
as to yᵉ Great Beauty: but we may see
particular beauties in yᵉ parts? That's
very true.)[1]

The marginal references are to the passages in the *Essay on Man*
and three of the Epistles, where Pope ultimately made use of the
ideas and phrases that he is here to be found discussing with Spence.
The reflection that this collation inspires is the length of time that
Pope required to give these poems their final polish. Spence's first
paragraph is essentially an outline of the argument of *To Cobham*
(which was not published until January 1733/4.) The second para-
graph is principally concerned with *To Burlington*, of which the
"piece" in which prodigality "flings away all in wrong tastes" and
"yᵉ Gardening Poem" must both be embryonic parts, and *To
Burlington* was not published until December 1731. The third para-
graph is largely made up of a series of fragmentary quotations from
To Bathurst, which was not published until January 1732/3. In
other words, between May 1730, when the poems were already in
process of composition, and the dates of the first editions there were
intervals of respectively $3\frac{1}{2}$, $1\frac{1}{2}$, and $2\frac{1}{2}$ years. In Pope's case, how-
ever, there was nothing unusual in this. "My *Essay on Criticism*," he
told Spence on another occasion, "was written in 1709; and pub-

---

1. Reprinted from Mr Sherburn's "Pope at Work" (in *Essays on the Eighteenth
Century presented to David Nichol Smith*, 1945, pp. 50–1) with corrections from the
more recent transcription by Professor Robert W. Rogers in *The Major Satires of
Alexander Pope* (1955). The original MS. is among the Spence Papers in the pos-
session of Mr J. M. Osborn of Yale University, who is now preparing them for
publication. S. W. Singer, in his edition of Spence, only printed two short
extracts from the 1–7 May notes (see Spence, pp. 15–16).

lished in 1711; which is as little time as ever I let any thing of mine lay by me."[1]

A point of some importance that emerges from Spence's notes is the degree to which the central ideas of the *Essay on Man* interpenetrate and determine the framework, if not the essential structure, of the Epistles. The theory of a "Ballance of things," the *rerum discordia concors* of traditional philosophy, is implicit in the whole argument of the *Essay on Man*,[2] and Spence's notes show Pope feeling his way, as it were, to the illustration of this theory in the socio-economic sphere. One epistle ($=To$ *Burlington*) is to be devoted to the vice of prodigality and the social function it unconsciously performs. "Prodigality scatters abroad money that may turn out to be useful in other hands." Another epistle ($= To$ *Bathurst*) will deal with avarice, the vice that is the opposite extreme from prodigality, though in its way equally useful to society. "Avarice lays up money that in other hands would be hurtful." Ethically the moral in either case is that of a golden mean, "The middle the point for Virtue".[3] Here indeed there is the first suggestion of what was later to have been the basis of the Fourth Book of the "*Opus Magnum*". "The fourth," Pope told Spence in 1744, "would have been on Morality; in eight or nine of the most concerning branches of it: four of which would have been the two extremes to each of the Cardinal Vir-

---

1. Spence, p. 170. Pope's habit of working away at several poems at the same time is illustrated by Mr Sherburn in the essay referred to in the note on p. xxii.

2. See Introduction to *E. on Man* in this edition, pp. i*ff*, xxiv*f*.

3. By November 1730 Pope was apparently contemplating a third epistle which was to be specifically devoted to the mean between the two extremes of prodigality and avarice. Among the notes that Spence passed on to Warburton after Pope's death is the following (now Brit. Mus. Egerton 1960, 1ᵛ): "Mr. Pope's new Poem (Novʳ 1730) grows upon his Hands. The first (4 or 5) Epistles will be yᵉ general Principles, or of yᵉ *Nature of Man*: The rest will be on Moderation, or *the Use of Things*. In yᵉ more particular part, each Class may take up three Epistles: e.g. On *Avarice*, on *Prodigality*, on yᵉ *Moderate Use of Riches*." In the plan of the "Ethic Epistles" of which Pope printed a few copies in 1734 (see Spence, p. 133, and *Essays on the Eighteenth Century presented to David Nichol Smith*, p. 58, where Mr Sherburn prints Spence's note in full from the MS.) there is "A View of the Equality of Happiness in the several Conditions of Man" immediately preceding "Of the Use of Riches". Presumably the prose notes on the "Happiness of Contentment", of which Pope had told Spence in May 1730, would have been utilized for this epistle.

tues."[1] In compliance with some such Aristotelian formula, when Pope reprinted *To Burlington* and *To Bathurst* in 1735, he dropped the titles of the first editions and both poems were called "Of the Use of Riches", the first—and, as it also proved, the last—instalment of this grandiose ethical scheme.[2]

But all this was a good deal easier to talk about than to translate into poetry. The logical contrasts and the symmetrical structure are much clearer in Spence's notes than they are in the poems themselves. Pope's trouble was that he was at least as interested in a lot of other things besides the "two Extremes of a Vice", that serve "like two opposite biasses to keep up yᵉ Ballance of things". Indeed to the poet—and therefore *a fortiori* to Pope's modern readers—the philosophical theory of plenitude may by this time have come to be primarily a technical device providing a formal scaffolding like that of the mock-heroic in *The Rape of the Lock* and *The Dunciad*, or Horace's text in the *Imitations*. There is an ominous sentence in Spence's record: "Tis there in particular yᵗ some of yᵉ Gardening Poem will be of Service." Of this gardening poem of Pope's nothing whatever is known.[3] His interest in landscape gardening was at its height in the years 1722–7, when (apart from his share in the translation of the *Odyssey*) he wrote little but occasional verse and most of his energy went into transforming his own little garden at Twickenham and helping Bridgman and Kent, the two professionals, to transform the grounds and parks of his aristocratic

1. Spence, p. 315. Date from Malone's edition. If "four" is not a slip or misprint, Pope may have meant that only four of the six extremes remained to be dealt with.

2. The cardinal virtue, of which prodigality and avarice were the extremes, was presumably prudence. *To Bathurst*, which is largely about avarice or the defective use of wealth, fits into the ethical scheme more comfortably than *To Burlington*, which is really about the aristocracy's bad taste rather than their extravagance. In Pope's letters a reference to the poem "on the Use of Riches" is always to *To Bathurst*, whereas *To Burlington* is referred to as such—which could be read as an unconscious realization on Pope's part of the artificiality of its inclusion in the scheme.

3. R. H. Griffith (Univ. of Texas *Studies in English*, 1952, xxxi 55–6) has identified it with James Gardner's translation of René Rapin, *Hortorum Libri IV*, of which the third edition (1728) had "The two first Books corrected by Mr. Pope". But Pope's corrections are trivial, and the poem is so unconnected with landscape gardening that it is difficult to see how it could "be of Service".

friends.[1] It is not impossible that the gardening poem was written
in this interval. What is certain is that in attempting later to marry
a poem on prodigality to a poem on gardening Pope was risking a
blurring of the lines of his philosophical argument. And gardening
was not the only alien element that found its way into this Epistle.
When *To Burlington* was published in 1731 it bore the following
title: *An Epistle To The Right Honourable Richard Earl of Burlington,
Occasion'd by his Publishing Palladio's Designs of the Baths, Arches,
Theatres, &c. of Ancient Rome*; the half-title providing a second title
"Of Taste" (which was changed in the second edition to "Of False
Taste"). It has always been assumed that Pope was paying a com-
pliment in his title to the magnificent *Fabriche Antiche disegnate da
Andrea Palladio Vicentino* that Burlington had issued in 1730. In
fact, however, Burlington's publication only included Palladio's
wash drawings of the principal Roman baths, and in a prefatory
note the Earl explains that he has also acquired Palladio's drawings
of arches, theatres, temples, and other ancient monuments which
he proposes publishing in a second volume.[2] The second volume
never appeared, but a hitherto unpublished letter of Pope's to
Burlington shows that the poem was at one time intended to appear
in it. The letter, which was accompanied by a MS. of the poem (in a
text considerably less polished than that of the printed editions),
runs as follows:

Twitenham Ap 4th [1731]

My Lord
    I send you the Inclosed with great pleasure to myself. It has
been above ten years on my conscience to leave some Testimony
of my Esteem for yr Lordship among my Writings. I wish it were
worthier of you. As to ye Thought wch was just suggested when
last I saw you, of its attending ye Book, I would have your Ldship
think further of it: & upon a considerate perusal, If you still
think so, the few Words I've added in this paper may perhaps
serve two ends at once, & ease you too in another respect. In
short tis all submitted to y^r own best Judgment: Do with it, &

---

1. Details about Pope's gardening, theory and practice, will be found in the
notes to *To Burlington*, especially ll. 47–98.
    2. These drawings are now in the Burlington-Devonshire collection deposited
at the Royal Institute of British Architects, London.

me, as you will. Only I beg your Ldsp. will not show the thing in manuscript, till ye proper time: It may yet receive Improvement, & will, to the last day it's in my power. Some lines are added tow.^d ye End on ye Common Enemy, the Bad Imitators & Pretenders, wch perhaps are properer there, than in your own mouth. I am with all truth,

> My Ld
>> Your most obed^t. & affectionate Servant
>> A. Pope.

I hope Lady B. thinks me as I am, her most faithful Servant.[1]

In the end, then, instead of being an "ethic epistle" on the vice of prodigality *To Burlington* turned out to be something of a hotch-potch, one third philosophy, one third gardening, and one third architectural compliment. Of its 184 lines, as many as 70 were taken up with the character of "Lord Timon", who exemplified in an amusing way the bad taste of the average eighteenth-century English nobleman. Not unnaturally, in this didactic miscellany, "Timon" stole the poem. And when a rumour began to circulate that "Timon" was really the Duke of Chandos, an unpopular millionaire whose pretentious seat Cannons at Edgware was well known to many Londoners, in the excitement of the scandal the more serious aspects of the poem were almost entirely overlooked. Indeed, it has only been in our own time that critical tribute has been paid to the fine lines in which Pope put into symbolic form the theory of a "Ballance of things". In the second volume of his *Works* (1735), where the text received its final form, they conclude the passage on "Timon":

> Another age shall see the golden Ear
> Imbrown the Slope, and nod on the Parterre,
> Deep Harvests bury all his pride has plann'd,
> And laughing Ceres re-assume the land.[2]

It is morally certain that "Timon" was not intended to carica-ture the Duke of Chandos, or indeed anybody in particular.[3] The

---

1. Devonshire Papers (Chatsworth) and Sherburn, III 187–8.
2. See W. Empson, *Seven Types of Ambiguity*, 1930, pp. 161–2, and F. R. Leavis, *Revaluation*, 1936, pp. 77–81.
3. A cancelled reading in the Pierpont Morgan MS.—an early autograph draft

reasons why "Timon" cannot be Chandos and why Pope was so irritated at the misidentification are discussed in Appendix B (pp. 170–4 below) and need not be repeated here.[1] Of the intensity of Pope's irritation there can be no doubt. The "Timon" incident is a recurrent theme in his correspondence of this period. His first public attempt to kill the rumour was in an unsigned open letter "To J.[ohn] G.[ay] Esq.", which was printed in *The Daily Post-Boy* for 22 December 1731 and reprinted in a more correct form in *The Daily Journal* for the following day with a postscript. The letter—which is dated 16 December, i.e. only three days after the poem had been published—is included in some editions of Pope's correspondence but without the postscript, where it is headed "Mr. Cleland to Mr. Gay".[2] Whoever did or did not sign the two letters, it is difficult to believe that anybody but Pope can have written them.[3] "Why, in God's Name," the letter-writer asks, "must a *Portrait*, apparently collected from 20 different Men, be apply'd to one only?" It can hardly be a coincidence that on 21 December Pope was making the same point in almost the same words in a private letter to Burlington: "nothing is so evident, to any one who can read yᵉ Language, either of English or Poetry, as that Character of Timon is collected from twenty different Absurditys & Improprieties: & was never yᵉ Picture of any one Human Creature."[4] The pained surprise that these letters exhibit had become

which shows the poem as it was before the architectural compliments to Burlington had been added—may confirm the impersonality of the satire. Here above "At Timon's" (also cancelled) is what appears to be "Vatia's". Servilius Vatia, who survived Sejanus's reign of terror by burying himself in his villa near Cumae, was an object of Seneca's philosophical contempt, who never passed the villa without saying "*Vatia hic situs est*" ("Here lies Vatia"). The *mot* was a favourite of Bolingbroke's, who quotes it in two letters (to Pope 18 August 1724, to Swift 27 June–6 July 1734). See Sherburn, II 252, III 413. For a possible parallel between Vatia and Chandos see p. 172 below.

1. Mr Sherburn has a remarkable article, " 'Timon's Villa' and Cannons", in the *Huntington Library Bulletin*, no. 8, October 1935, which should be consulted by everybody who is interested in this episode.

2. William Cleland, a close friend, acted as Pope's literary "ghost" on at least one other occasion. See Introduction to *The Dunciad*, vol. v of this edition, p. xxv.

3. Aaron Hill, who had read the letter in both *Post-Boy* and *Journal*, seems to have recognized Pope's hand in it at once. See Sherburn, III 261.

4. Devonshire Papers and Sherburn, III 259.

virtuous indignation by the time Pope prefixed an open letter to Burlington to the third edition of the Epistle:[1]

I was too well content with my Knowledge of that Noble Person's Opinion in this Affair, to trouble the publick about it. But since Malice and Mistake are so long a dying, I take the opportunity of this third Edition to declare *His Belief*, not only of *My Innocence*, but of *Their Malignity* of the former of which my own Heart is as conscious, as I fear some of theirs must be of the latter. His Humanity feels a Concern for the Injury done to *Me*, while His Greatness of Mind can bear with Indifference the Insult offer'd to *Himself*.

A letter Chandos wrote to Pope on 27 December 1731, that has only recently turned up, bears out the general truth of Pope's statements, and Johnson's ungenerous interpretation of the incident can now be dismissed as incorrect:[2]

Cannons 27th. Decr. 1731

Sir—

I am much troubled to find by your favour of ye 22^d. you are under any uneasiness, at ye application ye Town has made of Timon's Character, in Your Epistle to ye Earl of Burlinton. For my own part I have rec^d. so many instances of ye will they bear me, that I am as little surprized as I am affected with this further proof of it; It would indeed be a real concern to me, did I beleive One of your Judgment had designedly given grounds for their imbibing an Opinion, so disadvantageous of me. But as your obliging Letter, is sufficient to free me from this apprehension, I can with great indifference bear ye insults they bestow, and not find myself hurt by 'em: nor have I Reason to be much disturb'd, when I consider how many better persons are ye daily objects of their unjust censures.

---

1. The third edition of *To Burlington* was published 15 January 1731/2.

2. *Lives of the Poets*, III 153. The account of the affair that Pope gave Spence (p. 145) turns out to be substantially true: "When there was so much talk about the Duke of Chandos being meant under the character of Timon, Mr. Pope wrote a letter to that nobleman... The Duke in his answer, said, 'he took the application that had been made of it, as a sign of the malice of the town against himself;' and seemed very well satisfied that it was not meant for him."

I heartily lament ye Melancholly condition you are in on account of ye approaching loss, of so near and tender a Relation; Such strokes of Providence are great tryals of humane Nature, and exercise its utmost Fortitude, but they proceed from ye hand of One, whose power wee cannot resist, and whose will, it is our Duty to submit to: I need not I am confident enlarge on this subject to One, whose words have instructed many, and who hath so often upholden him that was falling, Religion and his own good Sense, will enable him to avoid ye reproach that follows; but now it is come upon thee and thou faintest, is this thy confidence and thy Hope?—

I earnestly wish you may soon be restored to that quiet of mind you have hitherto possest, and without wch no happiness can be enjoy'd. I am

Sir Your &c¹

Pope found it difficult to emulate Chandos's philosophical acceptance of the malicious gossip of "the Town". The satirical fragment, beginning

> The *Fop*, whose Pride affects a *Patron*'s Name,
> Yet *absent*, wounds an Author's honest Fame;

which was later worked into the *Epistle to Arbuthnot*, dates from this period.² When Pope was angry, really angry, as in these lines, his verse achieves a passionate surgical precision that is more French than English. What infuriated him was not the mud-slinging of the middle-class "dunces", like Welsted³ and Concanen; he could always pay them back in their own coin. It was "society" tittle-

---

1. Sherburn, III 262–3. The original, the Duke's own copy of the letter that he sent Pope, is in the Chandos Letter Books in the Huntington Library, California. The "approaching loss" Pope was expecting was of his mother, though she did not in fact die until June 1733.

2. Twelve lines were printed in *The London Evening Post*, 22–5 January 1731/2, "*inscrib'd to the Honourable Mr. —.*" See vol. IV of this edition, p. 116, vol. VI, pp. 338–40, and Mr Sherburn's contribution to *Essays on the Eighteenth Century presented to David Nichol Smith*, p. 57.

3. Mr Sherburn prints a letter from Chandos showing the Duke trying to dissuade Welsted from publishing his poem *Of Dulness and Scandal. Occasion'd by the Character of Lord Timon* (*Huntington Library Bulletin*, no. 8, October 1935, pp. 140–1).

tattle that was so difficult to suppress—and so infinitely more damaging—the scandal-monger,

> Who to the *Dean* and *Silver Bell* can swear,
> And sees at *C–n–ns* what was never there.[1]

A more elaborate, though much less successful, prose satire recently discovered by Professor Butt at Chatsworth was also directed against drawing-room gossip about "Timon". This is *A Master Key to Popery or A True and Perfect Key to Pope's Epistle to the Earl of Burlington,* an anonymous "irony" which is essentially a prolonged parody of the far-fetched satirical allusions that were then being read into the poem. By the courtesy of the Chatsworth Estates Company the tract is reprinted in Appendix C of this edition (see pp. 175–88 below). The MS. is in the hand of Lady Burlington and it is possible that it is the "Pamphlet" referred to by Pope in an undated letter of this period, not hitherto printed, addressed to the Earl:

> I have a favor to beg of my Lady B. (after having given me a Copy of Maister Johnson[2]) to give me the Copy of my Pamphlet wch she writ out, & to keep my Original among her papers of greater value: the bearer will bring it me, & also the Laurels, wch you (of all Mankind at this time) bestow upon me so liberally.[3]

Burlington's reply, also undated, may explain how it is that, in spite of Pope's request, the copy of the pamphlet has remained in the possession of Burlington's descendants:

> I told L^y B of your commands in relation to her copy. she says hers is locked up at Chiswick but when she goes back, shall be very desirous of the exchange. in the mean time not knowing what occasion you may have for the original, I now send it.[4]

---

1. See *To Burlington,* 141, 149, and the relevant notes (p. 151 below).

2. For "Maister Johnson" see *To Cobham,* 158*n*. Mr Sherburn suggests that the "Copy" Lady Burlington had given Pope of his neighbour James Johnstone (a Scot by origin) was a caricature drawing by herself.

3. Devonshire Papers, 143.28 and Sherburn, III 272. The "Laurels" are presumably the compliments that the Burlingtons paid Pope on *To Burlington,* when everybody else seemed to be abusing him.

4. Devonshire Papers, 143.29 and Sherburn, III 273.

There can be no doubt in any case that *A Master Key to Popery* is by Pope himself. Two small clues are provided in the following passage:

See Sportive Fate—Bids Babo build—

Here the Criticks differ. Some read, for Babo, Bubo. Others fix this on a Peer who I confess is noble enough for our Authors abuse; but (what I always take for a cause, to doubt it) one to whom he has no sort of Obligation. Tis certain Sh—d is this Noblemans Builder, but why should he satyrize Sh—d? Sh—d is none of his *Friends*.

Here the early editions all read "Babo" and "S—d" in *To Burlington*, ll. 20 and 18, whereas the only surviving MS. of the whole poem reads "Bubo" and "Sh x x".[1] Apparently then the author of *A Master Key* had seen Pope's MS. In addition to having access to Pope's MSS. he seems also to have known a great deal about Pope and Pope's friends. He knew, for example, that Pope had never been to Houghton, Sir Robert Walpole's country seat. He knew that Lord Bathurst "is so much an enemy to *nice Parterres*, that he never mows, but grazes them". He quotes a line by Bubb Dodding-ton,

In Power a Servant, out of Power a Friend,

that Pope was in the habit of making fun of,[2] as well as the Duke of Shrewsbury's *mot* about Blenheim that Pope had already repeated to Martha Blount.[3] And he has even included a sarcastic reference to the poet's "gentle Friend Lord Fanny",[4] who had apparently

---

1. The MS. is among the Devonshire Papers. It is in the hand of John Ferret, Burlington's agent, and is no doubt a copy of the MS. that Pope had sent Burlington with his letter of 4 April [1731] reproduced above. In addition to this Devonshire MS. of *To Burlington* a fragment of some 70 lines in Pope's hand is in the Pierpont Morgan Library, New York, and the Huntington Library, California, has a copy of Pope's *Works*, vol. II (quarto, 1735) with variant readings from the early drafts in a hand identified by Professor Maynard Mack as that of the younger Jonathan Richardson.

2. See *To Cobham*, 161n.   3. See *To Burlington*, 109–10n.

4. This antedates the reference in *Sat.*, II i, 6 which has hitherto been considered the first occasion on which Pope called Hervey "Lord Fanny". *Sat.*, II i was composed in January 1732/3, whereas *A Master Key* was almost certainly written in February 1731/2 at the latest.

been saying that "Villario", that inconstant landscape gardener, was Pope's friend Lord Bathurst.

A Master Key to Popery reads as though it had been written for publication. Perhaps, as in the parallel case of *A Letter to a Noble Lord*, when the first fury had passed, Pope may have realized that a retort of this kind would have been taken by his enemies as evidence that his armour had been pierced. And in any case, as he must have known, his proper satiric medium was not prose.

The letter prefixed to the third edition of *To Burlington* had concluded:

> Even from the Conduct shewn on this occasion, I have learnt there are some who wou'd rather be *wicked* than ridiculous; and therefore it may be safer to attack *Vices* than *Follies*. I will leave my Betters in the quiet Possession of their *Idols*, their *Groves*, and their *High-Places*; and change my Subject from their *Pride* to their *Meanness*, from their *Vanities* to their *Miseries*: And as the only certain way to avoid Misconstruction, to lessen Offence, and not to multiply ill-natur'd Applications, I may probably in my next make use of *Real* Names and not of Fictitious Ones.

The new poem, which is to be concerned with the "meanness" and "miseries" of the English aristocracy, was, of course, the poem on avarice that we have already met in Spence's notes. It was eventually published on 15 January 1732/3, some thirteen months after *To Burlington*, as *Of The Use Of Riches, an Epistle To the Right Honorable Allen Lord Bathurst*, the delay being certainly due to some extent to the reception that the earlier Epistle had had. "The Noise which Malice has raised about That Epistle," Pope wrote to Lord Oxford on 22 January 1731/2, "has caused me to suppress a much better, concerning the *Use of Riches*, in which I had payd some Respect, and done some Justice to the Duke of Chandos."[1] As the allusion to Chandos shows, by "to suppress" Pope really meant "to revise". The insertion of this compliment to Chandos, and its final suppression, was, as we can see from the autograph MSS. of the poem (now in the Huntington Library, California), another reason for the delay in the poem's publication. Pope had written to Oxford on 7 November 1731, only a few weeks before *To Burlington* was pub-

---

1. Sherburn, III 267.

lished, to say that he had "taken the Liberty to call at Your Door, in
my way to Moral Virtue",[1] and accordingly the first version of
what was eventually ll. 243–4 runs:

> There gracious Oxford, acting God's own part,
> Relieves th'Opprest, and glads the Orphan's heart.

After the "Timon" business, no doubt soon after he had got
Chandos's reassuring letter of 27 December, he seems to have
decided to fit the Duke in too, and after a number of false starts the
following couplet was achieved:

> OXFORD & CHANDOS, acting God's own part,
> Relieve th' Opprest, & glad the Orphans heart.

On second thoughts, however, Pope realized, as he put it to Oxford
in the letter of 22 January 1731/2, that "to print it, now, would be
interpreted by Malice . . . as if I had done it in attonement, or thro'
some apprehension, or sensibility of having meant that Duke an
abuse; which I'm sure was far from my Thought."[2] Once bitten,
twice shy. Pope, who was always exceptionally sensitive to the pos-
sible reactions of his readers—it was a source of his satiric strength
—had learnt one or two things about "the Town" in the "Timon"
episode that he had not known before and that he was not to forget.
But the decision to omit the compliment to Chandos was not the
end of the matter. To protect himself against a possible charge of
social presumption he wrote again to Oxford on 22 September 1732
to ask for his formal permission to introduce his name into the
poem, and it was only when Oxford had agreed in the friendliest
terms to this that the final version of the couplet (which is not repre-
sented in the surviving MSS.) was made public:

> Who copies Your's [=Bathurst's], or OXFORD's better part,
> To ease th' oppress'd, and raise the sinking heart?[3]

---

1. Sherburn, III 241.   2. Sherburn, III 267.

3. I have simplified considerably the textual evolution of this couplet. In the
two autograph MSS. there are altogether four attempts at the couplet. What
seems to be the earliest runs as follows:

> still may Laelius
> There ~~gracious~~ Oxford, acting God's own part,
> Ch—os and Ox —d   chear
> Relieve~~s~~ th' Opprest, and ~~glads~~ the Orphan's heart

This little incident is typical of the enormous amount of trouble that Pope took over *To Bathurst*. He later described it to Spence as being 'as much laboured as any one of my works",[1] and on 16 February 1732/3 he wrote to Swift, "I never took more care in my life of any poem."[2] It might have been a better poem if rather less care had been taken with it. As one of Pope's earliest biographers put it, it has been "*laboured* into *ease*".[3] There is in the final version curiously little spontaneity or real feeling. Pope's indignation with the wicked capitalists of the City of London is obviously second-hand and worked up, as it were, for the occasion. Far more than in the *Essay on Man* he is here simply Bolingbroke's mouthpiece. Compared with Fielding's contemporary "dramatic satires", like *Pasquin* and *The Historical Register*, in this poem Pope too often gives the impression that he doesn't know what he is talking about. Almost all of his information, for example, about the two great financial scandals of 1732—the misappropriations by the Commissioners for the sale of the Earl of Derwentwater's estates and by the Directors of the Charitable Corporation for the Relief of the Industrious Poor —seems to have been derived from the newspapers.

About the evolution of Epistle I (*To Cobham*), which was published on 16 January 1733/4, with a half-title reading, "Of the Knowledge and Characters of Men: To Richard Lord Cobham", much less is known. In a letter dated 6 January Pope promised Swift a copy "even before 'tis here publish'd" and explained that the poem was a "part of my *Opus Magnum*".[4] It is, indeed, the only one of the four Epistles that was written primarily to fit into the expanded *Essay on Man* scheme, and echoes of the terminology and arguments of the *Essay* (which had only just been completed) are frequent. Its *raison d'être* there was to introduce the series of epistles on morality that at one stage of the scheme's progress were to have constituted the Second Book, though in the final plan they were allocated to a Fourth Book. Pope's problem in this Epistle, as he had explained to Spence in May 1730, was to provide "wᵗ a Scale

1. Spence, p. 304. The comment was made in 1744, according to Malone's edition.
2. Sherburn, III 348.
3. Owen Ruffhead, *The Life of Alexander Pope* (1769), p. 293.
4. Sherburn, III 401.

is to a book of Maps". Here was his "greatest difficulty: not only in settling all ye parts, but in making them agreeable enough to be read with pleasure". The latter requirement he certainly succeeded in meeting. *To Cobham* may be rather superficial, but it is eminently readable. But to what extent is it what a scale is to a book of maps? How far, that is, does it provide a key by which the contrasting moral extremes of his scheme, such as prodigality and avarice, can be related to the problems of every-day conduct? Pope's professed key was the theory of the ruling passion. This was his "New Hypothesis, That a prevailing passion in ye mind is brought wth it into ye world, & continues till death". The theory of the ruling passion has been discussed in detail in the Introduction to the *Essay on Man* in vol. III i and there will be no need to go over the same ground again here. Two points about it, however, emerge in *To Cobham*, on which something must be said. The first is that, though Pope is entitled to claim that he has carried the hypothesis somewhat further than had been done before his time, it is not really new at all. The anecdotes with which he illustrates the ruling passion strong in death at the end of his Epistle are among the oldest stories in the world. The old gourmand, for example, who, when told that medicine can do nothing for him, cries "Alas!—then bring the jowl", has been traced back to a second-century compiler of anecdotes. Moreover, as Cobham himself pointed out to Pope in a letter of 8 November 1733, gluttony is an appetite "that from nature we indulg as well for her ends as our pleasure", and "a passion or habit that has not a natural foundation" would fit in better with Pope's argument.[1] Montaigne, from whom Pope has borrowed the psychological scepticism of the first half of the Epistle as well as, to some extent, the theory of the ruling passion itself, restricted the passion to acts of the conscious will, such as ambition, and excluded the instinctive appetites. As a peg for hanging anecdotes on no doubt Pope's hypothesis was adequate, but as the basis of an ethical system it would seem to be altogether too naïve.

Of the Characters of Women: an Epistle to a Lady, the last in order of appearance and much the most attractive of the four poems, was published on 17 February 1734/5. It was apparently in existence as early as January 1732/3, when Pope called it, in a letter to Caryll,

---

1. Sherburn, III 393.

"a prettier poem" than *To Bathurst*. Unfortunately, although MSS. of the poem certainly exist, it has not been possible to locate them.[1] The early editions are without the characters of "Philomedé", "Atossa", and "Cloe" which were only added in the "death-bed edition" of 1744. "Cloe" was printed separately in 1738[2] and may not have been a part of the original poem, but "Philomedé" and "Atossa" almost certainly were. The problems that these textual changes raise are discussed in the Textual Introduction to the poem (pp. 40–4 below). They are of considerable complexity and until one or more of the MSS. turn up a reconstruction of the poem's evolution must be largely a matter of guesswork. According to Ruffhead, who probably derived the information from Warburton, the poem was written rapidly:

> Mr. POPE . . . has been heard to declare, in private conversation, that what he wrote fastest, always pleased most.*[3]
>
> *An instance of which he gave, not only in the Rape of the Lock but in the Poem on the Characters of Women . . . which he wrote at once in a heat, not of malice or resentment, but of pure, though strong, poetical fire.[4]

There is no reason to doubt the general tenor of Ruffhead's account, but the whole of the poem cannot have been written in one "heat". The characters of "Rufa" and "Sappho" derive in part from "Artemisia" in the Pope-Swift *Miscellanies* of 1727, and "Calypso" and "Narcissa" come from "Sylvia, a Fragment" in the same collection. Ll. 243–8 had been printed in the version of "To Mrs. *M.B.* Sent on Her Birth-Day" also included in the *Miscellanies*, and there are a number of other couplets scattered through

---

1. Among the Pope MSS. "from the Library of Dr. Charles Chauncy" which were sold at Christie's on 30 July 1889, there were two autograph MSS. of *To a Lady*, both with "numerous corrections and alterations" by Pope. A cancel-sheet specially substituted in a set of Pope's works assembled by him in 1738 for the Prince of Wales has something of the status of a MS., since only one copy of the sheet—which includes the scandalous characters—would seem to have been printed. See Vinton A. Dearing, "The Prince of Wales's Set of Pope's Works", *Harvard Library Bulletin*, 1950, IV 320–38, and p. 159 below.

2. See vol. VI of this edition, p. 377.

3. Pope had told Spence *c.* 1734–6, "The things that I have written fastest, have always pleased the most" (p. 142).

4. *The Life of Alexander Pope* (1769), p. 293.

the poem that Pope had already made use of in epigrams, etc. There is also some reason to think that the character of "Atossa" had been written, though not printed, before the bulk of the poem.[1]

The ruling passion makes a brief appearance in ll. 207–10, but the poem cannot really be considered a serious contribution to the philosophical "*Opus Magnum*" in spite of its title (which seems to claim it as a companion piece to *To Cobham*). It is essentially a satirical portrait gallery in Pope's most accomplished Horatian manner. Bolingbroke, who with all his many faults was a man of taste, thought it, when he read the poem in manuscript early in 1733, Pope's *chef d'œuvre* at that time.[2]

III

"Epistles to Several Persons" is a better title than "Moral Essays", not only because it was the title of Pope's own choice, but because it describes more accurately the nature of the four poems. To a reader of the early eighteenth century the word "essay" had a more formidable connotation than it has today. The combination of "moral" and "essays", instead of suggesting, as it might to us, Addison's Saturday numbers of *The Spectator*, would then have been more likely to suggest some such dismal treatise as James Lowde's *Moral Essays wherein some of Mr. Lock's and Mons*[r]. *Malbranch's opinions are briefly examin'd* (1699). The effect of Warburton's title therefore was to put all the emphasis on the didactic elements in the poems. Here, it proclaimed, is another *Essay on Man*! It called attention, in other words, to all that is weakest and most pretentious in the four Epistles and ignored altogether the social satire and worldly wisdom in which their real strength lies.

If there is a certain convenience in the term "Moral Essays" as differentiating the Epistles that are associated with the *Essay on Man* from Pope's other letters in verse, such as those to Addison, Harley, Craggs, and Jervas,[3] this is more than counterbalanced by the

---

1. See Appendix A (Who was Atossa?). For "Artemesia", "Sylvia" and "To Mrs. *M.B.*", see vol. vi of this edition, pp. 48–9, 286–8, 244–7.

2. Pope to Swift, 16 February 1732/3, Sherburn, iii 349.

3. All reprinted in vol. vi of this edition.

reminder that the word "Epistle" conveys that Pope is using in these poems one of the accepted neo-classic forms. As a vehicle for political compliment, literary criticism, and social correction the Horatian epistle had long been a favourite of the Augustan poets, and Dryden, in "To My Honor'd Kinsman, John Driden", and Congreve, in "Of Improving the Present Time" (which had been addressed to the same Lord Cobham as Pope's epistle), had already shown that ethics could also be treated "in the Horatian way" in excellent English verse.

In *The Spectator*, no. 618, Ambrose Philips provides a long list of "The Qualifications requisite for writing Epistles, after the Model given us by *Horace*": "a good Fund of strong Masculine sense"; "a thorough knowledge of Mankind"; "an insight into the Business and the prevailing Humours of the Age"; a "Mind well seasoned with the finest precepts of Morality"; and a mastery of "refined raillery, and a lively turn of wit, with an easy and concise manner of expression". Philips adds that the illustrations and similes should be drawn from "common Life", and that "Strokes of Satyr and Criticism, as well as Panegyrics", are particularly desirable, provided that "a vulgar diction" and "too negligent" a versification are avoided. It will be seen that Pope's Epistles adhere closely to Philips's ideal recommendation, which is indeed only an elaboration of the prescription in Horace's tenth Satire that Pope used as an epigraph to the "death-bed" edition.[1] *To Burlington* was criticized on its publication as insufficiently "correct" in its versification. Sir Thomas Hanmer, for example, was informed by Dr Delany, Swift's friend, on 23 December 1731 (only ten days after the poem had come out) that "There is a general outcry against that part of the poem which is thought an abuse of ye Duke of Chandos—other parts are quarrelled with as obscure and unharmonious; and I am told there is an advertisement that promises a publication of Mr. Pope's Epistle versified . . ."[2] Except for an

---

1. See p. 1 below.
2. *The Correspondence of Sir Thomas Hanmer*, ed. Sir H. E. Bunbury (1838), p. 217. The charge of obscurity was also brought against *To Bathurst* by Lady [Anne] Irwin, in a letter to her father, Lord Carlisle, 18 January [1733/4]: "there are good thoughts wrapt up in obscurity, but that is so much the fashion that to be plain and intelligible is a meanness in writing the moderns are resolved not to be

occasional tiring of the ears with open vowels it is difficult to find
more than a line or two in *To Burlington* that could possibly be con-
sidered "unharmonious". But Aaron Hill refers to the same criti-
cism of the poem in a letter to Pope himself of 17 December (only
four days after publication):

> We have *Poets*, whom heaven *visits* with a *taste*, as well as
> planters and builders.—What other inducement could provoke
> some of them, to mistake your epistolary relaxation of numbers,
> for an involuntary defect in your versification?[1]

As Hill hints, a great deal more was in fact involved than the
precise degree of metrical negligence appropriate to a Horatian
epistle. The Dunces were moving in to the counter-attack, and
Pope was forced under this new pressure to reconsider the moral
basis of epistolary satire. Swift's satires provided an obvious con-
temporary criterion by which he could measure the extra-literary
validity of his own poems. "You call your satires, Libels," he wrote
in due course to Swift on 20(?) April 1733: "I would rather call my
satires, Epistles: They will consist more of morality than wit, and
grow graver, which you will call duller."[2] The implication here
that, as the writer of

> grave *Epistles*, bringing Vice to light,[3]

he is a more serious poet than Swift, becomes almost explicit in the
"Advertisement" to their joint imitation of Horace:

> His Manner, and that of Dr. *Swift* are so entirely different,
> that they can admit of no Invidious Comparison. The Design of
> the one being to sharpen the Satire, and open the Sense of the
> Poet; of the other to render his native *Ease* and *Familiarity* yet
> more easy and familiar.[4]

The difficulty was to define the difference between "satire",
especially if "sharp", and "libel". Was there really any difference?
Lady Mary Wortley Montagu wrote to Arbuthnot on 3 January

---

guilty on . . ." (Historical Manuscripts Commission, Report xv, App., pt vi, p.
97).

1. Sherburn, III 257.   2. Sherburn, III 366.
3. *Imit. Hor., Sat.*, II i, 151 (written January 1732/3).
4. *Imit. Hor., Sat.*, II vi (1738).

1735 (the day after the *Epistle to Arbuthnot* had been published):

> I wish you would advise poor Pope to turn to some more
> honest livelihood than libelling; I know he will allege in his ex-
> cuse that he must write to eat, and he is now grown sensible that
> nobody will buy his verses except their curiosity is piqued to it, to
> see what is said of their acquaintance...[1]

A delightfully feline comment! Did Arbuthnot show the letter to
Pope? At any rate when Pope reprinted his first *Imitation of Horace* in
April 1735[2] he added an "Advertisement" in which he takes up this
question of the distinction between libel and satire:

> And indeed there is not in the world a greater Error, than that
> which Fools are so apt to fall into, and Knaves with good reason
> to incourage, the mistaking a *Satyrist* for a *Libeller*; whereas to a
> *true Satyrist* nothing is so odious as a *Libeller*, for the same reason
> as to a man *truly Virtuous* nothing is so hateful as a *Hypocrite*.

Pope's point is that, as the virtuous man objects to hypocrites be-
cause they use virtue as the cloak for vice, so the satirist objects to
libellers because, under the pretence of writing "grave Epistles,
bringing Vice to light", they indulge in what is really personal
spite. But the difficulty still remained that there was no objective
criterion by which you could distinguish the exposure of vice from
the indulgence of spite. It all depended apparently on the poet's
motives.

Pope's answer, when anybody impugned his motives, was to
appeal to "virtue". Applying to himself the character that Horace
had attributed to Lucilius, he proclaimed himself (in capital
letters)

To virtue only and her friends, a friend.[3]

Pope's modern friends have found such passages, which are by no
means rare in his writings,[4] embarrassing and distressing. But for

---

1. Lady Mary's Letters, II 21.   2. In his *Works*, vol. II.
3. *Imit. Hor., Sat.*, II i, 121.
4. See Spence, pp. 301–2, Pope to Aaron Hill, 5 February 1730/1 (Sherburn,
III 172), Pope to Warburton, 12 November 1741 (Sherburn, IV 370), Pope to
Caryll, 27 September 1732 (Sherburn, III 316).

Pope "virtue" did not mean quite what it means to us. The most specific reference, though it does not quite amount to a definition, is in one of the later *Imitations of Horace*:

> Here, Wisdom calls: "Seek Virtue first! be bold!
> "As Gold to Silver, Virtue is to Gold."
> There, London's voice: "Get Mony, Mony still!
> "And then let Virtue follow, if she will."[1]

Here Pope seems to be saying that the opposite of the pursuit of virtue is the pursuit of money. And therefore presumably, if London symbolizes money, virtue must be symbolized by the country. (God made the country, in fact, and man made the town.) Virtue, on this interpretation, is a class-concept, the system of values of the "landed interest", the "Country Party". Vice is therefore the social philosophy of the urban capitalists, the rising middle classes who, with their champions in Parliament and at Court, were already a potential threat to the supremacy of the squirearchy.[2]

It is significant at any rate that Burlington, Bathurst, and Cobham were all prominent members of the landed aristocracy. They were at the opposite social and economic pole, that is, from such contemporary notabilities as Sir Gilbert Heathcote, who was one of the founders of the Bank of England, Sir John Blunt, the projector of the South Sea Company, Peter Walter, the moneylender, and the rest of the financiers and crooks who are satirized in *To Bathurst*. Politically Burlington was neutral (he is the exemplar of "Sense" rather than "Virtue"), but Bathurst was a prominent Tory and Cobham, who had voted against Walpole's Excise Bill in 1733, became from then one of the most influential of the Opposition Whigs. And their country seats at Chiswick, Cirencester, and Stowe were, of course, object lessons in the new gardening, at once picturesque and utilitarian,

---

1. *Ep.*, 1 i, 77-80.

2. This is not the place for a detailed exposition of the Augustan *Weltanschauung*, but some understanding of the social basis of Pope's poetry is essential if the modern reader is not to be unfair to him. Of course, it is not suggested that Pope himself would have accepted a class definition of "virtue", such as that given above, which is an attempt to get behind what he *thought* he meant to the basic implications of his satire.

> Whose ample Lawns are not asham'd to feed
> The milky heifer and deserving steed.

Pope's "virtue" was closely related therefore to Bolingbroke's "patriotism". (In Epistle I Cobham's last, and therefore most edifying, words are foretold to be "Oh, save my Country, Heav'n!") It was a quality that had little or nothing to do with the respectability of one's private life. Bathurst, the "Philosopher and Rake",[1] is held up as an example of the golden mean,

> There, English Bounty yet a-while may stand,
> And Honour linger ere it leaves the land.

"Virtue", in fact, is primarily a social quality, the positive element of which the negative is "vice", and Pope's satires are exercises in "contrast" (a pictorial term to which he often reverts) between the two elements. On the one hand, they applaud the exemplars of "virtue", the living representatives of what is to Pope the ideal social order. On the other hand, they attack and ridicule "vice", or the deviation from this social order. Each of the two aspects presented its own literary problem. The positive problem Pope solved, or thought he had solved, by piling up rhetorical compliments. And at any rate the recipients of the compliments seemed to have liked them. This is what Cobham, for example, had to say when he had read the Epistle addressed to him:

> Tho I have not modesty enough not to be pleasd with your extraordinary compliment I have wit enough to know how little I deserve it   you know all mankind are putting themselves upon the world for more then they are worth and their friends are dayly helping the deceits but I am afraid I shall not pass for an absolute Patriot   however I have the honour of haveing receivd a publick testimony of your esteem and friendship and am as proud of it as I coud be of any advantage which coud happen to me.[2]

But the positive social elements are not important in satire, except by implication. The literary problem presented by the nega-

---

1. *Imit. Hor.*, *Sat.*, I ii, 158.
2. Brit. Mus. Egerton MS. 1949, f. 1, and Sherburn, III 391. The letter is dated 1 November 1733.

tive elements was the crucial one. How was Pope to be the fearless social critic without seeming to be a libeller?

It is important to recognize that the basis of Pope's satire is *fact*. It was by stooping to Truth, i.e. the kind of evidence that would be accepted in a court of law, that he was able to moralize his song. Unlike his friend Young, whose five satires called *The Universal Passion* (1725/6) Pope had certainly read and admired, he was not content with what Charles Lamb, speaking of Restoration comedy, was to call "a speculative scene of things, which has no reference whatever to the world that is". His satire, in contradistinction to that of Wycherley and Congreve, is rooted in topical and contemporary life, and his progress as a satirist can best be measured by the degree of social actuality that each poem achieved. In *To Burlington*, for example, though the illustrative details are real, the satiric butts are personified abstractions, almost all without any living originals. The "Subject" of the poem, according to the letter that Pope prefixed to the third edition, was the "Pride" of his "Betters"; in other words, the extravagant ostentation of the Augustan aristocracy that a modern sociologist has called "the ritual of conspicuous waste". "Lord Timon" is obviously intended to personify this "Pride". (His villa is "proud" (l. 101), his chapel exhibits "the Pride of Pray'r" (l. 142), his "civil Pride" (l. 166) is sickening, though eventually "all his pride has plann'd" (l. 175) will pass away.[1]) On the other hand, some of the details that Pope introduces to illustrate "Timon's" pride can be traced to the actual grounds and mansions of contemporary noblemen. Blenheim Palace, for example, certainly contributed some items. It is not impossible either that, though "Timon" is not the Duke of Chandos, Cannons, the Duke's "place" at Edgware, may have provided one or two suggestions, e.g. the "Statues thick as trees" (l. 120). Chandos himself admitted to a friend, "I am not so ignorant of my own weakness, as not to be sensible of it's [Timon's Character's] Justness in some particulars."[2] Pope points out some of the topical allusions in the poem in his notes. To l. 75, for example,

---

1. "Pride" is a key-word in Pope. He uses it twice as often as Milton, surprisingly enough. The word occurs twenty-four times in the *E. on Man* alone.
2. See the letter to Anthony Hammond of 1 January 1731/2 printed by Mr Sherburn in the *Huntington Library Bulletin*, no. 8, October 1935, p. 140.

Or cut wide views thro' Mountains to the Plain,

Pope added the following note in 1735:

> This was done in Hertfordshire, by a wealthy citizen, at the expence of above 5000 l. by which means (merely to overlook a dead plain) he let in the north-wind upon his house and parterre, which were before adorned and defended by beautiful woods.[1]

Here Pope is clearly alluding to Moor Park, Rickmansworth, where the two vistas that Benjamin Styles, a successful South Sea speculator, cut through the hill can still be seen.

The presence of so much contemporary topical detail no doubt explains why the first readers of *To Burlington* jumped to the conclusion that "Timon" and the six other offenders against taste who are pilloried in the poem must be caricatures of real people. A catchpenny production called *A Miscellany on Taste* (1732) even provided a "Clavis" in which all the fictitious names are equated with contemporary notabilities. Not only is "Timon" the "Duke of C——", but "Villario" is "Lord *C–le–n*" (i.e. Castlemaine), "Bubo" is "Lord *C–d–n*" (i.e. Cadogan), and "Sir Shylock" is even identified with "Sir *R–W–*" (i.e. Walpole). It was all very annoying to Pope, not only because of the social hot water in which he found himself, but also because it meant that his satiric gun had misfired. What he had intended to be read as general "satire", illustrated by ideal types,[2] had been taken as topical and personal "libel".

In *To Bathurst* he succeeded in avoiding the mistake he had made in *To Burlington*. In the letter inserted in the third edition of *To Burlington* he had promised that his next poem would "make use of *Real* Names and not of Fictitious Ones", and he gave three reasons for this change of tactics, (i) "to avoid Misconstruction", (ii) "to lessen Offence", and (iii) "not to multiply ill-natur'd Applications". The first and third of these reasons were valid ones on the literary as well as the social plane. For an Augustan poet the first essential was to be

---

1. Pope's purpose in such notes has, I think, been misunderstood. They were not primarily for the benefit of the provincial reader who needed an explanation of the allusions. Their essential function is to supply the *evidence* on which Pope's satiric charges are based.

2. Pope's own description of his method in *To Burlington* was "telling truths, and drawing exemplary pictures of men and manners" (letter to Tonson, senior, 7 June 1732, Sherburn, III 291).

intelligible. But the second was really a betrayal of the satirist's function; satire only succeeds by being *offensive* to its victims. It is true that it might have been extremely dangerous at this stage for Pope to have attacked one of his "Betters", a Member of the House of Lords, for example, under his own name. In the end, therefore, he compromised. Of the thirty-one satiric butts introduced into *To Bathurst* sixteen appear under their own names and fifteen under fictitious names. Real names are used for all the middle-class victims such as Ward, Waters, Bond, etc., as well as for the Dukes of Buckingham and Wharton, who were both safely dead, and also for such disreputable aristocratic adventurers as Sir William Colepepper, Joseph Gage, and Lady Mary Herbert who were safe game, though still alive. The fictitious names fall into three categories, (i) parallel Latin or pseudo-Latin names of the Horatian type, (ii) pseudonyms sounding something like the victims' real names, and (iii) miscellaneous names, scriptural, national, etc. The first and second of these categories seem to include the "living examples, which inforce best" that Pope told Caryll he intended to restrict the poem to.[1] Most of the victims can be identified with some certainty because the real names, or at any rate one or more letters of the real names, often appear in the early drafts of the poem. They were almost all contemporary aristocrats, like the Herveys, the Wortley Montagus, General Cadogan, and Lord Selkirk.[2] The only ideal figure in these categories seems to be "Harpax" (l. 93).[3] The third category only includes two names, "Sir Morgan" (l. 49), which Pope assured Caryll "is a fictitious

---

1. Pope to Caryll, 22 September 1732 (Sherburn, III 316).

2. The exceptions are "Cato" (l. 68), who is certainly Sir Christopher Musgrave, who had died in 1704, and "Cotta" (ll. 179*ff*) who must be Sir John Cutler who was neither contemporary nor an aristocrat. Cutler comes in under his own name ll. 315–34, and his appearance as "Cotta" may be due to the fact that the point of the passage is the contrast between Cutler and his son-in-law the Earl of Radnor (whose successor was a neighbour of Pope's at Twickenham). Pope may have felt that if the son-in-law did not appear under his own name, the father-in-law should not either.

3. The ideality of "Harpax" seems to be guaranteed by *Imit. Hor., Sat.,* II i, 42–4:

> A hundred smart in *Timon* and in *Balaam*:
> The fewer still you name, you wound the more;
> *Bond* is but one, but *Harpax* is a Score.

name",[1] and "Balaam" (ll. 339*ff*), who may conceivably be Thomas Pitt but is more likely to be nobody in particular.

Although less consistently, Pope adheres on the whole to "living examples" in *To Cobham*. The fidelity to fact is underlined in a note to l. 251, which was added in 1735: "The rest of these Instances are strictly true, tho' the Persons are not named." And the central "example"—the character that plays the rôle in this poem that "Timon" played in *To Burlington*—is supplied by a contemporary, the Duke of Wharton, who appears in the final text under his own name.[2] But there are a number of figures that seem to be mere general types, e.g. the "gay Free-thinker" (ll. 162–5), "Catius" (ll. 136–9), and the politician (ll. 130–5), and others, which seem to derive from real people, are apparently in process of generalization. Thus Godolphin is called "Patritio" (l. 140), though he had been dead over twenty years and the reference is more complimentary than satirical, and James Johnston, who is "J**n" in the first edition, ends up as "Scoto".

Pope was, in fact, on the horns of a dilemma. If he used fictitious names for real people, how could he be sure that the reader identified them correctly?[3] If he used fictitious names for mere ideal

---

1. Pope to Caryll, 8 March 1732/3 (Sherburn, III 353).

2. In the earlier editions he had been called "Clodio"—a name that had been applied to his father, the first Marquis, by William Shippen in *Faction Display'd* (1704).

3. The copies of the Epistles that have been annotated in MS. by eighteenth-century readers show how difficult even the best informed of them, e.g. Horace Walpole, Wilkes, and William Cole, found it to make the correct identifications. Pope's intimate friend the second Earl of Oxford, recognized that "G—" stood for Gage, "Maria" for Lady Mary Herbert, and "Bl—t" for Sir John Blount in the first edition of *To Bathurst*, but failed apparently to identify any of the fictitious names. (His copy is now in the Bodleian.)

On the appearance of Faulkner's Dublin reprint of *To Bathurst* early in 1733 Swift reported to Pope "we have no objection but the obscurity of several passages by our ignorance in facts and persons, which makes us lose abundance of the Satyr. Had the printer given me notice, I would have honestly printed the names at length, where I happened to know them; and writ explanatory notes . . ." (Sherburn, III 343). In Faulkner's reprint of *To Cobham* a year or so later somebody (presumably Swift) has done exactly that; e.g. on "Clodio" (l. 180), "It is supposed the Author means the late Duke of *Wharton*." But the expansion of "J ** n" (l. 158) to "Jaunssen"—with a note on this South Sea millionaire—

types, how could he secure himself from the "ill-natur'd Applications" that the Dunces would be sure to propagate? The solution that he ultimately adopted in the later *Imitations of Horace* was to use real names for real people all the time, however influential and aristocratic they might be. For factual satire this was the course that logic demanded. Short of this, however, there were ways and means by which the reader could be helped to interpret a fictitious name correctly. One has already been noticed in discussing *To Bathurst*. Such names as Worldly (=Wortley Montagu), Shylock (=Lord Selkirk), and Bubo (=Bubb Doddington) told their own story. Another device, first used in the second volume of the *Works* (April 1735), was to retain the same fictitious name for a real person in a number of poems. Lady Mary Wortley Montagu was called "Sappho" so often by Pope—he had inherited the name from Peterborough[1]—that he could soon count on the reader making the correct identification. A similar case is that of "Bubo".[2] A more interesting device is exemplified by "Atossa" and "Philomedé" in *To a Lady*. Here the names, though Horatian in appearance, are much more specific than the run of Latin or pseudo-Latin names. There was only one Atossa in literary history, the Atossa of Herodotus, whose main claim to fame was that she was the daughter of Cyrus and the sister of Cambyses. And there was only one woman in England that the name could fit, viz. the Duchess of Buckinghamshire, who was enormously proud of being James II's illegitimate child and so half-sister of the Old Pretender. "Philomedé" is an equally unusual name, though a "Lover of the Mede" (if that is the sense intended) may mean more than one thing and could apply to many *grandes dames* of the period.[3]

Finally, if the worst came to the worst, it was always possible to tell the reader which fictitious names concealed a living original and which did not. This is what Pope does more than once in *To a*

---

illustrates the hazards of such identifications. By "J ** n" Pope had really meant his Twickenham neighbour James Johnston, and on learning the mistake Faulkner had to insert in the unsold copies a cancel leaf, which is without the note and just reads "J—n" in the text. See pp. 4 and 28 below.

1. See *To a Lady*, 24n. 2. See *To Burlington*, 20n.

3. "Philomedé" may also be an attempt to anglicize Φιλομμειδής ("laughter-loving"), the Homeric epithet for Aphrodite. Or the name may be derived from an unidentified French romance.

Lady. To the first edition he prefixed an "Advertisement" in which he declared "upon his Honour, that no one Character is drawn from the Life". This was true, or almost true,[1] of the first edition, which did not include the characters of "Atossa", "Philomedé", and "Cloe". And the "death-bed edition", which adds these characters, gives the reader a fairly broad hint in the note to l. 199 that there had been a good reason why they had not been included in the earlier editions.

Pope's satirical progress in the Epistles, from "Timon" to "Wharton", had been considerable. He had learnt, as he told Arbuthnot, that "General Satire in Times of General Vice has no force", and that "tis only by hunting One or two from the Herd that any Examples can be made."[2] Henceforth he was to avoid "harmless *Characters* that no one hit".[3] And, even more salutary, he had learnt the importance of fact. There is an interesting admission in a letter Pope wrote to the elder Tonson on 7 June 1732 to thank him for the biographical details he had collected about the Man of Ross:

> You know, few of these particulars can be made to shine in verse, but I have selected the most affecting, and have added 2 or 3 which I learnd fro' other hands. A small exaggeration you must allow me as a poet; yet I was determined the ground work at least should be *Truth*.[4]

He had allowed himself too much exaggeration in *To Bathurst*. *To a Lady* is a much better poem, not only because it is gayer, but because it is more honest and more accurate. When he claimed, in the "Advertisement" to the *Epistle to Arbuthnot*, that that poem included "not a Circumstance but what is true", he was pointing to what is its, and Pope's, real greatness. Veracity did not come easily to the *mens curva in corpore curvo*. In the *Epistles to Several Persons* we can trace the process of self-discipline, moral as well as technical, by which he eventually taught his Muse to stoop to Truth.

---

1. Pope's friend Lord Oxford thought "Arcadia's Countess" (l. 7) was the Countess of Pembroke. If she was, Pope might have excused himself by claiming that she had not been "drawn from the Life", as Pope had not known the Countess in question personally.

2. Pope to Arbuthnot, 2 August 1734 (Sherburn, III 423).

3. *Imit. Hor., Dia.* i, 65.   4. Sherburn, III 290.

GENERAL NOTE ON THE TEXT

POPE'S stylistic perfectionism, which at times approaches a *cacoethes corrigendi*, is reflected in the two hundred odd revisions of, and additions to, the text of the four Epistles included in this volume. The changes are sometimes structural (rearrangements in the order of paragraphs or couplets), but they are more often matters of wording or word-order within the line or couplet. Four consecutive phases or "states" can be distinguished in the Epistles' textual history: (i) each Epistle's separate publication by Lawton Gilliver[1] in a slim and elegant folio (price a shilling), followed within a few weeks by one or more authorized and/or unauthorized London reprints in various formats and a quasi-authorized Dublin reprint in octavo by George Faulkner;[2] (ii) their joint inclusion as four numbered "Ethic Epistles", or later "Epistles to Several Persons", in the second volume of Pope's *Works* (first edition folio 1735, second quarto 1735, third and fourth octavo 1735,[3] further octavos

---

1. Gilliver's agreement with Pope (B.M., Egerton MS. 1951) is endorsed with his acknowledgements of the receipt of three of the MSS. from Pope. *To Bathurst*, received 3 January 1732/3, was published on 15 January, *To Cobham*, received 1 January 1733/4, on 16 January, and *To a Lady*, received 4 January 1734/5, on 8 February (the delay in this case being no doubt due to Pope's second thoughts on the risks he might run if the three scandalous characters—see p. xxxvi above— were printed). January, the peak of the London social season in Georgian England, was the month in which Pope could count on their maximum circulation among the audience to whom the Epistles were primarily addressed.

2. English copyright did not include Ireland. Swift's letter to Pope, 3 September 1735 (Sherburn, v 17–18), summarizes the situation: "Mr. Faulkner tells me that he hath an Intention to print all your works, (except Homer) in two or three volumes in duodecimo, which although you cannot hinder, yet he desires you will not take ill, and he is ready to submit himself in all points to you. Here you are in my case, for it will be done by some other Printers, who may add spurious things, and make many blunders; whereas Mr. Faulkner hath many learned and ingenious Gentlemen who befriended him, and therefore I think you had better indulge what you cannot prevent." The relationship Swift is here recommending was in fact already in existence, as is clear from Faulkner's edition of *To Cobham* (1734). See note 1 in Note on the Text to that poem, p. 4 below.

3. The folio was obtainable in a large or small form, which are bibliographic-

D

xlix

1736 and 1739), which becomes *Works*, vol. II, part i in 1740 and 1743 (both octavo); (iii) a pre-publication issue for private distribution as *Epistles to Several Persons* in the "death-bed" instalment of the Pope–Warburton definitive edition of Pope's poems (quarto, May 1744); (iv) a posthumous re-emergence as "Moral Essays" in the third volume of Warburton's *The Works of Alexander Pope* (octavo, 1751), which proclaims itself the definitive edition begun by Pope and Warburton together and finished off after Pope's death in accordance with his instructions by Warburton on his own.

Later editions of the four Epistles have all descended from Warburton's (*1751*). Textually, however, *1751* is certainly inferior to the "death-bed" edition (*1744*), wherever their readings diverge. (The principal differences are the change of title and the division of *To Bathurst* into a dialogue between Pope and Bathurst; but there are also some verbal differences, e.g. the change to a subjunctive in *To a Lady*, l. 16, and *To Bathurst*, l. 38, as well as the reversal of the order of the lines in the couplet *To a Lady*, ll. 43–4, which may also be ascribed to Warburton rather than Pope or the printer.)

The special status of *1744*, which is confirmed by the literary superiority of most of its alterations, comes from its incorporation of Pope's final and sometimes long-meditated[1] revisions of both text and notes for what he intended to be the standard edition of his poetical works. As such, therefore, its readings might be presumed to be those in which he wished posterity to read the four poems.

The last version of a poem, however, is not always or necessarily the best version. *1744* was the victim, on the one hand, of Pope's increasingly feeble physical condition in the months when the text received its final form, and, on the other, of Warburton's attempts

---

ally identical. The folios and quarto were published simultaneously on 23 April 1735 (advertisement in *The Daily Post-Boy*, 22 April 1735), and the earlier of the two 1735 octavos on 30 July 1735. I call them respectively *1735a*, *1735b*, *1735c*, and *1735d*.

1. The change from Peter the Great to Julius Caesar in *To Cobham*, 83–4 must have been made in MS. in Pope's corrected copy of the poem soon after Aaron Hill had written to Pope, 15 January 1739 (Sherburn, IV 158), pointing out the unfairness of the original allusion. Warburton had seen, and had objected to, the revised couplet by 14 April 1741 (Sherburn, IV 339).

to foist into it his own ill-conceived improvements. The letters which have survived between them of this period are illuminating. Thus Pope's of 15 November 1743 (Sherburn, IV 480–1) begins: "Your Partiality to me is every way so great, that I am not surprized to find you take it for granted, that I observe more Method, and write more correctly, than I do." Warburton had made two suggestions, one of which was right ("as I see by casting my eye on the Original Copy"), but "the other, no such matter, the Emendation is wholly your own. (except that I find in the margin *How-ere*, instead of *Well then*, but cross'd over.)" The reference here is apparently to *To Bathurst*, l. 79, which reads in all the earlier editions,

> Well then, since with the world we stand or fall,

whereas *1744* has

> Since then, my Lord, on such a World we fall,

But whether the new reading is part of Warburton's rejected emendation after all, or Pope's own attempt to improve it, is not clear. The letter continues: "Upon the whole I will follow your Method, and therfore return the paper that you may accordingly refer the notes"—which must refer to the unfortunate transpositions in *To Bathurst* that are discussed in the Note on the Text (pp. 76–8 below). "Upon the whole", however, suggests a decidedly reluctant Pope. A Horatian epistle did not in fact require the author to "observe more Method" than he had done in the poem's first edition. Pope then passes on to defend a couplet (*To Bathurst*, ll. 159–60) that Warburton had wanted him to delete as illogical, and he ends "My health I fear will confine me, whether in town or here. . ."[1]

And Warburton was not *1744*'s only hazard, though its most serious one. The copy Pope sent Bowyer, the printer, can be reconstructed with some certainty from *1744*'s peculiarities of spelling, punctuation, and typography. With the exception of the scan-

---

1. A later letter to Warburton, written 21 February 1743/4, includes the confession "I have for some months thought myself going, and that not slowly, down the hill." As for his writings, "I would commit them to the Candor of a sensible and reflecting Judge, rather than to the Malice of every shortsighted and malevolent Critic or inadvertent and censorious reader" (Sherburn, IV 501)—a commendable attitude, no doubt, but not the spirit in which to undertake a final and meticulous revision of highly finished verse.

dalous characters then added to *To a Lady*, which were probably
printed from MS.,[1] Pope's practice seems to have been to revise
printed pages,[2] probably pasted on to larger sheets of paper, from
1735a or *1735b* (which are textually almost indistinguishable ex-
cept in *To a Lady*) and *1735c*. The case of *To Cobham* is complicated
by Pope's evident use of *1735c* in a few passages, though most of the
poem was set up from *1735ab*. With the three other Epistles, *1735c*
was used all the time.

It is not clear why Pope selected either *1735ab* or *1735c* as the
basis for the final revision.[3] *1735d*, *1736*, and *1739* all include a
number of new readings that are unquestionably Pope's work and
their punctuation is on the whole superior to that of *1735c*. (They
were themselves printed from corrected copies of *1735c*, a fact
which seems to confirm Pope's special confidence in that edition;
1740, which adds no new readings, was printed from *1739*, and
1743, which also adds nothing that must be ascribed to Pope, from
1740.) Whatever the reason for this neglect it raises the crucial
question whether Pope can be said to have *rejected* the revisions in
1735d, *1736*, and *1739*. Three readings from *1735d*—all within a
few lines of each other at the beginning of *To a Lady*—reappear in
1744, but the other revisions in these three editions seem to have
been not so much discarded by Pope as overlooked.[4] If one of them
had provided the pasted-up sheets he used in preparing *1744*,

---

1. See Pope to Warburton, 5 or 12 April 1744 (Sherburn, IV 515): "Pray send
me the Epistle on Women in Manuscript." The privately printed leaf included
in the Prince of Wales's set of Pope's *Works* now at Harvard (see p. xxxvi above)
differs so much from the *1744* text that the latter could hardly have been set up
from it, however drastically it was corrected.

2. Cf. the reference to "the Copies already printed" of *To Bathurst* in the letter
to Warburton of 15 November 1743 (Sherburn, IV 480).

3. *1735c* was the first edition with elaborate footnotes (all of which are retained
or expanded in *1744*), and its proofs may well have been read by Pope himself.
1735ab were respectively a folio and quarto; both, that is, provided more
generous margins than the octavos for MS. corrections and additions.

4. One or two other *1736d–43* revisions do turn up in *1744*. Pope may have
stored them away in his capacious memory, or they may have been available to
him in the collations that the younger Richardson prepared for him, though it
is difficult to prove that Pope made *any* use of the collations in 1743–4, The col-
lations of *To Bathurst* and *To Burlington* by Richardson now in the Huntington
Library are of the MSS. and not of the early editions.

instead of *1735ab* or *1735c*, it is a moral certainty that its punctuation, and with it the readings in a few passages, would be other than they are.

Similar considerations apply at an earlier stage of the four Epistles' textual evolution. For *To Cobham 1744* generally relies on *1735ab* and so by-passes, except for two or three pages, *1735c*, which was an independent revision of the poem's first edition. The fact that its *1735c* readings only appear in *1744* in passages which the spelling and punctuation show were actually printed from pasted-up sheets of that edition strongly suggests that Pope had forgotten the new and often brilliant readings he had introduced in *1735c*. And the passages in *To Cobham* that are based on *1735c* paste-ups show a similar ignorance of *1735ab*'s revisions. The *1735c* texts of *To Bathurst* and *To Burlington* derive from *1735ab* and so raise no problem of by-passings, but with *To a Lady* the position is much the same as with *To Cobham*. Its *1744* text derives from corrected paste-ups of *1735c*, and *1735c* is an independent revision of the poem's first edition which shows no awareness of the revisions in either *1735a* or *1735b* (*To a Lady* is the one Epistle where these two editions have substantially different texts).

The Overlooked Revision, as it may be called, raises a nice question of editorial policy. In the face of the evidence I have summarized—particular examples are discussed in the textual notes as well as in each Epistle's Note on the Text—*1744* cannot be considered sacrosanct, to be reproduced *verbatim et literatim*, even after Warburton's intrusions have been eliminated. On the other hand, mere eclecticism, with the editor picking and choosing as a variant catches his fancy, would be too erratic and subjective a way out. The compromise I have adopted is to give *1744*'s revisions the priority, where they are unquestionably Pope's and not Warburton's, but to print an Overlooked Revision where *1744* merely reproduces the text of the first edition. I share with Dr Johnson and Mr George Sherburn "the general opinion that Pope seldom altered without improvement".[1] Translated into a textual principle this

---

1. "Pope at Work" (*Essays on the Eighteenth Century presented to David Nichol Smith*, 1945, p. 62). Johnson's verdict on Pope's "parental attention" to his works was, "It will seldom be found that he altered without adding clearness, elegance, or vigour" (*Lives of the Poets*, III 221–2).

conviction might be stated as follows: *Other things being equal any revision conclusively attributable to Pope must normally be preferred to the original reading.*[1] During the last seven or eight months of his life, with Warburton and failing health both threatening his judgement, other things were not always equal, as the mere existence of so many Overlooked Revisions in these Epistles suggests, apart altogether from the external evidence. But the Overlooked Revisions themselves date from his most brilliant years—1734 to 1739—and their claims to admission into the text, when not actually superseded by an obviously superior reading in *1744*, appear to be conclusive.

Spelling and Punctuation. The *1744* spellings are generally sensible and consistent, and I have considered it an unnecessary pedantry to retain the occasional deviations, like "wou'd" (*To Cobham*, l. 33, but elsewhere "would", "could", "should") or "wast" (*To Burlington*, l. 3, but "waste" *To Burlington*, l. 15, and generally). Pope was careful, like Milton, to keep a decasyllabic façade in his versification, and an apostrophe regularly takes the place of the unstressed vowel in such words as *pow'r, Play'r, Av'rice, diff'rence, ev'n, Heav'n, Reas'ning, Dev'l,* or *Ven'son,* whenever the second syllable is not to "count" metrically. In such cases, where the apostrophe has been omitted or put in the wrong place, I have silently supplied it. Apostrophes were also often omitted in the eighteenth century at the close of a quotation or a piece of direct speech, but as Pope generally gives them I have inserted them wherever they are missing in *1744*. The punctuation of *1744* is always intelligible, though its reluctance to use a dash can lead to obscurities; I have hardly ever found it necessary to emend. I have also retained the conventional use of a question mark to indicate vague wonder, "a tone slightly different from exclamation".[2]

Capitals and Italics. Pope's note to Bowyer, of 3 March 1744, suggests a fairly cut-and-dried body of typographical convention:

On Second thoughts, let the Proof of the Epistle to Lord

---

1. It follows that a revision by Pope in the final text (*1744* for these Epistles) and an Overlooked Revision have, in general, equal authority. In cases like *To Bathurst*, 265 (p. 115 below) the editor must print the reading that seems preferable to him on stylistic grounds alone.

2. Sherburn, I xxvi.

Cobham, I, be done in the *Quarto*, not the *Octavo*, size: contrive the Capitals and evry thing exactly to correspond with that Edition.[1]

By "Edition" Pope must have meant format (though the *OED* does not recognize the sense). If I am right in thinking that the revision of the text for *1744* had been mainly carried out on sheets of *1735c* the point of these amended instructions to the printer is clear: *1735c* was an octavo, and the earlier volumes of the definitive edition (*The Dunciad, An Essay on Man, An Essay on Criticism*) had all been in quarto. Pope's "first thoughts" had overlooked the fact that *1735c*, following the octavo convention, was not only more heavily capitalized than the quartos but also made much use of italic type (which even the 1735 quartos use sparingly). Pope's readiness at this stage to leave whatever changes of style the new format required to Bowyer suggests that he did not take "the Capitals and evry thing" very solemnly. But the use of initial capitals in *1744* has a certain importance as a signpost to the words that the reader is required to emphasize. In the quartos of this period capital letters have something of the same function as italics in the octavos—in which the capitals are used so freely as to be almost meaningless—and they are generally confined to proper names, technical terms, and other key words (almost all of them nouns). Occasionally Bowyer and his men allowed themselves to be hypnotized by the functionless capitals of their octavo "copy", but as Pope and Warburton apparently did not mind I have preserved all the *1744* capitals.

Pope's notes, etc. The first editions have a few short explanatory notes, clearly by Pope himself, which are extended and elaborated in *1735c*. I have reprinted all of Pope's notes; the insertion of brackets has generally made it possible to show their precise textual evolution up to the final form reached in *1744*. These notes are all signed P. in this edition, as in Warburton's various editions and their successors, to distinguish them from later editorial comment. As explained in the Introduction, the verbose paraphrases added by Warburton in *1744* have normally been dropped—in spite of the probability that they must have received Pope's silent approval. They have little or no critical interest. *1735c* also disperses among

---

1. Sherburn, IV 504.

the notes separate sentences or clauses from the "Arguments" that were prefixed for the first time in *1735a*, where all four are grouped together before *To Cobham*. In most of the other editions before *1744* the "Arguments" appear in effect twice, as wholes preceding the separate Epistles and as parts in the notes. In *1744* this duplication was eliminated, *To a Lady*'s "Argument" only surviving dispersed through the notes and those of the other three Epistles immediately preceding each poem. The "Arguments" were part of the framework that the Epistles inherited from the *Essay on Man*; though these gestures towards philosophical rigour are of no importance they can scarcely be excluded from an edition of Pope's poems.

NOTE ON THE ILLUSTRATIONS

Frontispiece. Hogarth's print—generally referred to as "Taste" or "The Man of Taste" or "Burlington Gate", though it was actually issued without any title at all—is usually dated 1731. As *Of Taste, An Epistle to the . . . Earl of Burlington,* the poem by Pope that it caricatures, was only published on 13 December 1731, the print cannot have been on sale much before the end of that year. On the other hand, its re-engraving, not by Hogarth, for the Grub-Street attack on Pope's poem called *A Miscellany on Taste,* which was published on 15 January 1731/2, suggests that its date cannot be later than the first few days of 1732. The coach that Pope is bespattering is certainly that of the Duke of Chandos, whom Pope was suspected of satirizing in the poem as "Timon", and part of the Chandos coat-of-arms is to be seen on the coach's door at the edge of the print. The note "not a Duke's Coach as appears by yᵉ Crescent at one Corner" was perhaps intended to parody the somewhat lame disclaimers that Pope had sent to the newspapers. (See Appendix B, p. 172 below.) It will be noticed that there *are* ducal coronets on the other corners of the coach. The elaborate gate that provides the background of the print is that of Burlington House, Piccadilly—it was removed in 1868—and the labourer climbing up the ladder with more whitewash is probably Lord Burlington himself. Burlington and his gate had already appeared in Hogarth's earlier print "Masquerades and Operas" (1724). In both prints the gate is surmounted by a statue of William Kent, the painter, architect, and landscape gardener, who was Pope's friend and Burlington's protégé. Kent was a special *bête noire* of Hogarth's, because he had recently supplanted Sir James Thornhill, Hogarth's father-in-law and a much better painter than Kent, in the favour of the Court. John Nichols asserts (*Biographical Anecdotes of William Hogarth,* 1781, p. 18) that Hogarth, fearing retaliation by Pope, withdrew the print and destroyed the plate, but the assertion is not repeated in his second edition (1782), which was "enlarged and corrected". However, Nichols adds in this edition (p. 153) that a copy of the print had turned up endorsed as follows:

Boᵗ this book of Mr. *Wayte,* at *The Fountain Tavern,* in *The*

Strand, in the presence of Mr. *Draper*, who told me he had it of the
Printer, Mr. *W. Rayner*.   *J. Cosins*.

This attested memorandum may have been the first step in a pro-
jected prosecution of Hogarth by Pope. Cosins, according to
Nichols, "was an attorney"—perhaps the James Cosin, who was
described by the *London Magazine*, when he died in September
1746, as "an eminent Attorney at Law". In the end Pope and Kent
got their revenge by pulling strings at Court. "Queen Caroline was
prepared to patronize Hogarth, and had commanded him to paint
a conversation piece of the Royal Family, and also gave him per-
mission to make sketches of Princess Anne's wedding to the Prince
of Orange, from which he proposed publishing engravings. But
Kent used his influence to prevent Hogarth carrying out these pro-
jects, and the Lord Chamberlain in person insisted on Hogarth's
being turned out. These intrigues were, in Vertue's phrase (*Note-
books*, Walpole Society, vol. xxii, p. 68), 'sad mortifications to the
Ingenious Man. But its the effect of the Carricatures with which he
has hertofore Touch't Mr. Kent and diverted the town—which
now he is like to pay for when he has least thought on it' " (Margaret
Jourdain, *The Work of William Kent*, 1948, p. 39).

Portrait facing p. 48. By Jan van der Vaart (1647–1721), a Dutch-
man settled in London, who began by painting in the costumes and
landscape backgrounds in the portraits of his fashionable com-
patriot Willem Wissing, and later set up as a portraitist on his own.
The picture is described in Sir Nevile R. Wilkinson's *Wilton House
Pictures* (1907), vol. ii, p. 371. The low dress is blue in colour with
white sleeves. Wilkinson attributed the painting to Wissing, but
when cleaned in 1936 it was found to be by van der Vaart. Mar-
garet Sawyer (d. 1706) became the first wife of the eighth Earl of
Pembroke in 1684. As the companion picture of her husband *is* the
work of Wissing, who died in 1687, it is probable that van der
Vaart painted the Countess *c.* 1684–7. Both portraits are still at
Wilton.

CHRONOLOGICAL TABLE

The standard biographies are G. Sherburn's *The Early Career of Alexander Pope*, 1934, and W. J. Courthope's life in vol. v of the Elwin-Courthope edition of Pope's works, 1871–89. Sherburn's account stops in 1727.

1688 (May 21) Alexander Pope born in London of elderly parents.

c.1700 Pope's family moved to Binfield, in Windsor Forest, [?] to comply with anti-Catholic regulations.
Death of Dryden.

c.1705 Pope started to make acquaintance with the literary society of London.

1709 (May) The *Pastorals* published in the sixth part of Tonson's *Miscellanies*.

1711 (May) *An Essay on Criticism* published; praised in *The Spectator* by Addison, and damned by Dennis.

1712 (May) The *Messiah* published by Steele in *The Spectator*. Lintot's *Miscellany* published, containing the first version of *The Rape of the Lock*, and other poems by Pope. Pope was becoming acquainted with Swift, Gay, Parnell, and Arbuthnot, who together formed the Scriblerus Club.

1713 (March) *Windsor Forest*.
(April) Addison's *Cato* first acted, with a prologue by Pope. Pope was contributing to Steele's *Guardian*.
(October) Proposals issued for a translation of the *Iliad*.

1714 (March) The enlarged version of *The Rape of the Lock*.
(August) Death of Queen Anne.

1715 (February) *The Temple of Fame.*
(June 6) The *Iliad*, Books I–IV, published; followed two days
later by Tickell's translation of *Iliad* I. During this year [?]
Pope wrote his character of Addison, and became acquaint-
ed with Lady Mary Wortley Montagu.

1716 (March) *Iliad*, vol. II.
Pope's revenge by poison on Curll the publisher [Sherburn,
ch. VI].
(April) Pope's family sold the house at Binfield, and settled
at Chiswick, where their neighbour was Lord Burlington.

1717 (January) *Three Hours after Marriage* by Pope, Gay, and
Arbuthnot, first acted.
(June) *Iliad*, vol. III.
The collected volume of Pope's *Works*, containing *Verses to
the Memory of an Unfortunate Lady* and *Eloisa to Abelard.*
(October) Pope's father died.

1718 (June) *Iliad*, vol. IV.
Death of Parnell. Pope and his mother moved to Twicken-
ham late in the year.

1719 Death of Addison.

1720 (May) *Iliad*, vols. V and VI.

1721 (September) The *Epistle to Addison* prefixed to Tickell's
edition of Addison's *Works.*
(December) The *Epistle to Oxford* prefixed to Pope's edition
of Parnell's *Poems.*

1723 (January) Pope's edition of John Sheffield, Duke of Buck-
ingham's *Works* published, and seized by the Government
on suspicion of Jacobitish passages.
(May) Pope called before the House of Lords as a witness at
Atterbury's trial.

1725 (March) Pope's edition of Shakespeare published in six volumes.
(April) *Odyssey*, vols. I–III.
Bolingbroke returned from exile, and settled near Pope at Dawley Farm, Uxbridge.

1726 (March) Theobald's *Shakespeare Restored: or, a Specimen of the Many Errors ... Committed ... by Mr Pope.*
(June) *Odyssey*, vols. IV–V.
Pope visited by Swift. *Gulliver's Travels* published in October.

1727 (June) Pope-Swift *Miscellanies*, vols. I and II.
Swift's second visit to Pope.

1728 (March) Pope-Swift *Miscellanies*, "last" volume.
(May) *The Dunciad*, in three books, with Theobald as hero.

1729 (April) *The Dunciad Variorum.*

1731 (December) *Epistle to Burlington* [Moral Essay IV].

1732 (October) Pope-Swift *Miscellanies*, "third" volume.
(December) Death of Gay.

1733 (January) *Epistle to Bathurst* [Moral Essay III].
(February) The first *Imitation of Horace* [Sat. II i].
(February–May) *An Essay on Man*, Epistles I–III.
(June) Death of Pope's mother.

1734 (January) *Epistle to Cobham* [Moral Essay I].
An Essay on Man, Epistle IV.
(July) *Imitation of Horace* [Sat. II ii].
(December) *Sober Advice from Horace.*

1735 (January) *Epistle to Dr Arbuthnot.*
(February) *Of the Characters of Women* [Moral Essay II].
Death of Arbuthnot.
(April) The *Works*, vol. II.
(May) Curll's edition of Pope's letters.
Bolingbroke returned to France.

1737 (April) *Imitation of Horace* [Ep. II ii].
(May) Pope's edition of his letters.
Imitation of Horace [Ep. II i].
An Essay on Man attacked by Crousaz, Professor of Mathematics and Philosophy at Lausanne.

1738 (January–March) *Imitations of Horace* [Eps. I vi and I i].
(May–July) *Epilogue to the Satires.*
Warburton commenced his replies to Crousaz.
Pope visited by Bolingbroke.

1740 (April) Pope's first meeting with Warburton.

1742 (March) *The New Dunciad* [i.e. Book IV].

1743 (October) *The Dunciad* in four books with Cibber enthroned in the place of Theobald.

1744 (May 30) Death of Pope.

LIST OF THE PRINCIPAL POEMS
of Pope to be found in the other volumes

ABBREVIATIONS

used in the Introduction and in the footnotes

AUDRA = L'Influence française dans l'œuvre de Pope. Par E. Audra. Paris, 1931.

CARRUTHERS = Carruthers's notes on the *Moral Essays* in his edition of Pope's *Poetical Works* (4 vols., 1853), vol. III.

DILKE = A copy of Carruthers's edition of Pope with MS. notes by C. W. Dilke (British Museum, 12274 i. 15).

EC = Pope's Works. Ed. W. Elwin and W. J. Courthope. 10 vols., 1871–89.

GEC = The Complete Peerage. By G. E. C. Revised by Vicary Gibbs. 13 vols., 1910–40.

GRIFFITH = Alexander Pope. A Bibliography. By R. H. Griffith. 1 vol. in two parts, 1922, 1927.

HERVEY MEMOIRS = Memoirs of the Reign of George II. By John, Lord Hervey. Ed. R. Sedgwick. 3 vols., 1931.

JB = Information supplied by Professor J. Butt.

JOHNSON, LIVES OF THE POETS = Lives of the English Poets. By Samuel Johnson. Ed. G. Birkbeck Hill. 3 vols., 1905.

LADY MARY'S LETTERS = The Letters and Works of Lady Mary Wortley Montagu. Ed. Lord Wharncliffe. 2 vols., 1893.

NICHOLS = Literary Anecdotes of the Eighteenth Century. By John Nichols. The 9 vol. ed. of 1812–15 used.

OED = Oxford English Dictionary.

P = Note by Pope; usually followed by dates of the editions in which it was printed.

PERCY MS = notes apparently by Thomas Percy on Epistles I to III (Bodleian MS. Percy b2, ff. 63–4).

SHERBURN = The Correspondence of Alexander Pope. Edited by George Sherburn. 5 vols., 1956.

SHERBURN, EARLY CAREER = The Early Career of Alexander Pope. By George Sherburn, 1934.

SPENCE = Anecdotes . . . of Books and Men. By Joseph Spence. Ed. S. W. Singer. 1820.

Suffolk Letters=Letters to and from Henrietta, Countess of Suffolk. 2 vols., 1824.

Wakefield = Observations on Pope. By Gilbert Wakefield. 1796.

Walpole, Fraser Marginalia=Notes on the Poems of Alexander Pope, by Horatio, Earl of Orford, contributed by Sir William Augustus Fraser from the copy in his possession. 1876.

Walpole, Huntington Marginalia=Walpole's Marginalia in *Additions to Pope* (1776). By George Sherburn. Huntington Library Quarterly, vol. I, 1938.

Warburton =William Warburton's notes on the *Moral Essays* in the large octavo edition of Pope's works, 1751, vol. III.

Warton =Joseph Warton's notes on the *Moral Essays* in his edition of Pope's Works, 1797, vol. III.

Warton's Essay=An Essay on the Writings and Genius of Pope. By Joseph Warton. 2 vols., 1756, 1782.

EPISTLES
TO
SEVERAL PERSONS
[MORAL ESSAYS]

Est brevitate opus, ut currat sententia, neu se
Impediat verbis lassis onerantibus aures:
Et sermone opus est modo tristi, sæpe jocoso,
Defendente vicem modo Rhetoris atque Poetæ,
Interdum urbani, parcentibus viribus, atque
Extenuantis eas consultò.—HOR.
[*Sat.* I. x. 9–14]

EPISTLE I

To RICHARD TEMPLE, VISCOUNT COBHAM

NOTE ON THE TEXT

The first edition of *To Cobham* is a twenty-page folio, which, though dated 1733, was not in fact published until 16 January 1733/4. As in the case of *To Burlington* the poem was given two different titles. The title-page's is *An Epistle To The Right Honourable Richard Lord Visc*. *Cobham*, whereas the half-title has *Of The Knowledge and Characters of Men: To Richard Lord Cobham*. Octavo reprints (London and Dublin) followed in the same year, both apparently unauthorized,[1] and in 1735 the poem was grouped with *To a Lady*, *To Bathurst*, and *To Burlington* in *The Works of Mr Alexander Pope*, vol. II, as the first of the "Ethic Epistles, the Second Book". Pope took almost as much trouble with this collection as with its successor the "death-bed" edition, apparently employing the younger Jonathan Richardson as a kind of sub-editor.[2] The

---

1. The Dublin edition—by Swift's printer George Faulkner—should perhaps be described as semi-authorized. Pope's promise to send Swift a copy of the first edition before its publication in England, "which I conclude will be grateful to your bookseller on whom you please to bestow them so early" (Sherburn, III 401), suggests something more than a mere condoning of Faulkner's piracies. Moreover the Dublin edition's reading "quick" in l. 201 anticipates Pope's revision of the line in the 1735 collections. Perhaps Swift's copy had a MS. correction by Pope for this line? Faulkner or Swift, however, mistakenly assumed that "J**n" in l. 158 stood for Janssen (instead of Johnston) and inserted the following very Swiftian note:

   Sir Theodore Jaunssen, one of the Directors of the *South-Sea* Company in the year 1720, who amassed such vast sums of money that he settled upon each of his six children *only* sixty thousand pounds; and yet pleaded poverty, to the House of *Commons*, when under examination.

   There are copies in which the leaf containing this note has been cancelled and an insert pasted in of the same lines without any note. Presumably Pope had pointed the error out to Swift.

2. According to Richardson himself (*Richardsoniana*, 1776, p. 264) he had suggested to Pope the "making an edition of his works in the manner of *Boileau*'s", and Pope then set him to collate the MSS. of the *E. on Man* and the *E. on Criticism* with the printed editions. This is confirmed by a letter from Pope to the elder Richardson of 17 June [1737], from which it appears that Richardson junior had "mark'd, collated, and studied" Pope's poems by then (Sherburn, IV 78). Some of Richardson's collations, on the margins of pages of the quarto *Works*, vol. II, are now in the Huntington Library, including some of early drafts of *To Bathurst*

nature of the textual problems created by his extensive revisions of the poem both in the folio (*1735a*), quarto (*1735b*), and first octavo (*1735c*) editions of *The Works*, vol. II, and in the "death-bed" *Epistles to Several Persons* (*1744*), has already been summarized in the General Note on the Text. *1735a* adds six lines to *To Cobham* and emends the phrasing in eighteen other passages; *1735b* follows *1735a* minutely, though reverting to the readings of the first edition in three places (ll. 185, 198, 199); *1735c*, which appears to have been set up from a copy of the first edition, ignores most of *1735a*'s emendations and contributes four new readings. The omission of *1735a*'s changes by *1735c* presumably explains why Pope used pasted-up sheets of *1735a* as the main basis for the revision of 1744. The spelling, punctuation, and typography make it plain, how-ever, that some passages in *1744* must derive from pasted-up sheets of *1735c*.[1] Ll. 76*ff*, 125*ff*, and 195*ff* are certainly in this category, and there may well be others. (The variations in spelling, etc., are insufficiently frequent for exact termini to be identified; they do not generally coincide with either *1735a* or *1735c* pages.) It follows that Overlooked Revisions, in the sense defined in the General Note on the Text, may be expected (i) from *1735c* in passages where *1744* has been based on *1735a*, and (ii) from *1735a* in pas-sages where *1735c* has been the basis. The readings I have adopted are in fact all from passages of the second type (ll. 76, 126, and 201). In l. 121 *1735a*'s "that" might seem to qualify (instead of "who"), but the punctuation makes it clear that *1744* has been set up from *1735a* in this passage, and Pope must therefore have deliberately decided to return here to the reading of the first edition. Similar considerations seem to exclude "Acton" (l. 135), "a joke" (l. 185),

---

and *To Burlington*. The "Variations" collected at the end of the folio and quarto to *Works*, vol. II, apparently represent an earlier collation. Richardson may also have been responsible for the elaborate "Arguments" and analytical notes in the 1735 editions. The "Arguments" are competently done, but there are one or two slips and clumsinesses (see, for example, pp. 13 and 22 below) that make it virtually certain they were not compiled by Pope. Richardson, or whoever the collator was, may also have contributed some, though certainly not all, of the explanatory notes.

1. This edition was the first to include the elaborate footnotes with which Pope gradually filled out his *Works*, vol. II. Its partial use as the "copy" for *1744* must have saved much laborious transcription.

and the couplet about "Affections" (after l. 161) from the Over-looked Revisions, though an element of uncertainty remains in all these instances. I have also excluded from the text the four lines about Marlborough that were added in *1735a* and retained in all the editions of *Works*, vol. II, and its successors until *1744* when the page was cancelled (see note on l. 143) and a new leaf printed and pasted in.

This cancel was probably ordered by Pope, so as not to offend the Dowager Duchess of Marlborough, though the corrected proof was not actually checked by Warburton until 20 June 1744, when Pope had been dead for four weeks. About Warburton's respon-sibility, however, for the transposition of five passages in *1744*—involving in all seventy-five lines (more than a quarter of the whole poem)—there can be little doubt. No explanation is offered of the transpositions in *1744*, but Warburton has prefixed a character-istic note to the 1751 *Works*: "Whoever compares this with the former Editions of this poem, will observe that the order and dis-position of the several parts are entirely changed and transposed, tho' with hardly the Alteration of a single Word. When the Editor, at the Author's desire, first examined this Epistle, he was surprised to find it contain a number of fine observations, without order, connexion, or dependence: but much more so, when, on an atten-tive review, he saw, that, if put into a different form, on an idea he then conceived, it would have all the clearness of method, and force of connected reasoning. Indeed the observations then appeared to him so jumbled and confounded in one another, as if the several parts of a regular poem had been rolled up in tickets, drawn at ran-dom, and then set down as they arose. The author appeared as much struck with the observation as the editor, and agreed to put it in the present form, which has given the poem all the justness of a true composition. The introduction of the epistle on Riches was in the same condition, and underwent the same reform."

This note makes it clear that it was Warburton who was pri-marily responsible for the transpositions. It was Warburton, not Pope, who spotted, or thought he had spotted, the incoherence of the original version. And it was Warburton, again without any help from Pope, who got the "idea" which was to bring order into the earlier chaos. All that Pope did was to agree "to put it [the poem] in the present form". Warburton's statement that the change was made "with hardly the Alteration of a single Word" is literally true. A small emendation was made in l. 31, and in l. 51 the change of "the grave" to "the Sage" may have been dictated by Warburton's "idea". But otherwise the only alterations are the transpositions. This fact alone makes it almost certain that Pope's rôle in the business was merely one of passive acceptance. It is true that the reshuffling of couplets and passages was an old habit of Pope's, both before and after publication, but in the poems that he himself recast the way is smoothed for the structural alterations by verbal emendations. The changes of order are accompanied by more or less elaborate changes of phrase or epithet. If Pope had made the Warburton transpositions his own instead of accepting them cut-and-dried from his mentor, it is inconceivable that he would not have made the minor textual adjustments which are required to smooth out some awkwardnesses that resulted.[1]

The transpositions, then, were Warburton's and Warburton's only. What was the "idea" from which they originated? Briefly it was to continue and elaborate the distinction in the poem's opening lines between the philosopher and the man of the world. In the early editions Pope, having made this distinction and having shown that both types are fallible, had passed on to discuss the general complexity of mental phenomena. Warburton's "idea" was to break up this part of the poem (ll. 1–173) into two sections, ll. 1–98 treating of "the difficulties in coming at the *Knowledge* and true *Characters of Men*", and ll. 99–173 dealing with "the *wrong means* which both *Philosophers* and *Men of the World* have employed in surmounting those difficulties". And by the drastic use of scissors and paste, and by pretending that ll. 51*ff* refer to the philosopher (as opposed to the man of the world) and ll. 87*ff* to the man of the world (as opposed to the philosopher), he does manage, with the help of his "Commentary", to give the division a certain air of plausibility.

But Warburton's complacency with his "idea" has not been shared by later editors. Carruthers considered that "the whole of this boasted emendation is not of the slightest value" and regretted that "Pope yielded such implicit submission to the pedantic sug-

---

1. For some examples see pp. 9–10 below.

gestions of his friend".[1] And Dilke[2] and Courthope[3] are equally explicit. But, though the editors have grumbled, they have continued to reprint Warburton's text. In this edition I have preferred to restore the poem to the order it was in before Warburton began to "reform" it.

The case for the Warburton transpositions can be put in one sentence. The transpositions are undeniably all in *1744* which Pope apparently intended to be the final and authoritative edition of the poem. Pope must therefore have approved of them. And the case against the transpositions consequently is that Pope was wrong in approving of them. As with most of Warburton's other suggestions this can be shown by two different lines of argument: (i) that the transpositions spoil the poem; (ii) that at the time they were made Pope was in no condition to stand up to Warburton and what Mr Sherburn has nicely called his "ratiocinative virtuosity".

Warburton's initial premise was that Pope's poem was "without order, connexion, or dependence". This is simply not true. There is perhaps no formal logical structure, but this would have been inappropriate in a Horatian epistle and the poem evolves sufficiently clearly and comprehensibly. The argument of ll. 1–173, before Warburton's rearrangement, can be summarized as follows:

I. Generalizations upon mental phenomena, whether by the philosopher (ll. 1–8) or the man of the world (ll. 9–14), are equally fallible.

II. Reasons for this.
(i) Each individual mind is in some respects unique (ll. 15–18).
(ii) Even a single mind is variable and not self-consistent (ll. 19–22).
(iii) The temperamental differences between observers complicate matters (ll. 23–8).

---

1. I 371.

2. Dilke's MS. note on the passage in his copy of Carruthers (now in the British Museum) runs as follows: "Where is the proof beyond Warburton's assertion, that Pope did yield. Warburton has said enough to awaken attention, & whoever reprints should I think compare Warburton's edit. with the last edit. pub. by P. & consider from which he should reprint."

3. EC, III 50–1.

(iv) The fluctuating character of mental phenomena makes permanently valid generalizations impossible (ll. 29–40).

(v) We are not even trustworthy observers of our own mental processes, many of which are subconscious (ll. 41–50).

III. Illustrations from history and common experience of typical errors.

(i) Actions are no reliable guide to motives (ll. 51–70).

(ii) Difficulty of discriminating between more and less significant actions (ll. 71–84).

(iii) The historian tends to attribute exalted motives to personages of exalted station (ll. 85–100).

(iv) In the middle classes moral characteristics become attached to particular professions (ll. 101–9).

IV. Examples of inconsistencies of character.

(i) Although some characters can be easily read (ll. 110–21), most are puzzlingly inconsistent (ll. 122–9).

(ii) Illustrations of this in an M.P. (ll. 130–5), Catius (ll. 136–9), Patritio (ll. 140–5), and some well-known historical figures (ll. 146–53).

(iii) Human nature is essentially unstable (ll. 154–7).

(iv) What men say or do not say is equally no guide to their characters (ll. 158–67).

V. Conclusion. The various false clues (nature, actions, passions, opinions) are summed up and dismissed (ll. 168–73).[1]

Warburton's transpositions make nonsense of this scheme. His first alteration is to put II (iv) before II (iii), which obscures the fact that what Pope is stressing is the difficulty of *observing* mental processes accurately. His second major transposition is to remove the whole of III to follow l. 157. This upsets the logical order altogether by interrupting the natural transition from II to III, i.e. from the general complexity of mental phenomena to the typical errors which that complexity leads the observer into. The order of the

---

1. This analysis conflicts with Pope's "Argument"—if it was Pope's and not, as I suspect, Jonathan Richardson's or another's (see pp. 4–5 above)—in one or two details. The most serious difference is over the interpretation of ll. 101–9, which is discussed in the note on that passage.

items in v also becomes meaningless now. Clearly Pope had meant "Nature" there to refer to II, "Actions" to refer to III, and "Passions" to refer to IV; the transposition of the sections should have been followed by a revision of the conclusion. Finally there is the transposition, which Courthope thought "fortunate", of ll. 166–7 (which originally summed up the instability of men's political or religious opinions) to the end of v:

> Manners with Fortunes, Humours turn with Climes,
> Tenets with Books, and Principles with Times.

As an explanation of the different tunes Scoto and the "gay Freethinker" play under different circumstances the lines are admirable. But Warburton tries to make them sum up the whole of the previous two hundred lines of argument, and as such they are, it is clear, grotesquely inadequate.[1]

The transpositions, then, interfere with the course of Pope's argument. They also interfere with the effectiveness of the poetry. Thus Warburton transferred ll. 31–2:

> Life's stream for Observation will not stay,
> It hurries all too fast to mark their way,

out of its context of "depths", "shallows", "whirls", and "eddies" (to which "their" refers), with the result that the image loses all its vividness and the grammar becomes obscure. Another transposition led to an unnecessary clumsiness. In Warburton's text the "smart Free-thinker" is only divided by four lines from the "gay Free-thinker", although the two characters are totally disconnected. Pope had originally had over fifty lines between the two free-thinkers, and detached like this their repetition would not be noticed.[2]

---

1. The transposition of ll. 248–51 to precede l. 228 does not seem to have been part of Warburton's "idea". The motive in this case was apparently to tidy up the eight examples of the Ruling Passion "strong in death". Two of the eight episodes are strictly more concerned with old age than with death, and the transposition has the effect of grouping them together at the head of this section. This officious tidiness bears all the marks of the Warburtonian beast, but I cannot prove it against him and have therefore adopted the *1744* order. It has the advantage of providing examples of "our follies and our sins" (l. 226) in that sequence.

2. The "gay Free-thinker" (ll. 162–5) was one of the two passages added in

Why then did Pope consent to the transpositions? Partly no
doubt it was simply a particular instance of the unnecessary awe in
which he stood of his formidable commentator. This aspect of the
problem is discussed more fully in the Introduction (pp. xiv–xvi).
But Pope's subservience may also, I suspect, have been due to his
physical and mental condition when Warburton conceived his
"idea". The Pope-Warburton letters do not contain any references
to the transpositions in *To Cobham*, but they enable their approxi-
mate date to be ascertained. They cannot be later than 3 March
1743/4 when the MS. of the Epistle was in the printer's hands
(Sherburn, IV 504), and they are unlikely to be earlier than October
1743 when Warburton, having completed the commentary on the
Essay on Criticism, turned to the four Epistles (Sherburn, IV 474,
480). Apparently Pope did not see Warburton's notes on *To Cobham*
until January 1743/4 (Sherburn, IV 495). By then his health was
already failing, and he was tending to leave everything more and
more to Warburton. "I own," Pope wrote to him on 21 February
1743/4, "the late Encroachments upon my Constitution make me
willing to see the End of all further Care about *Me* or my *Works*.
I would rest, for the one, in a full Resignation of my Being to be
dispos'd of by the Father of all Mercy; and for the other (tho indeed
a Triffle, yet a Triffle may be some Example) I would commit them
to the Candor of a sensible and reflecting Judge, rather than to the
Malice of every short-sighted, and malevolent Critic or inadver-
tent and censorious reader; And no hand can set them in so good
a Light, or so well turn their best side to the day, as your own"
(Sherburn, IV 500–1). Warburton himself states that when he ex-
plained his "idea" Pope had "appeared as much struck with the
observation" as he had been. The qualification is significant. Was
it only *appearance*? The tone of Pope's letters later suggests that
other and more serious topics than his commentator's perverse in-
genuities were then occupying his time and his thoughts. With
death becoming daily more imminent he may well have given

1744. The lines must therefore have been inserted before Pope had heard about
Warburton's "idea". Pope's practice seems to have been to make his own re-
visions first and then send the emended text to Warburton to be fitted up with
notes and commentary, further revisions only being made at Warburton's sug-
gestion (see Pope to Warburton, 12 January [1743-4], Sherburn, IV 491).

Warburton what was virtually a textual *carte blanche*. But it seems unnecessary for the modern reader to extend to Warburton the same immunity.

The text printed here represents an attempt to reproduce Pope's final revisions *minus* the intrusions of Warburton. Apart from the correction of a few slips and misprints, the spelling, punctuation, and capitalization follow the British Museum's copy of *1744*, but the order of the paragraphs is that of the early editions. It is believed that in this way the poem is presented here in a sounder text than any that has hitherto been available.[1]

KEY TO THE CRITICAL APPARATUS

1733 = First edition, Griffith 329 (and a textually identical reprint, Griffith 330).

1734 = Dublin edition (Griffith 335)

1735*a* = Works, vol. II, large and small folio, Griffith 370, 371.

1735*b* = Works, vol. II, quarto, Griffith 372.

1735*c* = Works, vol. II, octavo, Griffith 388.

1735*d* = Works, vol. II, octavo, Griffith 389.

1736 = Works, vol. II, octavo, Griffith 430.

1739 = Works, vol. II, octavo, Griffith 505.

1740 = Works, vol. II, part i, octavo, Griffith 523.

1743 = Works, vol. II, part i, octavo, Griffith 583.

1744 = Epistles to Several Persons, Griffith 591.

1751 = Works, ed. Warburton, vol. III, large octavo, Griffith 645.

1. In order to facilitate references to the Warburton text line-numbers are given to it in brackets by the side of the line-numbers to the present text.

Readers who prefer the Warburton text can claim Dr Johnson as an ally. Edmond Malone, who had begun to prepare a new edition of Pope, which he abandoned when learning that Joseph Warton was already engaged on one, consulted Johnson on 15 March 1782 and received *inter alia* the following advice: "He said he thought whatever Warburton had done ought to be retained. Add as much as you will to his notes—but suppress nothing. He supposed that the new arrangement that W. had made of P's works was concerted between them before the death of Pope—& that therefore I had no right to alter it." (See James M. Osborn, "Johnson on the Sanctity of an Author's Text", *PMLA*, September 1935, L 928–9.)

ARGUMENT
OF
THE FIRST EPISTLE[1]
Of the Knowledge *and* Characters *of* MEN

THAT *it is not sufficient for this knowledge to consider Man in the* Abstract: Books *will not serve the purpose, nor yet our own Experience singly,* v. 1. *General maxims, unless they be formed upon both, will be but notional,* v. 9. *Some Peculiarity in every man, characteristic to himself, yet varying from himself,* v. 15. *The further difficulty of separating and fixing this, arising from our own Passions, Fancies, Faculties, &c.* v. 23. *The shortness of Life, to observe in, and the uncertainty of the* Principles of Action *in men, to observe by,* v. 29, &c. *Our own Principle of action often hid from ourselves* v. 41. *No judging of the* Motives *from the actions; the same actions proceeding from contrary Motives, and the same Motives influencing contrary actions,* v. 51. *Yet to form Characters, we can only take the strongest actions of a man's life, and try to make them agree: The*

5

10

Argument] *add. 1735a and reprinted in all the later editions except 1739. 1735c–43 also insert the separate sentences, with occasional minor changes, as footnotes to the poem. Errors and changes in the line numbers are not recorded below.*

1 *it . . . knowledge*] *for this Knowledge it is not sufficient 1735c–43.*
2–3 Experience] Observation *1735a–43.*
5–6 *The further . . . arising*] *Difficulties arising 1744–51.*
9 *No judging*] *1744–51 transfer ll. 16–19* Some few . . . Nature *to precede this.*
11 *Yet to*] *1744–51 prefix* II.

---

1 This seems to mistake the sense of ll. 29–40 (where the real point is the rapidity of succeeding impressions on the stream of consciousness and not the brevity of human life) as well as that of ll. 101–9 (see note on the passage). Jonathan Richardson may be responsible for the analyses (see p. 5). Warburton's transpositions involved some rearrangement of the Argument, but the work was done in a very perfunctory way. Thus although "Clodio" becomes "Wharton" in the text, "Clodio" is retained in the Argument.

utter uncertainty of this, from Nature *itself, and from* Policy, v. 71. Characters *given according to the* rank *of men in the world,* v. 87. *And some reason for it,* v. 93. Education *alters the* Nature, *or at least* Character *of many,* v. 101. *Some few Characters plain, but in general confounded, dissembled, or inconsistent,* v. 122. *The same man utterly different in different places and seasons,* v. 130. *Unimaginable weaknesses in the greatest,* v. 140, &c. *Nothing constant and certain but* God *and* Nature, v. 154. Actions, Passions, Opinions, Manners, Humours, *or* Principles *all subject to change. No judging by* Nature, *from* v. 158 to 173. *It only remains to find (if we can) his* RULING PASSION : *That will certainly influence all the rest, and can reconcile the seeming or real inconsistency of all his actions,* v. 174. *Instanced in the extraordinary character of* Wharton, v. 179. *A caution against mistaking* second qualities *for* first, *which will destroy all possibility of the knowledge of mankind,* v. 210. *Examples of the strength of the* Ruling Passion, *and its continuation to the last breath,* v. 222, &c.

2 *in the world*] of the world *1744–51* (*no doubt to support Warburton's interpretation of the passage ; see Note on the Text, p. 7.*)

2 v. 87] *1735a–43* om.

8 v. 154] *1735a–43 read Of Man we cannot judge, by his* Nature, *his* Actions, *his* Passions, *his* Opinions, *his* Manners.

9 *change*] change, 160 &c. *1735a–43.*   *No* . . . Nature] *Add. 1744–51.*

9–10 *It only*] *1744–51 prefix* III.

11 *and can*] and only can *1735a–43.*

13 Wharton] Clodio *1735a–51.*

EPISTLE I.

To Sir RICHARD TEMPLE,
Lord Viscount COBHAM

Y ES, you despise the man to Books confin'd,
    Who from his study rails at human kind;
    Tho' what he learns, he speaks and may advance
Some gen'ral maxims, or be right by chance.
The coxcomb bird, so talkative and grave,   5
That from his cage cries Cuckold, Whore, and Knave,

Heading] An Epistle to the Right Honourable *Richard* Lord Visc.ᵗ
Cobham 1733–4; Epistle I. to Sir *Richard Temple*, Lord *Cobham*
1751.

The line numbers in brackets are those of Warburton's editions and the
reprints descending from them, including EC.

Heading] First printed in 1733. [P. *1739–43*.] Sir Richard Temple (1675–1749),
Whig politician and soldier (Lieutenant General 1710), was raised to the peer-
age as Viscount Cobham on the Hanoverian succession, and became a Field
Marshal in 1742. He opposed the Government in the debates on the Excise Bill
(1733) and was deprived of his regiment a few months later for protesting against
Walpole's refusal to allow further inquiry into the affairs of the South Sea Com-
pany. From this time onwards until Walpole's fall, Cobham was one of the
Opposition Whigs.

The intervals of Cobham's active life were passed at the family seat of Stowe,
where he entertained his friends and erected monuments and temples to their
memories in the elaborate landscape gardens. Pope made Cobham's acquaint-
ance about 1725 (see a letter to Caryll, dated 17 July 1735), and in later years
Stowe became a frequent house of call on his summer travels. Pope told Caryll
that he did not write letters to Cobham, "yet esteem as much as any friend he
has" (Sherburn, III 474). Cobham's two surviving letters to Pope (Egerton MS.,
1949, ff. 1, 2 and Sherburn, III 391–2, 393–4), both full of the shrewd casual com-
ments of a clever man of the world, show that this esteem was mutual.

5–8. Cf.   If he call Rogue and Rascal from a Garrat,
               He means you no more Mischief than a Parat.
Dryden, *Absalom and Achitophel. The Second Part*, 425–6 [Wakefield]. Johnson
(*Lives of the Poets*, III 187) assumed the bird is a magpie. The epithet "coxcomb"
would be particularly appropriate to a cockatoo (G. K. Hunter).

Tho' many a passenger he rightly call,
You hold him no Philosopher at all.
　　And yet the fate of all extremes is such,
Men may be read, as well as Books too much.　　　　10
To Observations which ourselves we make,
We grow more partial for th' observer's sake;
To written Wisdom, as another's, less:
Maxims are drawn from Notions, these from Guess.

9　is] are *1735b* (*but corrected in Errata*).
14　these] those *1733–35b* (*but 1735ab Errata correct to* these), *1744–51*.

---

14. *Notions*] Defined by Locke as complex ideas, with "their original and constant existence more in the thoughts of men than in the reality of things" (*Essay on Human Understanding*, bk II, ch. 22, § 2). Locke, however, treats "notions" and "maxims" as convertible terms (ibid., bk IV, ch. vii, § 12). The whole of this passage reflects Pope's interest in Locke. Pope considered him a closer and more accurate reasoner than any classical or French philosopher (Spence, p. 199). He also admired Locke's style (Spence, p. 291). Compare too the English translation of La Rochefoucauld, *Moral Maxims and Reflections*, 1694, p. 147: "There is no Man, but may find great Advantage from *Learning*; but then it is as true, that there are few who do not find great prejudice too, from the Notions they acquire by Studies."

these] i.e. observations. Warburton's idea that the passage is an oblique criticism of La Rochefoucauld is unlikely. If Pope had intended to reflect upon *Les Maximes* he would not have used the word *maxim* for the *a priori* generalizations of the "man to Books confin'd", which he contrasts with the *guesses* of the man-of-the-world observer (like La Rochefoucauld). It is just possible, however, that l. 10 is a reminiscence of the maxim which appears in the 1706 English translation (p. 94) as " 'Tis more necessary to Study Men, than Books." See Audra, pp. 512–13. The general sceptical argument developed in the first half of the Epistle derives from Montaigne rather than La Rochefoucauld. The notes that Spence took of Pope's conversation in the first week of May 1730, when the poem was being drafted, make this clear. (They are printed in full in the Introduction, pp. xx *ff* above.) After reciting some examples of human inconsistency, Pope said, "Montaigne hence concludes Pyrrhonically, That nothing can be known of the Workings of men's minds," and he then referred Spence to the first essay of Book II (in Cotton's translation, the form in which Pope probably generally read Montaigne, "Of the Inconstancy of our Actions"). It is possible that Pope also used Jacques Esprit's *La Fausseté des Vertus Humaines*, which had been translated into English in 1691 and again in 1706. A more specific source was Prior's short "Essay upon Opinion", which Pope had certainly read in MS. (see Spence,

There's some Peculiar in each leaf and grain,   15
Some unmark'd fibre, or some varying vein:
Shall only Man be taken in the gross?
Grant but as many sorts of Mind as Moss.
        That each from other differs, first confess;
Next, that he varies from himself no less: 20
Add Nature's, Custom's, Reason's, Passion's strife,
And all Opinion's colours cast on life.
        Yet more; the diff'rence is as great between   (31)
The optics seeing, as the objects seen.
All Manners take a tincture from our own,   25
Or come discolour'd thro' our Passions shown.
Or Fancy's beam enlarges, multiplies,   (35)
Contracts, inverts, and gives ten thousand dyes.
        Our depths who fathoms, or our shallows finds,   (23)
Quick whirls, and shifting eddies, of our minds?   30

23–8 *1744–51 transfer to follow l. 40.*

p. 48); it was only printed in 1907 (*Dialogues of the Dead and Other Works in Prose and Verse*, ed. A. R. Waller, pp. 190–201). Geoffrey Tillotson sees Swift's account of madness in *A Tale of a Tub* as second only in importance to Montaigne as Pope's point of departure here (*Pope and Human Nature*, 1958, p. 131).

18. There are above 300 sorts of Moss observed by Naturalists. [P. *1733–43.*] Pope's note on *Dunciad*, IV 450 is to the same effect. See vol. V of this edition, p. 384.

20. Cf. Prior, "An Essay upon Opinion", ed. A. R. Waller, p. 190, "no Man is so different from another as the same Man is from Himself", and La Rochefoucauld, *Moral Maxims and Reflections*, 1694, p. 37, "A man at sometimes differs as much from himself, as he does from other people." No doubt all three passages have a common origin in Montaigne, II i, "there is as much difference betwixt us and ourselves, as betwixt us and others" (Cotton's translation, fourth edition, 1711, vol. II, p. 11).

23–4. Cf. *E. on Man*, II 127–30 and the note on the passage in vol. III i of this edition, p. 70.

24. Cf. Prior, "An Essay upon Opinion", ed. A. R. Waller, p. 201, "We look upon the different Objects without finding that we have insensibly turned the Tube". In Pope's time "optics" could mean either the human eye or magnifying glasses; no doubt both senses are intended here. Marjorie Nicolson has surveyed, in a series of special studies, the influence both of Newton's *Opticks* (1704) and of the newly discovered telescope and microscope on Pope and his contemporaries.

Life's stream for Observation will not stay,   (37)
It hurries all too fast to mark their way.
In vain sedate reflections we would make,
When half our knowledge we must snatch, not take. (40)
On human actions reason tho' you can,   35 (25)
It may be reason, but it is not man:
His Principle of action once explore,
That instant 'tis his Principle no more.
Like following life thro' creatures you dissect,
You lose it in the moment you detect.   40 (30)
    Oft in the Passions' wild rotation tost,
Our spring of action to ourselves is lost:
Tir'd, not determin'd, to the last we yield,
And what comes then is master of the field.
As the last image of that troubled heap,   45
When Sense subsides, and Fancy sports in sleep,
(Tho' past the recollection of the thought)
Becomes the stuff of which our dream is wrought:
Something as dim to our internal view,
Is thus, perhaps, the cause of most we do.   50

31–4 *1744–51 transfer to precede l. 41.*
31 Life's stream . . . not] Nor will Life's stream for Observation
    1744–51.
50 most] all *1733–4, 1735c–43;* half *1735ab.*

---

33. *sedate reflections*] As Geoffrey Tillotson has pointed out (*Pope and Human Nature*, 1958, p. 132n), Pope had already used this phrase in a letter to Caryll, 28 March 1727 (Sherburn, II 429).

39. Stephen Hales the physiologist was a neighbour and friend of Pope's. See *To a Lady*, 198n.

43. *not determin'd*] without having reached a conclusion.

46. *Sense*] consciousness (including also a general connotation of good sense).

48. *the stuff of which our dream*] No doubt a reminiscence of *The Tempest*, IV i 156–7, a passage marked by Pope with marginal commas as one of "the most shining passages" in his edition of Shakespeare (vol. I, 1725, p. 60). In spite of his professed admiration, imitations of Shakespeare are few and far between in Pope. E. A. Abbott (*A Concordance to the Works of Alexander Pope*, 1875, p. x) notes only seven.

In vain the Sage, with retrospective eye,   (99)
Would from th' apparent What conclude the Why,
Infer the Motive from the Deed, and show,
That what we chanc'd was what we meant to do.
Behold! If Fortune or a Mistress frowns,   55
Some plunge in bus'ness, others shave their crowns:
To ease the Soul of one oppressive weight,   (105)
This quits an Empire, that embroils a State:
The same adust complexion has impell'd
Charles to the Convent, Philip to the Field.   60

51–109 *1744–51 transfer to follow l. 157.*
51 Sage] grave *1733–43.*

51–86. Pope is here elaborating or confuting points touched on in *The Spectator*, 408 (18 June 1712): ". . . by observing the Nature and Course of the Passions, we shall be able to trace every Action from its first Conception to its Death; We shall no more admire at the Proceedings of *Catiline* or *Tiberius*, when we know the one was actuated by a cruel Jealousie, the other by a furious Ambition; for the Actions of Men follow their Passions as naturally as Light does Heat, or any other Effect flows from its Cause; Reason must be employed in adjusting the Passions, but they must ever remain the Principles of Action." Similar sentiments are also to be found in *The Spectator*, 224 (16 November 1711), which adumbrates a theory of the ruling passion. Both issues have been recently attributed to Pope by Norman Ault in his edition of *The Prose Works* (vol. 1, 1936), but the MSS., now at Blenheim, are not in Pope's hand.

51. *Sage*] The change from "grave" (see textual note) was perhaps made to help out the rearrangement of this part of the poem that Warburton had persuaded Pope to adopt. See Note on the Text, pp. 6–12 above.

56. *shave their crowns*] become monks.

59. *adust complexion*] originally a medical term; "characterized by dryness of the body, heat, thirst, burnt colour of the blood and little serum in it" (*OED*). "In hot and adust Tempers it [gin] makes Men Quarrelsome" (Mandeville, *Fable of the Bees*, ed. F. B. Kaye, 1924, 1 89).

impell'd] The rhyme with *field* appears to be one of the very few false rhymes in Pope. *field* could be pronounced *filled* (see E. J. Dobson, *English Pronunciation 1500–1700* (1957), 11 478).

60. Charles V [and] Philip II. [P. *1733–43.*] The atrabilaire complexion of Philip II. is well known, but not so well that he derived it from his father Charles V. whose health, the historians of his life tell us, was frequently disorder'd by bilious fevers. But what the author meant principally to observe here was, that this humour made both these princes act contrary to their Character; Charles,

     Not always Actions show the man: we find
Who does a kindness, is not therefore kind;   (110)
Perhaps Prosperity becalm'd his breast,
Perhaps the Wind just shifted from the east:
Not therefore humble he who seeks retreat,   65
Pride guides his steps, and bids him shun the great:
Who combats bravely is not therefore brave,   (115)
He dreads a death-bed like the meanest slave:
Who reasons wisely is not therefore wise,
His pride in Reas'ning, not in Acting lies.   70
     But grant that Actions best discover man;
Take the most strong, and sort them as you can.   (120)
The few that glare each character must mark,

---

65 therefore] always *1733–4*.

---

who was an active man, when he retired into a Convent; Philip, who was a man
of the Closet, when he gave the battle of St. Quintin [Warburton, *1744–51*].
   62. Cf. La Rochefoucauld, *Maximes*, no. xvi, "Cette clémence, dont on fait une
vertu, se pratique, tantôt par vanité, quelquefois par paresse, souvent par crainte,
et presque toujours par tous les trois ensemble." See too Jacques Esprit, *La
Fausseté des Vertus Humaines* (Paris, 1693), *passim*.
   65–6. Audra (p. 515) compares La Rochefoucauld, *Maximes*, no. ccliv:
"L'humilité n'est souvent qu'une feinte soumission dont on se sert pour sou-
mettre les autres; c'est un artifice de l'orgueil qui s'abaisse pour s'élever."
   67. "This alludes to Monsr. Auverquerque a Dutch General in Qu. Anne's
wars. Having a painfull chronical disorder he was always trying to get killed;
one day having led the D. of Marlb. too near to the Enemy, to show him a new
battery, one of the Duke's aid-de-camp's advertised his Grace of the danger: he
took no notice; being again admonished, he replied peevishly, 'Why do you tell
me of it? don't you see that old Fool there?' This story was probably told to Pope
by Lord Cobham . . . who one day related it as an Instance of the D. of Marl-
borough's resolution" (Horace Walpole, Fraser marginalia, pp. 22–4). On
the other hand a literary allusion may be intended—to Horace, *Epistles*, ii ii
26–40 (see Pope's *Imitation*, 32–51), or to Rochester's "Satyr against Mankind",
ll. 157–8:   Meerly for safety, after Fame we thirst,
                For all Men, wou'd be *Cowards* if they durst.
   71–6. "They chuse the general Air of a Man, and according to that interpret
all his Actions, of which, if some be so stiff and stubborn, that they cannot bend
or writh them to any Uniformity with the rest, they are presently imputed to
Dissimulation" (Cotton's Montaigne, 4th edition, 1711, ii 2) [EC].

You balance not the many in the dark.
What will you do with such as disagree?   75
Suppress them, half, or call them Policy?
Must then at once (the character to save)   (125)
The plain rough Hero turn a crafty Knave?
Alas! in truth the man but chang'd his mind,
Perhaps was sick, in love, or had not din'd.   80
Ask why from Britain Cæsar would retreat?
Cæsar himself might whisper he was beat.   (130)
Why risk the world's great empire for a Punk?
Cæsar perhaps might answer he was drunk.
But, sage historians! 'tis your task to prove   85
One action Conduct; one, heroic Love.
   'Tis from high Life high Characters are drawn;   (135)
A Saint in Crape is twice a Saint in Lawn;

76 them, half, or call] them, or miscall *1733–4, 1735c–51*.
78 The] A *1733–4, 1735c–36*.
81 why] how *1733–35b*.   would] made *1733–43*.
82 himself might whisper] perhaps had told you *1733–43*.
83 Why . . . for] The mighty *Czar* what mov'd to wed *1733–43*.
84 Cæsar perhaps] The mighty *Czar 1733–43*.

79–84. "Ces grandes et éclatantes actions qui éblouissent les yeux sont représentées par les politiques comme les effets des grands desseins, au lieu que ce sont d'ordinaire les effets de l'humeur et des passions. Ainsi la guerre d'Auguste et d'Antoine, qu'on rapporte à l'ambition qu'ils avaient de se rendre maîtres du monde, n'était peut-être qu'un effet de jalousie" (La Rochefoucauld, *Maximes*, no. vii).

83–4. The substitution of Caesar for Peter the Great (see textual note) has landed Pope in a historical mis-statement. Drunkenness was never one of Caesar's vices. And "Punk"—though perhaps the right word for Peter's Martha Skavronsky, the Lithuanian peasant girl who was successively his lover, consort, and successor (as Catherine I)—does not seem to suit Cleopatra. The change had been made in deference to Aaron Hill, an enthusiastic admirer of both Peter and Catherine (letter to Pope, 15 January 1738/9, Sherburn, IV 158). Warburton disapproved of it (see Pope's letter to him, 14 April 1741, Sherburn, IV 339).

88. *Lawn* is the fine linen used for the sleeves of bishops; *crape* is the thin worsted that the inferior clergy generally wore in the eighteenth century.

A Judge is just, a Chanc'lor juster still;
A Gownman, learn'd; a Bishop, what you will;   90
Wise, if a Minister; but, if a King,
More wise, more learn'd, more just, more ev'rything. (140)
Court-virtues bear, like Gems, the highest rate,
Born where Heav'n's influence scarce can penetrate:
In life's low vale, the soil the virtues like,   95
They please as Beauties, here as Wonders strike.
Tho' the same Sun with all-diffusive rays   (145)
Blush in the Rose, and in the Diamond blaze,
We prize the stronger effort of his pow'r,
And justly set the Gem above the Flow'r.   100
    'Tis Education forms the common mind,
Just as the Twig is bent, the Tree's inclin'd.   (150)
Boastful and rough, your first son is a 'Squire;
The next a Tradesman, meek, and much a lyar;
Tom struts a Soldier, open, bold, and brave;   105
Will sneaks a Scriv'ner, an exceeding knave:

No favy

100 justly] always *1733–4, 1735ᶜ–43.*
101 common] vulgar *1733–4, 1735ᶜ–43.*

---

93. An allusion to the vulgar error that precious stones and metals are created by the sun's rays. Pope is particularly fond of the conceit. See notes to *To a Lady*, 289, *To Bathurst*, 12.

95. *life's low vale*] Apparently a reminiscence of Cowley's translation of Virgil, *Georgic* II, ll. 486–8 [EC]:

    In Life's cool vale let my low Scene be laid.

(*Essays, Plays, and Sundry Verses*, ed. A. R. Waller, 1906, p. 409).

101–9. The "Argument" and Warburton take this paragraph at its face value. But to do so, as Courthope points out (EC, III 64), is to make nonsense of Pope's argument. Like the previous paragraph the lines are clearly to be taken ironically. Pope is satirizing both a vulgar error and the prevalent neo-classic notion—which reaches its *reductio ad absurdum* in Rymer's criticism of Iago—that all members of a single profession must share the same characteristics.

106. *Scriv'ner*] Notary; but also (because of the opportunities the profession provided) one who "received money to place out at interest, and who supplied those who wanted to raise money on security" (OED). Pope's favourite butt, Peter Walter (see *To Bathurst*, 125), was a scrivener.

Is he a Churchman? then he's fond of pow'r: ⎫   (155)
A Quaker? sly: A Presbyterian? sow'r: ⎬
A smar Free-thinker? all things in an hour.   ⎭

    True, some are open, and to all men known; 110 (51)
Others so very close, they're hid from none;
(So Darkness strikes the sense no less than Light)
Thus gracious CHANDOS is belov'd at sight,
And ev'ry child hates Shylock, tho' his soul   (55)

---

112 strikes the sense] fills the eye *1733–43*.

---

109. *Free-thinker*] A "society" Deist or atheist. The word (a translation from the French) had only been introduced in 1692. It had been popularized by Anthony Collins's *A Discourse of Free-thinking, occasioned by the Rise and Growth of a Sect called Free-thinkers* (1713), and the replies this provoked. Berkeley's *Alciphron* (1732) was directed "against those who are called *Free-thinkers*". See also ll. 162–5.

113. James Brydges, first Duke of Chandos (1673–1744). A Whig millionaire and M.P. for Hereford, 1698–1714; paymaster of the forces abroad, 1707–12; succeeded as ninth Baron Chandos and created Earl of Carnarvon 1714, and Duke of Chandos 1719. Chandos was a lavish patron of all the arts and his mansion at Cannons, near Edgware, was one of the most magnificent in England. See C. H. Collins Baker and Muriel I. Baker, *The Life and Circumstances of James Brydges First Duke of Chandos* (1949). Pope only knew Chandos slightly, but they had many friends in common, including Bolingbroke (who had borrowed money from Chandos), Bathurst, Burlington, and Arbuthnot. Pope and his friends were irritated and distressed by a whispering campaign which identified the character of Timon (*To Burlington*, 99–176) with Chandos. See Appendix B (pp. 170–4 below). The compliment here was apparently intended to remove the impression that Pope had satirized the Duke as Timon.

114. *Shylock*] "On a printed leaf of this Essay among the Warburton papers, Pope has crossed out 'Shylock', and written over it the real name 'Selkirk'" (EC, III 58). The Shylock of *To Bathurst*, 117, was S–l–k in the first edition. Charles Douglas, Earl of Selkirk (1663–1739), was a warm supporter of the Revolution and represented the Scottish peers in four Parliaments, 1713–15, 1722–39. Selkirk does not appear to have excited much affection; Lord Hervey wrote of him in a poetical epistle to the Queen (*Memoirs*, p. 583):

    Let nauseous Selkirk shake his empty head
    Through six courts more, when six have wish'd him dead.

Pope is continually sneering at Selkirk in *Imit. Hor.* [JB]; "a great Miser" (Percy MS.).

Still sits at squat, and peeps not from its hole.   115
   At half mankind when gen'rous Manly raves,
All know 'tis Virtue, for he thinks them knaves:
When universal homage Umbra pays,
All see 'tis Vice, and itch of vulgar praise.   (60)
When Flatt'ry glares, all hate it in a Queen,   120
While one there is who charms us with his Spleen.

120 Who but detests th'Endearments of *Courtine 1733–43.*
121 who] that *1735ab.*

---

   115. Cf.   him there they found
                Squat like a Toad.
Par. Lost, IV 799–800. Another reminiscence of this passage is in *Epistle to Arbuthnot,* 319.

   116. *Manly*] The "plain dealer" in Wycherley's comedy (1676). "Probably Richard, Earl of Scarboro' " (Percy MS.). Pope introduced complimentary references to Richard Lumley, Earl of Scarborough (1688?–1740) into *Dia.* ii, 65 and *1740,* 78, but in 1735 he was still a loyal Whig and as such unlikely to commend himself to Pope.

   118. *Umbra*] The Umbra in *Miscellanies. The Last Volume* (1727) is identified in *Characters of the Times* (1728), pp. 36–9, as Walter Carey, a prominent Whig official, who as chief secretary to the Duke of Dorset when Lord Lieutenant of Ireland had recently incurred Swift's wrath:
                In the Porch *Briareus* stands,
                Shews a Bribe in all his Hands:
                Briareus the Secretary,
                But we Mortals call him *Cary.*
"The Legion Club" (1736) (Swift, *Poems,* ed. H. Williams, 1937, III 833). Pope's reasons for disliking Carey are discussed in vol. VI of this edition, pp. 112, 141. Umbra in *Donne, Imit.,* IV, 177, and Lord Umbra in *E. on Man,* IV, 278, seem to be unconnected with this Umbra and with each other.

   120. *a Queen*] Queen Caroline (see *To a Lady,* 182). Her sin of flattery does not seem to have amounted to more than common politeness. The charge was no doubt conditioned by the reading of the earlier editions (see textual note). Caroline died in 1737.

   121. *his Spleen*] His misanthropy. The word was used in a variety of senses in the eighteenth century (see O. Doughty, "The English Malady of the Eighteenth Century", *Review of English Studies,* 1926, II 257–69). Swift, for whom the compliment appears to be intended, generally uses the word in an unfavourable sense (e.g. *Tale of a Tub,* preface, *Gulliver's Travels,* part IV, ch. vii). Walpole (Fraser marginalia, p. 24) took the reference to be to Cobham; Wilkes (Car-

But these plain Characters we rarely find;
Tho' strong the bent, yet quick the turns of mind:
Or puzzling Contraries confound the whole,   (65)
Or Affectations quite reverse the soul.   125
Or Falshood serves the dull for policy,
And in the Cunning, Truth itself's a lye:
Unthought-of Frailties cheat us in the Wise,
The Fool lies hid in inconsistencies.   (70)
    See the same man, in vigour, in the gout;   130
Alone, in company; in place, or out;
Early at Bus'ness, and at Hazard late;
Mad at a Fox-chace, wise at a Debate;
Drunk at a Borough, civil at a Ball,   (75)
Friendly at Hackney, faithless at Whitehall.   135
    Catius is ever moral, ever grave,

124–5 Or ... Or] Here ... There *1733–4*.
126 Or Falshood serves the dull] The Dull, flat Falshood serves
  1733–4, 1735c–51.
127 And] Or *1735ab*.   135 Hackney] Acton *1735ab*.

ruthers, I 375) thought General James Dormer (1679–1741) was intended. The *locus classicus* on the spleen is Matthew Green's poem (published 1737, though written earlier), of which Pope said, "there was a great deal of originality in it" (*The Gentleman's Magazine*, 1780, L 122). Pope may have had Boileau's line in mind: "Un Esprit né chagrin plaist par son chagrin mesme" (*Epistres*, IX 88).

126. The meaning must be that *flat falsehood* is often, if unexpectedly, to be met with in the stupid. The ambiguity was due to the reconstruction entailed by the textual changes in ll. 124–5 (see textual note).

135. "... that is, full of professions, when a candidate for a seat in Parliament; (for the Middlesex members are put into nomination at *Hackney*) and faithless to those professions when the object of them is secure" [Wakefield]. A particular Whig M.P. for Middlesex may be intended. The Middlesex M.P.s, 1727–34, were James Bertie and Sir Francis Child, the banker. Acton, the reading of some of the early editions, has not been explained. Were the Middlesex candidates sometimes nominated there?

136. *Catius*] The epicure in Horace, *Sat.*, II iv. Carruthers's suggestion (i 375) that Pope meant Charles Dartineuf (1663–1737) is unlikely. Dartineuf, though an epicure, was far from "grave". Swift describes him as a great punster and gossip (*Journal to Stella*, 22 March 1711).

Thinks who endures a knave, is next a knave,
Save just at dinner—then prefers, no doubt,
A Rogue with Ven'son to a Saint without.   (80)
    Who would not praise Patritio's high desert,   140
His hand unstain'd, his uncorrupted heart,
His comprehensive head! all Int'rests weigh'd,
All Europe sav'd, yet Britain not betray'd.

---

140. *Patritio*] Sidney, first Earl of Godolphin (1645–1712). Swift alludes to
Godolphin's love of cards, dice, and racing in *The Examiner*, nos. 27, 30 (1711).
Burnet confirms this: "He loved gaming the most of any man of business I ever
knew" (*History of his Own Time*, 1833, II 245). It is not clear why Pope calls
Godolphin Patritio; possibly a compliment is intended to Godolphin's patriot-
ism. He told Spence (p. 272) that Clarendon and Godolphin were the only
"honest" ministers of the Stuart period. The Percy MS. identification—"Lord
Godolphin (rather Robert Earl of Oxford Lord Treasurer)"—may be correct.

143. *Britain not betray'd*] The Tories had accused Marlborough of prolonging
the war against France to serve his own interest. The second of the four omitted
lines (see textual note) refers to the annual £6,000 that Sir Solomon Medina
paid Marlborough "to have the employment of providing bread for the army"
(Swift, *Journal to Stella*, 23 January 1712). Marlborough claimed this was "a
perquisite of the general or commander-in-chief in the Low Countries; and it has
been constantly applied to one of the most important parts of the service there,
I mean the procuring intelligence, and other secret service" (*Parliamentary His-
tory*, VI 1088). The whole agitation against Marlborough's alleged peculations
was primarily a party move. See Sir Winston Churchill, *Marlborough his Life and
Times*, 1938, IV, ch. xxxi. The innuendo of the last of the omitted lines derives
its sting from Marlborough's reputation for meanness. "The D^c of Marlboro'
seriously ownd & lamented to Sir J: Vanburgh, that he c^d not part with half-a-
crown, without Pain" (D. C. Tovey, *Gray and his Friends*, 1890, p. 283) is a typical
contemporary anecdote. Gray derived it from Mrs Bonfoy. At the end of *1735ab*
Pope has the following note: "These four Verses having been misconstrued, con-
trary to the Author's meaning, they are suppressed in as many Copies as he cou'd
recall." No copies, however, have so far turned up in which the passage is can-
celled (see Griffith, p. 290). The note was perhaps intended as a sop to the
Duchess of Marlborough, who had joined the opposition to Walpole in 1734. It
is possible the lines were also originally included in the "death-bed" edition
(1744). Leaf A4 in all the copies of the edition now extant is an insert and the sup-
pression of these lines is the most probable explanation of the cancel. Their inclu-
sion in what was intended to be the authoritative edition of his poems would have
been inept in the extreme in 1744. In 1735 the Duchess was a *grande dame* to be
placated on political grounds, but nothing more. In 1744, on the other hand,

He thanks you not, his pride is in Picquette,   (85)
New-market-fame, and judgment at a Bett.   145
    What made (say Montagne, or more sage Charron!)
Otho a warrior, Cromwell a buffoon?

144 is] was *1733, 1735a–43.*
145 *1735a–43 add:*
    Triumphant Leaders at an Army's head,
    Hemm'd round with Glories, pilfer Cloth or Bread,
    As meanly plunder as they bravely fought,
    Now save a People, and now save a Groat.

Pope and the Duchess were close and congenial friends. Warburton's note to Bowyer, the printer, dated 20 June 1744, appears to refer to the suppression of this passage: "I have looked over the corrected proof of the half-sheet, title, &c. and of the leaf that was ordered to be cancelled, and find them right: so desire they may be printed off" (Nichols, II 165). It is not clear if it was Pope or Warburton who "ordered" the cancel. The *possibility* that it may have been Pope—who only died on 30 May—has prevented the restoration of the four lines to the text in this edition. But see Introduction, p. xiv above.

146. "Charron was an admirer of Montaigne; had contracted a strict friendship with him; and has transferred an infinite number of his thoughts into his famous book *De la Sagesse*; but his moderating every-where the extravagant Pyrrhonism of his friend, is the reason why the poet calls him *more sage Charron*" [Warburton]. Pope, however, shows few signs of knowing Charron's book well —if he read it at all it was probably in Dean Stanhope's translation (1696), which reached its third edition in 1729—and he was no doubt merely repeating Bolingbroke's often expressed preference for Charron to Montaigne (see Audra, pp. 461–5). Pope certainly knew Montaigne's *Essais* intimately. The whole argument of the first half of this Epistle is derived from Montaigne's "Of the Inconstancy of our Actions" (bk II, ch. i)—the essay that Pope told Spence was "the best in his whole book" (see p. xxi above)—and the theory of the Ruling Passion seems to be adumbrated in "The Story of Spurina" (bk II, ch. xxxiii).

147. M. Salvius Otho, Roman emperor from January to April 69, had been a companion of Nero in his debaucheries. On the news of the revolt of Vitellius reaching Rome, Otho is said by Tacitus to have led his army against the enemy in person and on foot. After his defeat by Vitellius's generals he committed suicide.

Cromwell's buffooneries are a relic of royalist prejudice. Unlike the Opposition Whigs (e.g. Lyttleton and James Thomson), who eulogized Cromwell as a champion of liberty, Pope and the Tories still looked upon him as
    damn'd to evelasting fame (*E. on Man,* IV 284).

A perjur'd Prince a leaden Saint revere,
A godless Regent tremble at a Star?   (90)
The throne a Bigot keep, a Genius quit,   150
Faithless thro' Piety, and dup'd thro' Wit?
Europe a Woman, Child, or Dotard rule,
And just her wisest monarch made a fool?
   Know, God and Nature only are the same: (95)
In Man, the judgment shoots at flying game,   155
A bird of passage! gone as soon as found,
Now in the Moon perhaps, now under ground.
Ask men's Opinions: Scoto now shall tell

---

153 wisest] *ablest 1733–4, 1735c–43.*
156 gone] lost *1733–4, 1735c–43.*
158 Scoto] *J**n 1733. Jaunssen 1734 (but cancel leaf corrects to J——n).*

---

148. Louis XI of France wore in his Hat a leaden image of the Virgin Mary, which when he swore by, he feared to break his oath. [P. *1744–51. 1735a–43 merely read:* Lewis XI. of France.]

revere] Pope seems to have pronounced this *revar*. H. C. Wyld's belief that he used the modern pronunciation (*Studies in English Rhymes*, 1923, p. 123) is not borne out by the rhymes.

149. Philip Duke of Orleans, Regent of France in the minority of Louis XV. superstitious in judicial astrology, tho' an unbeliever in all religion [P. *1744–51*].

150–1. Philip V. of Spain [d. 1746], who, after renouncing the throne for Religion, resum'd it to gratify his Queen; and Victor Amadeus II, King of Sardinia [d. 1732], who resign'd the crown, and trying to reassume it, was imprisoned till his death. [P. *1744–51. Briefer note in 1735c–43*] Pope very much admired Victor Amadeus (see Spence, p. 300). He inherited the king's watch from Lord Peterborough, and it is mentioned in his will. It was "a common plain gold one, not worth twenty guineas" (Sir J. Prior, *Life of Malone*, 1860, p. 397).

152–3. The "Child" is, of course, Louis XV, and the "wisest monarch" no doubt Victor Amadeus II again. Walpole (Fraser marginalia, p. 27) identified the "Woman" as the Czarina Elizabeth (Empress 1741–62) and the "Dotard" as Benedict XIII (Pope 1724–30). EC is probably right in thinking the references are to the Czarina Anna Ivanovna (Empress 1730–40) and to Clement XII (Pope 1730–41).

155. *flying game*] Cf. *E. on Man*, 1 13 and the note on the passage in vol. III i of this edition, p. 14.

158–61. The reading of the first edition makes it clear that the allusion is to James Johnston (1655–1737), a Twickenham neighbour of Pope's, who had been

How Trade increases, and the World goes well;
Strike off his Pension, by the setting sun,   160
And Britain, if not Europe, is undone.
      That gay Free-thinker, a fine talker once,
What turns him now a stupid silent dunce?
Some God, or Spirit he has lately found,
Or chanc'd to meet a Minister that frown'd.   165
      Manners with Fortunes, Humours turn with Climes,
Tenets with Books, and Principles with Times.
      Judge we by Nature? Habit can efface,
Int'rest o'ercome, or Policy take place:
By Actions? those Uncertainty divides: 170
By Passions? these Dissimulation hides:
Opinions? they still take a wider range:
Find, if you can, in what you cannot change.

---

161 *1735ab add:*
      Trust their *Affections*: soon Affections end;
      "In pow'r your Servant, out of pow'r your Friend."
162–5 *Add. 1744.*   166–7 *1744–51 transfer to follow l. 173.*
166 turn] change *1733–43.*
172 Opinions] *Affections 1733–4, 1735c–43.*

Secretary of State for Scotland, 1692–6. Johnston's "Pension" was the grant of
£5,000 that he had received in 1697 and which was paid out of the annual tithes
in the rents of the nonjuring Scotch bishops (see *DNB*). Johnston was a Whig and
a great favourite of Queen Caroline. Pope sneers at "Maister Johnson" in letters
to the Burlingtons (Sherburn, III 272) and other friends. See also Pope's imitation
of Spenser, 50 (vol. VI of this edition, p. 44 and note), and *Epistle to Arbuthnot*, 363.
      161. In most of the early editions Pope inserted an additional couplet here (see
textual note), which included a sarcastic quotation from Bubb Dodington's
Epistle to The Right Honourable Sir Robert Walpole (1726, p. 9):
                In Power, a Servant; out of Power, a Friend.
The line is also quoted in *Epilogue to the Satires*, II 161—a fact which perhaps
explains its ultimate omission here—and in an undated letter to Fortescue (Sher-
burn, II 294, V 2), as well as in the anonymous *A Master Key to Popery* (see Appendix
C, p. 186 below). The couplet was first put to ironic purpose in *The Craftsman*,
14 October 1727.
      162. *Free-thinker*] See note to l. 109 above.

> Search then the Ruling Passion: There, alone,
> The Wild are constant, and the Cunning known;   175
> The Fool consistent, and the False sincere;
> Priests, Princes, Women, no dissemblers here.
> This clue once found, unravels all the rest,
> The prospect clears, and Wharton stands confest.
> Wharton, the scorn and wonder of our days,   180
> Whose ruling Passion was the Lust of Praise;
> Born with whate'er could win it from the Wise,
> Women and Fools must like him or he dies;

174 Search then] 'Tis in *1733–43*.
179, 180 Wharton] *Clodio 1733–43*.

---

174. Pope had already outlined his theory of the Ruling Passion in *E. on Man*, II 123–44, and a discussion of his sources will be found in the notes on that passage and in the Introduction to vol. III i of this edition, pp. xxxviff. It appears that, in spite of all its by no means recondite antecedents, Pope really thought the theory was his own discovery. "New Hypothesis" was the term he used when he outlined the theory to Spence in May 1730 (see Introduction, p. xxi above). For anticipations of the theory, perhaps by Pope himself, in *The Spectator*, see note on ll. 51–86 above.

179. *Wharton*] Philip, Duke of Wharton (1698–1731), son of the Whig politician, Thomas, Marquis of Wharton, succeeded to the marquisate, 1715; visited Old Pretender at Avignon and Marie Beatrix at St Germain, 1716; created Duke of Wharton 1718, to retain him in the Whig interest; adopted in 1726 the cause of "James III", urging a Spanish invasion of England, and became a Roman Catholic; served against Gibraltar, 1727, and outlawed, 1729; died in Catalonia.

Pope's disapproval of Wharton's vagaries may possibly have had some personal origin. Lady Mary Wortley Montagu "told Lady Pomfret, that when she became acquainted with the Duke of Wharton, Mr. Pope grew jealous, and that occasioned the breach between them" (Spence, p. 237). Another account is that Wharton wrote a satire on Pope which Lady Mary showed him (Lady Mary's *Letters*, I 30). It is just possible that this satire is "To Mr. Pope, on his second Subscription for Homer", which accuses Pope of being as mercenary a poet as Marlborough was a general. It is printed in *Whartoniana* (1727), I 144.

Clodio, the reading of the early editions, was the name under which Wharton's father, Thomas Wharton, first Marquis of Wharton (1649–1715), had been satirized in William Shippen's *Faction Display'd* (1704, pp. 7–9). The implied comparison with P. Clodius Pulcher, the gangster politician of republican Rome, was more telling in the father's case than the son's and Pope did well to drop it.

Tho' wond'ring Senates hung on all he spoke,
The Club must hail him master of the joke.   185
Shall parts so various aim at nothing new?
He'll shine a Tully and a Wilmot too.
Then turns repentant, and his God adores
With the same spirit that he drinks and whores;
Enough if all around him but admire,   190
And now the Punk applaud, and now the Fryer.
Thus with each gift of nature and of art,
And wanting nothing but an honest heart;
Grown all to all, from no one vice exempt,
And most contemptible, to shun contempt;   195

185 the joke] a *Joke 1735a*.

184. He was created Duke of Wharton in 1718 as a reward for his services in debate in the Irish Parliament. He was then nineteen years old. His most dazzling parliamentary performance was his defence of Pope's friend Atterbury in the House of Lords in May 1723.

185. He was president of one of the short-lived Hell-Fire Clubs and of an equally disreputable organization called the Schemers. See R. J. Allen, *The Clubs of Augustan London*, 1933, pp. 119–23.

187. *Wilmot*] John Willmot, Earl of Rochester, famous for his Wit and Extravagancies in the time of Charles the Second. [P. *1744–51*.] Pope tended to underrate Rochester, thinking him a mere "holiday-writer" (Spence, p. 281). Wharton's few occasional poems have little to recommend them. "The Drinking Match at Eden Hall" is a facetious imitation of "Chevy Chase". See *Whartoniana*, 2 vols., 1727.

188–9. "He has public devotions twice a day, and assists at them in person with exemplary devotion; and there is nothing pleasanter than the remarks of some pious ladies on the conversion of so great a sinner" (Lady Mary Wortley Montagu to the Countess of Mar, *c.* 1725, Lady Mary's *Letters*, I 479).

191. *Fryer*] Wharton became a Roman Catholic in 1726 and entered a convent for a brief period in 1729. "His Resolution in the Circumstances he was reduced to, was not absolutely to quit the World; but to retire from it; he propos'd to lodge himself in a Convent, and there to apply himself to some sort of Study. . . The Duke of Wharton was look'd upon in the Convent for a Devotee. He talk'd so well upon all Points of Religion that the pious Fathers beheld him with Admiration . . . they esteem'd him little less than a Saint" ("Memoirs of the Life Of His Grace Philip late Duke of Wharton", 1731, pp. 30, 42. Prefixed to *The Life and Writings of Philip Late Duke of Wharton*, 2 vols., 1732).

G

His Passion still, to covet gen'ral praise,
His Life, to forfeit it a thousand ways;
A constant Bounty which no friend has made;
An angel Tongue, which no man can persuade;
A Fool, with more of Wit than half mankind,   200
Too quick for Thought, for Action too refin'd:
A Tyrant to the wife his heart approves;
A Rebel to the very king he loves;
He dies, sad out-cast of each church and state,

198 A] His *1733–35b*.   which no] no one *1733–35b*.
     has] had *1735a*.
199 An] His *1733–35b*.   which no man] no mortal *1733–35b*.
     can] could *1735a*.
201 quick] rash *1733, 1735c–51*.

198. One beneficiary of Wharton's "Bounty" was Pope's friend Edward
Young, who dedicated his tragedy *The Revenge* (1721) to the Duke and was said
(see Spence, p. 255) to have received £2,000 for the compliment.

202. His first wife (by a Fleet marriage in 1715, when Wharton was only six-
teen) was Martha Holmes (d. 1726). Although he abandoned or neglected her
for most of their married life, he had occasional fits of affection. Lady Mary
Wortley Montagu reported to the Countess of Mar in 1725, "The Duke of
Wharton has brought his duchess to town, and is fond of her to distraction"
(Lady Mary's *Letters*, 1 278). A passage in Mrs Haywood's *Memoirs Of a Certain
Island Adjacent to the Kingdom of Utopia* (1725) appears to relate to this episode:
"After some Years of one continu'd Extravagance, the Duke . . . falling into the
Conversation of the sober Part of Mankind . . . was persuaded by them to take
home his Dutchess . . . Love had no part in his Resolution.—He liv'd with her
indeed, but she is with him as a Housekeeper, as a Nurse" (pp. 220–1). His
second wife, Maria Theresa O'Byrne, seems to have been better treated.

203. A bill of indictment was preferred against him for High Treason; "the
Fact was appearing in Arms before, and firing off Canon against, His Majesty's
Town of *Gibraltar*" ("Memoirs", 1731, p. 27). He had been aide-de-camp to the
Conde de los Torres at the unsuccessful siege of Gibraltar by the Spanish in 1727.
He was outlawed by a resolution of the House of Lords on 3 April 1729.

204. This is an overstatement. Wharton died a member of the Church of
Rome, in a Franciscan convent at Poblet in Catalonia, and attired in the habit
of the Order. In its original form Pope's character of Wharton appears to have
contained several such overstatements, but Caryll persuaded him to omit them.
"I have left out of the character of the D. of Wharton (which I showed you)

And (harder still) flagitious, yet not great!   205
Ask you why Wharton broke thro' ev'ry rule?
'Twas all for fear the Knaves should call him Fool.
    Nature well known, no prodigies remain,
Comets are regular, and Wharton plain.
    Yet, in this search, the wisest may mistake,   210
If second qualities for first they take.
When Catiline by rapine swell'd his store,
When Cæsar made a noble dame a whore,
In this the Lust, in that the Avarice
Were means, not ends; Ambition was the vice.   215
That very Cæsar, born in Scipio's days,

206, 209 Wharton] *Clodio 1733–43.*
208 prodigies] Miracles *1733–43.*
210 this] the *1733–43.*

those lines you thought too hard" (Pope to Caryll, 23 October 1733; Sherburn, III 390).

208. *prodigies*] Warburton persuaded Pope "to alter *Miracles* to *Prodigies*, not only for the religion, but the reason of the thing. It was not only declaring against Miracles, but it was arguing inconclusively: prodigies being natural effects, whose causes we being ignorant of, we have made them ideal creatures of a distinct species: as soon as we come to the knowledge of the causes, prodigies are no longer a distinct species, but rank with all other natural effects. But it is *no consequence* that when nature is known no *miracles* remain; because miracles imply supernatural effects; therefore these are consistent with the whole knowledge of nature. Yet this was one of the *speciosa dictata* of Bolingbroke, who was fond of the impiety, and yet did not see the blunder" (letter to Hurd, *c.* May 1752, *Letters from a Late Eminent Prelate*, 1809, p. 110).

209. The study of comets had been notably advanced in Pope's time by Newton (*De Systemate Mundi*, 1687) and Halley (*Synopsis Astronomiae Cometicae*, 1705).

212. *Catiline*] L. Sergius Catilina, the notorious conspirator.

213. *noble dame*] Servilia, the sister of Cato and mother of Brutus. Pope is perhaps borrowing from Montaigne, who also shows that Caesar's amorousness was subsidiary to his ambition (*Essais*, bk II, ch. xxxiii).

216. *Scipio*] P. Cornelius Scipio Africanus Major, the conqueror of Hannibal.

216–17. Pope made the same point in conversation with Spence (p. 315): "Facts in Antient History, are not very instructive now; the principles of acting vary so often and so greatly.—The actions of a great man were quite different, even in Scipio's and Julius Caesar's times."

Had aim'd, like him, by Chastity at praise.
Lucullus, when Frugality could charm,
Had roasted turnips in the Sabin farm.
In vain th' observer eyes the builder's toil,   220
But quite mistakes the scaffold for the pile.
    In this one Passion man can strength enjoy,
As Fits give vigour, just when they destroy.
Time, that on all things lays his lenient hand,
Yet tames not this; it sticks to our last sand.   225
Consistent in our follies and our sins,
Here honest Nature ends as she begins.
    Behold a rev'rend sire, whom want of grace   (232)

228   *1744–51 transfer ll. 248–51 to precede this.*

218. *Lucullus*] L. Licinius Lucullus, the conqueror of Mithridates, devoted his
retirement to the exploitation of a natural genius for luxury.

223. One of Pope's "Thoughts on Various Subjects" (EC, x 521) runs: "Our
passions are like convulsive fits, which, though they make us stronger for the
time, leave us weaker ever after."

224. *lenient*] softening.

225. "It is no lesse worthy to observe, how little Alteration, in good Spirits,
the Approaches of *Death* make; For they appeare to be the same Men, till the
last Instant. *Augustus Caesar* died in a Complement . . . Tiberius in dissimulation
. . . *Vespasian* in a Jest . . . *Galba* with a Sentence . . . *Septimius Severus* in dispatch"
(Bacon, "Of Death", *The Essays*, 1625). According to Warton (*Essay*, I 129) Pope
"is known to have been remarkably fond" of Bacon's essays. He commends
Bacon's style more than once (Spence, p. 310, *Imit. Hor., Ep.*, II i, 168), and in
general thought him "the greatest genius that England (or perhaps any country)
ever produced" (Spence, pp. 169–70).

228–33. Walpole (Fraser marginalia, p. 28) believed this was intended for
Lancelot Blackburne (1658–1743), the disreputable Archbishop of York whom
Pope refers to as "moral Ebor" in *1740*, 58. There is a more specific allusion in
Sober Advice, 43–4:

    Better than lust for Boys, with *Pope* and *Turk*,
    Or others Spouses, like my Lord of —.

If the identification is correct, "reverend" and "grace" must be deliberate puns.
The episode was originally longer. "Dont you think," Cobham wrote to Pope,
I November 1733, "you have bestowd too many lines upon the old Letcher the
instance it self is but ordinary and I think shoud be shortnd or changd" (Egerton
MS. 1949, f. 1 and Sherburn, III 392). On 8 November he wrote again, "I like
your Leachour better now 'tis shorter" (ibid., f. 2 and Sherburn, III 393).

Has made the father of a nameless race,
Shov'd from the wall perhaps, or rudely press'd   230
By his own son, that passes by unbless'd: (235)
Still to his wench he crawls on knocking knees,
And envies ev'ry sparrow that he sees.
  A salmon's belly, Helluo, was thy fate:
The doctor call'd, declares all help too late.   235
Mercy! cries Helluo, mercy on my soul!   (240)
Is there no hope? Alas!—then bring the jowl.
  The frugal Crone, whom praying priests attend,

---

230 Shov'd ... perhaps] Crawl thro' the Street, shov'd on *1733–43*.
231 son ... passes] Sons ... pass him *1733–43*.
232 crawls] creeps *1733–43*.
238–41 *Add. 1744*.

234–7. This anecdote derives ultimately from the account of the poet Philoxenus in Athenaeus, VIII 341 [Warton]. Pope may have met with it in John Hales: "When *Philoxenus* the *Epicure* had fallen desperately sick upon glutting himself on a delicate and costly fish, perceiving he was to die, he calls for the remainder of his fish, and eats it up, and dies a true Martyr to his belly" (*Golden Remains, The Second Impression*, 1673, p. 21 of the appended "Sermons"). The episode is also in La Fontaine, "Le Glouton", 11–14 (*Contes et Nouvelles en vers*, Amsterdam, 1685, II 96):

          Et puis qu'il faut que je meure,
          Sans faire tant de façon
          Qu'on m'apporte tout à l'heure
          Le reste de mon poisson.

Pope had dipped into La Fontaine, but was not apparently much influenced by him. See Audra, p. 146. The tradition that Sir Godfrey Kneller was the original Helluo (see Walpole's *Anecdotes of Painting*, ed. R. N. Wornum, 1849, III 592) can be safely rejected, as can the identification with Dartineuf (see l. 136 above) in the Percy MS. Helluo is the Latin word for glutton. There is another Helluo in *To a Lady*, 79.

236. The rhyme *soul–jowl* was a good one, *soul* being still pronounced as modern *foul*. See E. J. Dobson *English Pronunciation 1500–1700* (1957), II 694.

238–41. "A fact told him, by Lady Bolingbroke of an old Countess at Paris" [Warton]. Bolingbroke's second wife, whom he married in 1722, was Marie Clare, Marquise de Villette (1675–1750). (It was this Lady Bolingbroke who once wittily described Pope as "un politique aux choux et aux raves", Johnson, *Lives of the Poets*, II 200.) Pope read the lines to the Richardsons before they were published: "I remember Mr *Pope*'s repeating to my father and me, in his library

Still tries to save the hallow'd taper's end,
Collects her breath, as ebbing life retires,   240
For one puff more, and in that puff expires.   (245)
    "Odious! in woollen! 'twould a Saint provoke,
(Were the last words that poor Narcissa spoke)
"No, let a charming Chintz, and Brussels lace
"Wrap my cold limbs, and shade my lifeless face: 245
"One would not, sure, be frightful when one's dead—(250)
"And—Betty—give this Cheek a little Red."

---

at *Twickenham*, four verses, designed for his epistle *on Riches*, which were an ex-
quisite description of an old lady dying, and just raising herself up, and blowing
out a little end of a candle that stood by her bed side, with her last breath"
(*Richardsoniana*, 1776, p. 221). Richardson's statement that the lines were
intended for *To Bathurst*, though not impossible, is probably just a slip.

242. *Odious*] Like *frightful* (l. 246) this was fashionable feminine slang. Con-
greve's Millamant—another of Mrs Oldfield's rôles—uses both words. See also
To a Lady, 40.

242–7. This story, as well as the others, is founded on fact, tho' the author had
the goodness not to mention the names. Several attribute this in particular to a
very celebrated Actress, who, in detestation of the thought of being buried in
woollen, gave these her last orders with her dying breath. [P. *1744–51.*] The
actress was Anne Oldfield (1683–1730), who is attacked, perhaps because she
was Cibber's ally, more than once by Pope. (See *Sober Advice*, 4–5, *Imit. Hor.*,
Ep., II i, 331, and vol. VI of this edition.) Narcissa in Cibber's *Love's Last Shift* was
one of her stock parts. A series of Acts of Parliament making it illegal to bury the
dead in anything but woollens had been passed from 1666 onwards as a protec-
tive measure against foreign linen. Pope had probably been reading "William
Egerton's" *Faithful Memoirs of Mrs. Anne Oldfield*, 1731. According to this Curll
production (p. 144), Mrs Oldfield was "nicely dressed after her Decease; being
by Mrs. *Saunders*'s Direction then laid in her Coffin. She had on a very fine
Brussels Lace Head; a Holland Shift with a Tucker, and double Ruffles of the
same Lace; a pair of New Kid-Gloves, and her Body wrapped up in a Winding
Sheet." Mrs Oldfield, however, was not the first to evade the Act—a regular
charge was made at St Martin's-in-the-Fields "for persons buried in linen, con-
trary to Act of Parliament" (see Steele, *Plays*, ed. G. A. Aitken, 1903, p. 81)—
and the whole thing had long been a satirical commonplace. Thus in Steele's
The Funeral (1700), v iii, Lady Brumpton exclaims, "Harkee, hussy, if you should,
as I hope you won't, outlive me, take care I ain't buried in flannel; 'twould never
become me, I'm sure." See, too, *The Tatler*, 118 (10 January 1709/10).

247. *Betty*] A generic name in the eighteenth century for the lady's maid. Com-
pare *Rape of Lock*, I 148, Swift, "A Description of the Morning, 1709", l. 3, and

Old Politicians chew on wisdom past,   (228)
And totter on in bus'ness to the last;
As weak, as earnest, and as gravely out,   250 (230)
As sober Lanesb'row dancing in the gout.
      The Courtier smooth, who forty years had shin'd
An humble servant to all human kind,
Just brought out this, when scarce his tongue could stir,
"If—where I'm going—I could serve you, Sir?"   255
      "I give and I devise, (old Euclio said,
And sigh'd) "My lands and tenements to Ned."
Your money, Sir? "My money, Sir, what all?
"Why,—if I must—(then wept) I give it Paul."
The Manor, Sir?—"The Manor! hold," he cry'd,   260
"Not that,—I cannot part with that"—and dy'd.

---

249 totter] blunder *1733–43*.
251 Lanesb'row] *L**w 1733–4*; La–w *1735ab*.

Young, *Love of Fame*, 1725–8, Satire v, 438. The whole couplet may be a half-reminiscence of Swift's "The Journal of a Modern Fine Lady" (1729), ll. 48–9 (*Poems*, ed. H. Williams, 1937, II 446):

> *Betty*, pray
> Don't I look frightfully to Day?

249. *in bus'ness*] in the conduct of public affairs. Cf. Burnet's comment on Godolphin quoted in the note on l. 140.

251. *Lanesb'row*] An ancient Nobleman, who continued this practice long after his legs were disabled by the gout. Upon the death of Prince George of Denmark, he demanded an audience of the Queen, to advise her to preserve her health and dispel her grief by *Dancing*. [P. *1735a–51. 1735c–43 add*: The rest of these Instances are strictly true, tho' the Persons are not named.] James Lane, second Viscount Lanesborough (1640–1724), is "often alluded to as the dancing peer in the Irish pasquinades of that day" (Carruthers, I 381).

256–61. Euclio is the miser in Plautus' *Aulularia*. Pope's original has been variously identified as Sir Godfrey Kneller (1646–1723), the painter and eccentric, Sir Charles Duncombe (d. 1711), the banker who died the richest commoner in England, and Sir William Bateman, a London merchant who was knighted by Charles II in 1660. See respectively *Richardsoniana*, 1776, p. 92, Wakefield, p. 206, and Sir J. Prior, *Life of Malone*, 1860, pp. 252–3. Percy MS. adds "Supposed to be Auditor [Thomas] Foley" (d. 1737). Auditor of the Imprests and M.P. for Stafford. I suspect Pope had no particular living original in mind.

And you! brave COBHAM, to the latest breath
Shall feel your ruling passion strong in death:
Such in those moments as in all the past,
"Oh, save my Country, Heav'n!" shall be your last.   265

262–5. These lines are still to be seen inscribed on a plaque on the south side of the 115-foot pillar erected at Stowe by Cobham's widow. Cobham wrote to Pope, 1 November 1733, to thank him for the compliment: "Tho I have not modesty enough not to be pleasd with your extraordinary compliment I have wit enough to know how little I deserve it   you know all mankind are putting themselves upon the world for more then they are worth and their friends are dayly helping the deceit, but I am afraid I shall not pass for an absolute Patriot however I have the honour of having receivd a publick testimony of your esteem and friendship and am as proud of it as I coud be of any advantage which coud happen to me" (Egerton MS. 1949, f. 1, and Sherburn, III 391). Cobham's last words were somewhat different from Pope's anticipation: "In his last moments, not being able to carry a glass of jelly to his mouth, he was in such a passion, that he threw the jelly, glass and all in the face of his niece, Hester Grenville, and expired!" (William Roberts, *Memoirs of the Life and Correspondence of Mrs Hannah More*, 2 vols., 1834, cit. Carruthers, 1 428). Pope's epitaph on Atterbury, who died in 1732, concludes with the attribution of exactly the same sentiment to Atterbury:

          Is there on Earth one care, one wish beside?
          YES—SAVE MY COUNTRY, HEAV'N,—

                              He said, and dy'd.
The Atterbury epitaph was originally included in the quarto *Works*, vol. II (1735), but was cancelled at the last minute—no doubt because of the identity of its final couplet with that in *To Cobham*. The sentiment derives from Atterbury's last letter to Pope, 23 November 1731: "After all I do and must love my country with all its faults and blemishes. . . My last wish shall be like that of Father Paul, *Esto perpetua* . . ." (Sherburn, III 247–8). For a full discussion of the lines see vol. VI of this edition, pp. 343–5.

EPISTLE II

To a LADY.
Of the CHARACTERS *of* WOMEN.

NOTE ON THE TEXT

Of the Characters of Women: an Epistle to a Lady was published as an eighteen-page folio on 8 February 1734/5. A second edition, a mere reprint of the first, and a Dublin edition in octavo by Faulkner also followed later in the same year.[1] In *The Works of Mr. Alexander Pope. Volume II (1735) To a Lady* is grouped with *To Cobham, To Bathurst*, and *To Burlington* as "Epistle II" of "Ethic Epistles, the Second Book". Some of the textual problems raised by the various editions of this collection (*1735abcd*) and their relationship to the "death-bed" edition (*1744*) have been discussed in the General Note on the Text. Changes of phrasing that are certainly to be ascribed to Pope are to be found in all four of the 1735 editions, but *1744* derives from a corrected copy of *1735c*, which was itself a direct revision of the first edition. Overlooked Revisions therefore abound from *1735a, 1735b*, and *1735d*. They are not, however, of much interest, though I have adopted all of them[2]; the "Argument", which was added in *1735a* and translated into analytical footnotes in *1735c*, may not be Pope's work.[3]

The principal difference between *1744* and the earlier texts is that *1744* has been expanded to 292 lines by the addition of ll. 69–86 (Philomedé), 115–50 (Atossa), and 157–98 (Cloe, and the passage on Queen Caroline). Some at least of this new matter had formed part of the original draft of the poem, as is clear from Pope's

---

1. Faulkner (or Swift?) has spelled out "Chartres" in l. 64. Cf. p. 4n above. The "shall" (for "should") in l. 155 may perhaps derive from Pope.

2. *1735a*'s "creates this" in l. 272 may seem an Overlooked Revision that I have excluded; but its correction in that edition's *Errata* to "it forms a" (almost the reading of the first edition) shows that Pope immediately recognized the change was for the worse. Pope's principal objective in revision was a greater verbal precision. Thus Papillia's spark, who has bought a whole park to satisfy her rural longings, becomes "doating" (l. 37) instead of merely "am'rous".

3. If Pope had compiled the notes himself he would not perhaps have been so cavalier in his treatment of them. There is a curious oversight. Up to l. 100 the analysis is almost pedantically complete (though not always very accurate), and there are notes on the principal transitions from l. 207 to the end. But for ll. 101–206 there is not a single note. In the *1744* revision, only one alteration was made in the analytical notes. Jonathan Richardson has been suggested as editor of the folio *Works*, vol. i. (1735) (see Griffith, p. 282, and pp. 4–5 above).

note to Warburton, 27 January [1743/4], "I have gone over all y^r. Papers on ye 2 Epistles, to my Satisfaction, and I agree with you to make shorter work with those to the Lady, & to Ld Burlington (tho' I have replaced most of ye omitted lines in the former)."[1] Unfortunately Pope's MSS. of this poem have not been traced,[2] and the history of his omissions and restorations must be largely conjectural. Pope's only explicit public statement on the matter is to be found in his note on l. 199. In its first form, in the octavo *Works*, vol. II (*1735c*), the note apologizes for "a want of Connexion" at this point, "and also in some following Parts", due to "the omission of certain *Examples* and *Illustrations* to the Maxims laid down". In *1744* and *1751* the note concludes, "some of these have since been found, viz. the Characters of *Philomedé*, *Atossa*, *Cloe*, and some verses following, others are still wanting, nor can we answer that these are exactly inserted."

The question immediately arises, "Were the additions made in 1744 all part of the original draft or not?" A possible clue is provided in a postscript to an undated letter from Pope to Warburton, "I have just run over ye Second Epistle frō Bowyer. I wish you c^d add a Note at ye very End of it, to observe ye authors Tenderness in using no *living Examples* or *real Names*."[3] The note Pope was here suggesting eventually appeared in the 1744 edition at l. 7. Significantly, however, although he prides himself there on "real names" not being used, nothing is said about there being no "living Examples". I interpret this discrepancy to mean that in the final

---

1. Brit. Mus. Egerton MS. 1946, f. 78^r, and Sherburn, IV 495. Rumours of Pope's intention were in circulation the preceding autumn. On 24 October 1743 Elizabeth Wyndham wrote to the Countess of Denbigh, ". . . mais pour le Dunciad, il n'est pas encore imprimé, non plus que la nouvelle edition des 'Caractères des Femmes', auxquelles il en a ajouté quelques autres" (Hist. MSS. Comm., Denbigh MSS., pt V, p. 244).

2. Two autograph MSS. of the poem from the library of Dr Charles Chauncy were sold at Christie's on 30 July 1889. Some idea of what the original MS. may have been like is provided by the specially printed sheet containing the scandalous characters in the Prince of Wales's set of Pope's works assembled in 1738. See Vinton A. Dearing, *Harvard Library Bulletin*, 1950, IV 320–8, and pp. 159–70 below. Since the sheet exists in only one copy and was never published, I have excluded its variant readings from the textual apparatus below.

3. Brit. Mus. Egerton MS. 1946, f. 96^v, and Sherburn, IV 516. The letter must be either late March or early April 1744.

revision a "living Example" had crept into the text; and as it happens one of the new "characters", that of Cloe, can properly be so described. It is likely that some features in the character of Cloe are based upon Mrs Howard (see note to l. 157), and Mrs Howard did not die until 1767. Clearly with a recognizable caricature of Mrs Howard in the poem a note in which the author proclaimed his "Tenderness in using no *living Examples*" would have been inept.

It follows that, if Pope could say he had "replaced most of ye omitted lines" in an expansion of the poem that did not include the Cloe lines, Cloe was not one of the offensive "Examples and Illustrations" in the first draft.[1] And there is independent confirmation for this conclusion. The Cloe lines were first printed as "*Cloe*: a character" in *Works*, vol. II, part ii (1738) without Mrs Howard or anybody else complaining. If the lines could be printed in 1738 they could have been printed in 1735 in the first edition of the poem. That they were not proves that they were not part of its original scheme. The lines were probably, in my opinion, a last-minute addition to the final revision of the poem in 1744. They are quite irrelevant, indeed an interruption to the evolution of the argument, and a bolder editor might relegate them to the notes. Stylistically too they jar. They are in the more diffuse, more conversational, and less rhetorical manner of Pope's later years, and I find it difficult to believe that they can date from the same period as the characters of Philomedé and Atossa. My guess is that Pope, anxious to pad the poem out to a respectable length and finding the Cloe fragment to hand, inserted the lines where they could do least harm, somewhat as he had used his earlier fragments (Artimesia, Sylvia, Erinna, etc.) in the first edition (see notes to ll. 23, 45, 53, 241, 253).

The other new passages in the suppressed edition—the character of Philomedé, the character of Atossa, and the lines on Queen Caroline—undoubtedly derive from the original draft, although some of the Atossa lines were apparently revised in 1743 (see note to l. 115). They are in the harsh elliptic style of the *Essay on Man* period; they are all "Examples and Illustrations to the maxims laid down"; they fit into the poem's general argument; and (if my identifications are correct), though they would have been exceedingly scan-

---

1. Independent confirmation is provided by the absence of the Cloe lines in the Prince of Wales's version. See note 2 on p. 159.

dalous in 1735, the deaths of all their originals would make it natural for Pope to wish to publish them in 1744.

There is no reason to think every line of the original draft reappears in the "death-bed" text. Pope told Warburton in 1744 that he had "replaced most of yᵉ omitted lines"; *most* but not *all*. Among the omitted lines that were certainly not restored are eight lines which once followed l. 198 that Warburton has preserved among the "Variations" in the 1751 *Works*. Two other lines, according to Warburton, originally followed l. 122, and he also supplies four that once followed l. 148 but were finally rewritten as a couplet. A discarded couplet not recorded by Warburton has also survived in the unique set of Pope's writings that once belonged to Frederick, Prince of Wales.[1]

Were there any other lines that were not replaced in the final text? I am inclined to think not, primarily because of the eccentric line-numbering of one passage in the folio *Works*, vol. II (1735). L. 107 in that edition is followed by l. 194. This suggests that between l. 109 of the folio text ("Each is a sort of *Virtue*, and of *Vice*", l. 206 of the final text), where the paragraph ends, and l. 196 ("In sev'ral Men we sev'ral Passions find", l. 207 of the final text), where the next paragraph begins, there were originally eighty-six lines that were presumably cancelled almost at the last moment.[2] Now the character of Philomedé runs to eighteen lines, Atossa amounts to thirty-six lines, and the character of Queen Caroline to eighteen lines—a total of seventy-two lines. Add the twelve rejected lines that Warburton printed as "Variations", plus the extra couplet in the Prince of Wales's set, and a grand total is reached of exactly eighty-six lines. Apparently Pope, acting on a principle he once avowed to Warburton,[3] had at first intended to introduce the three scandalous characters in this collected edition of his "Ethic

---

1. See note 1 on p. xxxvi.

2. By eliminating these 86 lines Pope was able to cancel the whole of gathering G. H (which has 84 lines) follows F (94 lines). F may perhaps have been re-set (it has more lines than the other gatherings).

3. "Mr. Pope used to tell me, that when he had any thing better than ordinary to say, and yet too bold, he always reserved it for a second or third edition, and then nobody took any notice of it" (Warburton to Hurd, 22 September 1751, *Letters from a Late Eminent Prelate*, 1809, p. 86).

Epistles", but decided at the last moment that discretion was the better part of valour.

With the exception, then, of the Overlooked Revisions, the text that follows is that of the suppressed edition of 1744. In addition to inserting the scandalous characters, thirteen verbal changes were made by Pope that are not in any of the earlier editions.

KEY TO THE CRITICAL APPARATUS

1735 = First edition, Griffith 360, 361.

1735*a* = Works, vol. II, large and small folio, Griffith 370, 371.

1735*b* = Works, vol. II, quarto, Griffith 372.

1735*c* = Works, vol. II, octavo, Griffith 388.

1735*d* = Works, vol. II, octavo, Griffith 389.

1736 = Works, vol. II, octavo, Griffith 430.

1738 = Works, vol. II, part ii, octavo, Griffith 507.

1739 = Works, vol. II, octavo, Griffith 505.

1740 = Works, vol. II, part i, octavo, Griffith 523.

1743 = Works, vol. II, part i, octavo, Griffith 583.

1744 = Epistles to Several Persons, Griffith 591.

1746 = Verses Upon the Late D—ss of M – – –, Griffith 613, 614, 615.

Harl. Misc. = The Harleian Miscellany, ed. W. Oldys (1744–6, VIII 212 ("The Character of a certain Great Duchess deceas'd by a certain great Poet lately deceas'd. MS.").

1751 = Works, ed. Warburton, vol. III, large octavo, Griffith 645.

ARGUMENT

OF the Characters of *Women* (consider'd only as contradis-
tinguished from the other Sex.) That these are yet more
inconsistent and incomprehensible than those of Men,
of which Instances are given even from such Characters as are
plainest, and most strongly mark'd; as in the *Affected*, Ver. 7, &c. 5
The *Soft-natur'd*. 29. the *Cunning*, 45. the *Whimsical*, 53. the *Wits and
Refiners*, 87. the *Stupid* and *Silly*, 101. How Contrarieties run thro'
them all.

But tho' the *Particular Characters* of this Sex are more various than
those of Men, the *General Characteristick*, as to the *Ruling Passion*, is 10
more uniform and confin'd. In what That lies, and whence it *pro-
ceeds*, 207, *&c.* Men are best known in publick Life, Women in pri-
vate, 199. What are the *Aims*, and the *Fate* of the Sex, both as to
Power and *Pleasure?* 219, 231. &c. Advice for their true Interest,
249. The Picture of an esteemable Woman, made up of the best 15
kind of Contrarieties, 269, *&c.*

"Argument" added 1735a, but to 1743 grouped with arguments of To
Cobham, To Bathurst, *and* To Burlington *before text of* To Cobham.
*1739, 1744–51 om. The line-numbers vary from edition to edition. They
have been corrected above to conform with 1744's text.*
1 (consider'd . . .)] *1735ab om.*
5 Ver. 7, &c.] VER 7 to 21 *1735ab.*
6 *Soft-natur'd.* 29] *Soft natur'd, 29 to 37 1735ab.*

45

EPISTLE II

To a LADY
Of the CHARACTERS *of* WOMEN[1]

N OTHING so true as what you once let fall,
     "Most Women have no Characters at all".
     Matter too soft a lasting mark to bear,
And best distinguish'd by black, brown, or fair.

Heading] Of The Characters of Women : An Epistle To A Lady *1735*;
Epistle II. *To a* Lady *1735a–43. Most copies of 1735 have an additional
sheet, evidently inserted as an afterthought, on the first page of which
(immediately preceding the text) is*

ADVERTISEMENT.[2]

The Author being very sensible how particular a Tenderness is due to the
FEMALE SEX, *and at the same time how little they generally show to each
other ; declares, upon his Honour, that* no one Character *is drawn from the*
Life, *in this Epistle. It would otherwise be most improperly inscribed to a*
Lady, *who, of all the Women he knows, is the last that would be entertain'd
at the Expence of Another.*

This "*Advertisement*" *was dropped in 1735a and later editions.*

---

[1] Of the CHARACTERS of WOMEN, [a Corollary to the former Epistle] *treating of this Sex only as contradistinguished from the other.* [P. *1735c–43. 1739 adds*] First
publish'd in 1735.

The lady was Martha Blount. Pope wrote to Swift, 16 February 1733: "Your
Lady friend is *Semper Eadem*, and I have written an Epistle to her on that quali-
fication in a female character; which is thought by my chief Critick [Boling-
broke], in your absence to be my *Chef d'Œuvre*" (Sherburn, III 349). And to
Caryll, 8 February 1735, enclosing a copy of the first edition: "The lady to whom
it is addressed had the great modesty to insist on my suppressing her name. So I
must leave you with the rest of the world to guess at her" (Sherburn, III 451). The
"Advertisement" also makes it clear that a real woman was addressed, and
William Ayre (*Memoirs of the Life and Writings of Alexander Pope*, 1745, II 30),
Walpole, Warton, and others agree that she was Martha Blount. Warburton,
however, in revising his notes in the "death-bed" edition (1744) for the 1751
Works added some sentences to the notes on ll. 1 and 269 to the general effect that
the lady was "imaginary". Warburton's motive appears to have been partly to

46

deprive Martha Blount (his principal rival in Pope's affections) of literary glory;
and partly to propitiate Mrs Allen, whose niece Warburton had married and
who had quarrelled with Martha. Details of the quarrel will be found in Spence,
pp. 358–60.

Martha ("Patty"; 1690–1763) and her elder sister Teresa Blount (b. 1688)
belonged to an old Catholic family and were educated at Catholic schools in
Hammersmith and Paris. They were the granddaughters of Anthony Engle-
field, of Whiteknights, who was a neighbour of the Popes at Binfield and had
encouraged the young Pope in his literary ambitions. It was at Whiteknights
that they first met Pope, apparently about 1705, although Pope's earliest letters
to the sisters only date from 1711. Pope flirted with both sisters impartially until
about 1718 when less is heard of Teresa and his relations with Martha became
more serious. In the following years Martha spent much of her time with or near
Pope and they were expected to marry. It is not improbable that she was Pope's
mistress. Horace Walpole, who described her as "red-faced, fat, and by no means
pretty", told Malone "She was the decided mistress of Pope, yet visited by re-
spectable people" (Sir J. Prior, *Life of Malone*, 1860, p. 437). A remark by Wil-
liam Cheselden, the surgeon, to Spence appears to confirm this (Spence, p. 339);
Cheselden attended Pope professionally. And an anecdote recorded by Gray the
poet about Pope's last visit to Prior Park is significant: "Mrs. Warburton re-
members that she lay at that time in the next room to Pope, & that every Mor^g
between 6 & 7 o'clock, Mrs Blount used to come into his Chamber, when she
heard them talk earnestly together for a long time. & that when they came down
to breakfast, M^{rs} B: usd alys to ask him how he had rested that night" (D. C.
Tovey, *Gray and his Friends*, 1890, p. 281). Gray's informant was William Mason,
who had been told the story by the Warburtons themselves. Pope's devotion to
Martha remained unbroken to the end. Warburton told Spence that, when Pope
was dying, "It was very observable, during that time, that Mrs. Blount's coming
in gave a new turn of spirits, or a temporary strength to him" (Spence, p. 357). By
his will Pope left her £1,000, all his goods and chattels and a life-interest in the
rest of his estate.

2 "There is nothing in Mr. Pope's works more highly finished than this Epistle:
Yet its success was in no proportion to the pains he took in composing it. Some-
thing he chanced to drop in a short Advertisement prefixed to it, on its first pub-
lication, may perhaps account for the small attention given to it. He said, that
no one character in it was drawn from the life. The Public believed him on his word,
and expressed little curiosity about a Satire in which there was nothing per-
sonal" [Warburton]. The question how far the satire in this Epistle is personal
is discussed in the Introduction (p. xlvii).

1. That their particular Characters are not so strongly mark'd as those of Men,
seldom so fixed, and still more inconsistent with themselves. [P. *1735c–43*.]

2. EC (III 95) compares Butler's "Women" (*Satires and Miscellaneous Poetry and
Prose*, ed. R. Lamar, 1928, p. 220):

> The Soules of women are so small
> That Some believe th'have none at all.

H

> How many pictures of one Nymph we view,   5
> All how unlike each other, all how true!
> Arcadia's Countess, here, in ermin'd pride,

But, as this poem was only printed in *The Genuine Remains*, ed. R. Thyer, vol. I, 1759, neither Pope nor Martha Blount (if the *mot* really was hers) is likely to have seen it. A more plausible parallel is Congreve's confession to Dennis (letter of 10 July 1695), "I have never made any observation of what I Apprehend to be true Humour in Women", where "Humour" really means "character". The observation is, of course, something of a commonplace. See, for example, Lord Chesterfield's letter to his son (19 December 1749), "Women are much more like each other than men."

7–13. Attitudes in which several ladies affected to be drawn, and sometimes one lady in them all.—The poet's politeness and complaisance to the sex is observable in this instance, amongst others, that, whereas in the *Characters of Men* he has sometimes made use of real names, in the *Characters of Women* always fictitious. [P. *1744–51*.] Although signed P. in *1751* Warburton appears to have had a finger in this note. Its genesis will be found in the postscript to an undated note (early 1744?) from Pope to Warburton (Egerton MS. 1946, f. 96ᵛ): "I have just run over yᵉ Second Epistle frō Bowyer [the printer], I wish you cᵈ add a Note at yᵉ very End of it, to observe yᵉ authors Tenderness in using no *living Examples* or *real Names* of any one of yᵉ softer [Female *erased*] Sex, tho so free with those of his own in all his [?] other satyrs." The significance of the words "living Examples", and of their omission in the printed note, is discussed in the Note on the Text (p. 41 above), and see Sherburn, IV 516. Earlier poems using a gallery of portraits as the inclusive structural metaphor are listed in Jean H. Hogstrum's discussion of this poem in *The Sister Arts* (Chicago, 1958).

Arcadia's Countess] "It is said this hints at the countess of Pembroke, who used to be drawn in these several attitudes" (MS. note by Edward Harley, second Earl of Oxford, in a copy of the first edition, now Bodley M. 3. 19). The full title of Sir Philip Sidney's romance was (in compliment to his sister Mary) *The Countesse of Pembrokes Arcadia* (1590). Pope's countess may have been, as Walpole suggests (Fraser marginalia, p. 30), another Mary, a Mary Howe (d. 1749), who became the third wife of Thomas Herbert, eighth Earl of Pembroke (see *To Burlington*, 8 and note there) in 1725. The Earl was an enthusiastic collector and patron of the arts who might have been expected to commission portraits of the young wife he doted on (see Lady Hervey to Mrs Howard, 30 July 1725, *Suffolk Letters*, I 191–2), but I have been able to locate only one portrait of this Countess —a head and shoulders at Wilton by Pope's friend Jervas—which represents her in ordinary eighteenth-century costume. It seems more likely that Pope had the Earl's first wife in mind, Margaret Sawyer, whose portrait with a lamb by van der Vaart (here reproduced by the kindness of the present Earl) is still at Wilton. Pope may have seen it when he visited Wilton in 1724 (Sherburn, II 240). This would explain "Pastora". The other "attitudes" may be due to a confused

'ARCADIA'S COUNTESS . . . . . IS THERE, PASTORA'
(*Margaret Sawyer, Countess of Pembroke, by Jan van der Vaart, c. 1687*)

Is there, Pastora by a fountain side:
Here Fannia, leering on her own good man,
Is there, a naked Leda with a Swan.   10
Let then the Fair one beautifully cry,
In Magdalen's loose hair and lifted eye,
Or drest in smiles of sweet Cecilia shine,
With simp'ring Angels, Palms, and Harps divine;
Whether the Charmer sinner it, or saint it,   15
If Folly grows romantic, I must paint it.
    Come then, the colours and the ground prepare!

8 Is there, Pastora] There, *Pastorella 1735–35c*.
10 Is there] And there *1735–35c, 1744–51*.
16 If . . . paint it] When Folly grows romantic, we must paint it
    1735–35b; If Folly grows romantic, must I paint it? *1735c*;
    If Folly grow romantic, I must paint it *1751*.

recollection by Pope of two fine double portraits of a husband and wife (Fannia)
and a version of Leonardo's "Leda and the Swan", which are also at Wilton. See
Sir Nevile R. Wilkinson, *Wilton House Pictures*, 2 vols., 1907.

8. *Pastora*] There is no Pastora in Sidney's *Arcadia*. Pope may have got the name
from Congreve's *The Mourning Muse of Alexis* (1695), a pastoral elegy on Queen
Mary with the refrain
          I mourn PASTORA *dead, let* ALBION *mourn,*
          And Sable Clouds her Chalkie Cliffs adorn.

9. *Fannia*] "In this passage the poet meant to display the contrast between
Fannia looking at her husband in the attitude of a modest matron; and Fannia
in the looser posture of an unattired wanton. By the use of the epithet *leering*, the
poet marks the lubricity of Fannia" (Owen Ruffhead, *The Life of Alexander Pope*,
1769, pp. 279–80). Ruffhead may be wrong; *leering* in Pope's time could still
connote an innocent side-glance. Fannia was the name of an important Roman
plebeian gens, the most famous Fannia being the adulteress who saved Marius's
life. But Pope may only have intended a latinized form of Fanny, a common
upper-class abbreviation in the eighteenth century.

16. *romantic*] extravagant, theatrical, a *poseuse*. For the full *nuance* of the word in
Pope's time, see Logan Pearsall Smith, *Four Words*, S.P.E., 1924.

17. "Pope's pleasure in painting was apparently keen, but experience of the
art affected his poetry hardly more than in the occasional use of technical terms
from painting" (Sherburn, *Early Career*, p. 103). See also "Pope and the Techni-
calities of the Arts", *Spectator*, 20 September 1919, pp. 364–5. For a statement of
the opposite point of view see Norman Ault, *New Light on Pope* (1949), ch. v. Pope

Dip in the Rainbow, trick her off in Air,
Chuse a firm Cloud, before it fall, and in it
Catch, ere she change, the Cynthia of this minute.   20
    Rufa, whose eye quick-glancing o'er the Park,
Attracts each light gay meteor of a Spark,

---

19 it fall] it falls *1735, 1735b*.

---

had taken lessons in painting from his friend Charles Jervas from March to about October 1713, but only one or two of his paintings survive, including a very clever copy of Kneller's portrait of Betterton. The passage is perhaps a reminiscence of La Bruyère, "De la Mode" (*Caractères*, Paris, 1714, p. 525): "Les couleurs sont préparés, et la toile est toute prête; mais comment le fixer, cet homme inquiet, léger, inconstant, qui change de mille et mille figures". In the English translation: "The colours are all prepar'd, and the Pallet is ready; but how shall I fix this restless, light, and inconstant man, who changes himself into a thousand and a thousand figures?" (2nd edition, 1700, p. 281). See Audra, p. 556. Cf. too *Rape of the Lock*, II 95–7.

18. *Dip*] Immerse in a colouring solution (a technical sense).

trick her off] Sketch or draw in outline.

19. *a firm Cloud*] Perhaps a reference to the use of clouds in Renaissance paintings to help disguise the nudity of such modest deities as Diana (Cynthia).

20. *Cynthia of this minute*] Geoffrey Tillotson (vol. II of this edition, pp. 360–1) has pointed out that, like Drayton and Herrick, Pope associated fairies, and daintiness in general, with the short *i*.

21. Instances of contrarieties [this Position *1735c–44*], given even from such Characters as are most strongly mark'd and seemingly therefore most consistent. As I. In [As first, Contrarieties in *1735c–44*] the *Affected*, v. 21 &c. [P. *1735c–51*.]

"This character of Rufa, and the succeeding ones of Silia, Papillia, Narcissa, and Flavia, are precisely and entirely in the style and manner of the portraits Young has given us in his Fifth Satire on Women" [Warton]. Young's *Love of Fame, the Universal Passion, in seven characteristical Satires* (1725–8) certainly influenced Pope (see Charlotte E. Crawford, *ELH*, September 1946, XIII, 157–67), and the parallels are especially close with Young's Satires V and VI (both "On Women"). Young's Clarinda, Zara, Xantippe, Delia, Daphne, etc. are generalized types and it seems unnecessary to assume that this group of Pope's characters had any living originals either.

Rufa] Red-head. There is a disreputable Rufa in *Sober Advice*, 29. Rufus was a common Roman name, but Pope's main point is certainly the lubricity popularly ascribed to women with red hair (cf. the female Yahoo in *Gulliver's Travels*) (G. K. Turner).

Agrees as ill with Rufa studying Locke,
As Sappho's diamonds with her dirty smock,

24 Sappho's] *Flavia's 1735, 1735a.*

23–4. Rufa and Sappho both derive in part from Pope's Artimesia ("said to mean Q. Caroline" [Warton]), which is reprinted in vol. vi of this edition, pp. 48–9. The first stanza runs:

> Tho' *Artimesia* talks, by Fits,
> Of Councils, Classicks, Fathers, Wits;
> Reads *Malbranche, Boyle,* and *Locke*:
> Yet in some Things methinks she fails,
> 'Twere well if she would pare her Nails,
> And wear a cleaner Smock.

In his annotated copy of Pope's *Works*, vol. ii (1736) (recently presented to the Bodleian Library by the late B. H. Newdigate) William Cole wrote against Rufa "Lady Mary Wortley Montagu". "George Paston" (*Life of Pope*, 1909, ii 512) has suggested that Rufa is Margaret Rolle, who married Walpole's eldest son, Robert, Baron Walpole. Both of these identifications appear to be mere guesses.

24. *Sappho*] In the early editions (see textual note) Sappho is Flavia, perhaps the same Flavia as in l. 87. The change to Sappho was from an ideal to a real character. Lady Mary Wortley Montagu (see Biog. App. in vol. iv) was apparently the Sappho of Pope's lines to Erinna (1722) and of Peterborough's "I said to my heart" (1723?). (The marginal note "Lady Mary Wriothesley" in Bodley MS. Add. B. 105, f. 104 of Peterborough's lines is apparently only the transcriber's misreading of "Lady Mary Wortley M".) But both of these references were complimentary. The passage in *Imit. Hor., Sat.,* ii i (1733), 83–4,

> From furious *Sappho* scarce a milder Fate,
> P–x'd by her Love, or libell'd by her Hate,

was the first occasion on which Pope attacked Lady Mary as Sappho. For her attempts to get the couplet suppressed see vol. iv of this edition, pp. xvii, xviii. Lady Mary is the Sappho, Sapho or Sa** of Pope's later satires (*Epistle to Arbuthnot,* 101, 369, *Imit. Donne,* ii 6, *Epilogue to Satires,* i 15). The change here from Flavia is paralleled in *To Bathurst,* 121, where Sappho had originally been Lesbia. Both of these changes, as well as the reference in *Imit. Donne,* ii, are first found either in the folio or quarto *Works,* vol. ii, which were both published 23 April 1735. Was there any special reason just then why Pope should wish to rub in that Sappho was Lady Mary? A letter from Lady Mary to Arbuthnot, 3 January [1734/5], suggests a possible answer: "I have perused the last lampoon [*Epistle to Arbuthnot*] of your ingenious friend, and am not surprised you did not find me out under the name of Sappho, because there is nothing I ever heard in our characters and circumstances to make a parallel; but as the town (except you, who know better) generally suppose Pope means me, whenever he mentions that

Or Sappho at her toilet's greazy task,   25
With Sappho fragrant at an ev'ning Mask:
So morning Insects that in muck begun,
Shine, buzz, and fly-blow in the setting-sun.
    How soft is Silia! fearful to offend,
The Frail one's advocate, the Weak one's friend: 30
To her, Calista prov'd her conduct nice,
And good Simplicius asks of her advice.
Sudden, she storms! she raves! You tip the wink,
But spare your censure; Silia does not drink.

25 Or Sappho . . . task] Or *Flavia*'s self in glue (her rising task)
    1735, 1735a; Or Sappho's self in glue (her rising task) *1735b–35c*.
26 With Sappho fragrant at] And issuing flagrant to *1735–43* (*pre-
    sumably a misprint for* fragrant).
30 the Weak] and weak *1735–35b*.
31 Calista] Calisto *1735b* (*a misprint?*).

name, I cannot help taking notice of the horrible malice he bears against the lady
signified by that name" (Lady Mary's *Letters*, II 20–1). Pope may well have seen
this letter—indeed, Lady Mary specifically asked Arbuthnot to show it him—
and seeing it may well have decided to give Lady Mary more of the same medi-
cine. See also Appendix I ("Pope's Quarrel with Lady Mary and Lord Hervey")
in Robert W. Rogers, *The Major Satires of Alexander Pope*, 1955, pp. 127–33.

dirty smock] Lady Mary was notoriously slovenly. Horace Walpole describes her
in a letter to Conway, 25 September 1740: "She wears a foul mob, that does not
cover her greasy black locks, that hang loose, never combed or curled; an old
mazarine blue wrapper, that gapes open and discovers a canvas petticoat"; and
Pope sneers at "Linnen worthy Lady Mary" in *Imit. Hor., Ep.*, I i (1737), 164.
29–40. Contrarieties in the *Soft-natured*. [P. *1735c–51*.]

31. *Calista*] Calista was the guilty heroine of Rowe's famous "she-tragedy"
The Fair Penitent (1703), one of the most popular plays of the eighteenth century.
Callisto (see textual note) was the Arcadian princess or nymph, a companion of
Artemis, whose pregnancy (by Zeus) was discovered by the goddess when
they were bathing.

nice] Punctilious. In Pope, however, the word normally has a flavour of con-
tempt. Compare l. 205 below, and *Rape of Lock*, IV 124,
        And the nice Conduct of a *clouded Cane*.
32. *Simplicius*] The historical Simplicius was a sixth-century neo-platonist
whose commentary on Epictetus Pope may well have read in George Stanhope's
translation (1694). But Pope may only intend a general connotation of *simplicity*.

All eyes may see from what the change arose,   35
All eyes may see—a Pimple on her nose.
    Papillia, wedded to her doating spark,
Sighs for the shades—"How charming is a Park!"
A Park is purchas'd, but the Fair he sees
All bath'd in tears—"Oh odious, odious Trees!"   40
    Ladies, like variegated Tulips, show,
'Tis to their Changes that their charms they owe;
Their happy Spots the nice admirer take,
Fine by defect, and delicately weak.
'Twas thus Calypso once each heart alarm'd,   45

---

37 doating] am'rous *1735–35a, 1735c–51*.
42 that their charms they] half their charms we *1735–35a, 1735c–51*.
43–4 Their . . . weak] Such . . . weak *1735, 1735a, 1735c–43; 1751
retains 1744's reading and punctuation but inverts the order of the lines.
The change is clearly for the worse; the defects and weaknesses are a* non
sequitur *unless preceded and explained by the ambiguity of* Spots. *The
transition must be from* Tulips *to* Spots *and from* Spots *to defect. The
odd punctuation in 1751 suggests a printer's error.*
45 each heart] our hearts *1735–43*.

---

37. *Papillia*] *Papilio* is Latin for butterfly.
40.   Such *Fulvia's* Passion for the Town, fresh Air
        (An odd Effect!) gives Vapours to the Fair:
        Green Fields, and shady Groves and Chrystal Springs,
        And Larks, and Nightingales, are odious Things.
                 Young, *Love of Fame*, Satire v, ll. 239–42.
Odious was fashionable feminine slang. Narcissa uses it in *To Cobham*, 242. Con-
greve's Millamant was fond of the word: "that odious Man" (*The Way of the
World*, iii x), "Odious Endeavours!", "I toast Fellows, Odious Men! I hate your
odious *Proviso's*" (*ibid.*, iv v).
    45–52. III. Contrarieties in the *Cunning* and *Artful*. [P. *1735c–51*.] Walpole
(Fraser marginalia, p. 31) identified Calypso with Anne Griffith who married
William Stanhope the politician (later created first Earl of Harrington). Their
son the second Earl was an intimate friend of Walpole's and there may have been
a family tradition to this effect. On general grounds it is most unlikely. Anne had
died as early as 1719 and Pope never knew her well. Moreover the character of
Calypso is not original but represents a rewriting of the opening lines of Pope's
"Sylvia, a Fragment" (vol. vi of this edition, pp. 286–8):

Aw'd without Virtue, without Beauty charm'd;
Her Tongue bewitch'd as odly as her Eyes,
Less Wit than Mimic, more a Wit than wise:
Strange graces still, and stranger flights she had,
Was just not ugly, and was just not mad;   50
Yet ne'er so sure our passion to create,
As when she touch'd the brink of all we hate.
  Narcissa's nature, tolerably mild,

Sylvia my Heart in wond'rous wise alarm'd,
Aw'd without Sense, and without Beauty charm'd,
But some odd Graces and fine Flights she had,
Was just not ugly, and was just not mad:
Her Tongue still ran, on credit from her Eyes,
More pert than witty, more a Wit than wise.

Sylvia herself (see vol. VI) was clearly drawn from the life. Walpole's and War-
ton's notes on Narcissa (see l. 53) suggest that Sylvia may perhaps have been
intended for Elizabeth Gerard, second wife of the Duke of Hamilton who was
killed in the duel with Lord Mohun. The Duchess (d. 10 February 1744) was a
lively disreputable woman of the world, and Swift and Pope knew her well.
Horace Walpole describes her (Huntington marginalia, p. 486) as "a Woman of
great Debauchery & Wit. I have led her out in a morning when she has sat up
all night drinking to be in time for my Father Sr R. Walpole's Levée." Pope once
received a letter from her amanuensis beginning, "Sir,—My Lady Dutchess
being drunk at this present and not able to write herself . . ." (Sherburn, I 404).

  53–68. IV. In the *Whimsical*. [P. *1735c–51*.] Walpole (Fraser marginalia, p. 31)
and Warton (III 215) agree that Narcissa is a caricature of the Duchess of Hamil-
ton. But Narcissa, like Calypso, has simply been made up from the *disjecta membra*
of "Sylvia, a Fragment" (see note to ll. 45–52), and Pope can hardly have in-
tended the lines to be read as a portrait. The original Sylvia *may* have been meant
for the Duchess of Hamilton. The relevant lines in "Sylvia" are:

Good Nature, she declar'd it, was her Scorn,
Tho' 'twas by that alone she could be born.
Affronting all, yet fond of a good Name,
A Fool to Pleasure, yet a Slave to Fame . . .
Now deep in *Taylor* and the *Book of Martyrs*,
Now drinking Citron with his *Gr*— and *Ch*— . . .
Frail, fev'rish Sex! their Fit now chills, now burns;
Atheism and Superstition rule by Turns;
And the meer Heathen in her carnal Part,
Is still a sad good Christian at her Heart.

The Narcissa in *To Cobham*, 247, is Mrs Oldfield the actress.

To make a wash, would hardly stew a child,
Has ev'n been prov'd to grant a Lover's pray'r,   55
And paid a Tradesman once to make him stare,
Gave alms at Easter, in a Christian trim,
And made a Widow happy, for a whim.
Why then declare Good-nature is her scorn,
When 'tis by that alone she can be born?   60
Why pique all mortals, yet affect a name?
A fool to Pleasure, and a slave to Fame:
Now deep in Taylor and the Book of Martyrs,
Now drinking citron with his Grace and Chartres.
Now Conscience chills her, and now Passion burns;   65
And Atheism and Religion take their turns;
A very Heathen in the carnal part,
Yet still a sad, good Christian at her heart.
    See Sin in State, majestically drunk,

62 and] yet *1735–35ᵃ, 1735ᶜ–51.*
64 Chartres] *Ch** 1735.*   69–86 *Add. 1744.*

---

54. *wash*] Washes for the hair or the skin were normally home-made in the eighteenth century.

63. *Taylor*] Jeremy Taylor's *Holy Living and Holy Dying* had reached its twenty-fourth edition in 1727.

Book of Martyrs] John Foxe's martyrology, *Actes and Monuments*, was published in 1563 and reached a ninth edition in 1684. It was not reprinted in Pope's lifetime.

64. *citron*] Citron-water, brandy flavoured with citron- or lemon-peel.

his Grace] Philip Duke of Wharton (see note to *To Cobham*, 179). The identification is made by Pope's friend the second Earl of Oxford in his copy of the poem now in the Bodleian Library, as well as by Walpole, Warton, and others, and seems certain. Percy MS. adds that Wharton was "very intimate at one time with Chartres: who won Hornby Castle of him: i.e. bôt it at 7 years' purchase".

Chartres] Francis Charteris (see note to *To Bathurst*, 20).

69–87. V. In the *Lewd* and *Vicious*. [P. *1744–51.*] The character of Philomedé was one of the passages added in 1744. There is no reason to suspect Pope's statement that the character was a part of the original draft which was suppressed in 1735 as dangerously scandalous. (See Note on the Text, p. 41 above.) But the nature of the scandal is obscure. According to Warton (III 215) Philomedé was "Designed for the Duchess of Marlborough, who so much admired

Proud as a Peeress, prouder as a Punk;   70
Chaste to her Husband, frank to all beside,
A teeming Mistress, but a barren Bride.
What then? let Blood and Body bear the fault,
Her Head's untouch'd, that noble Seat of Thought:
Such this day's doctrine—in another fit   75
She sins with Poets thro' pure Love of Wit.
What has not fir'd her bosom or her brain?
Cæsar and Tall-boy, Charles and Charlema'ne.

Congreve", i.e. Henrietta Churchill (1681–1733), wife of the second Earl of Godolphin, later Duchess of Marlborough in her own right. Walpole (Fraser marginalia, p. 31) believed Henrietta Churchill to be the original of Flavia (ll. 87–100), and he does not attempt to identify Philomedé. The name might be taken to imply exotic tastes (a lover of the Medes), and Henrietta was an enthusiastic patron of Buononcini (Lady Mary's *Letters*, I 459). Her mother told Mrs Boscawen she would not leave Marlborough House to Henrietta to "bee filled with poets Jades & fidlers" (Evelyn MSS. at Christ Church, Oxford, 1894; cit. K. M. Lynch, *Philological Quart.*, July 1953, p. 339n.) The ambiguous intimacy with Congreve may be referred to in l. 76. And the phrase in the suppressed character of Marlborough (see vol. vi), "Madness & lust (said God) be you his heirs," goes to show Pope's contempt at this time for Henrietta and her surviving sister the Duchess of Montagu (see l. 107n). But, on the other hand, (i) Henrietta was a generous patron of Gay which should have made her *persona grata* to Pope, (ii) she had three children and so was not "a barren Bride", though the father of the youngest, Mary, *may* have been Congreve (see J. C. Hodges, *William Congreve the Man*, New York, 1941, pp. 109ff), (iii) her husband, if politically a "cypher" (Chesterfield to Mrs Howard, 15 July 1734), was "a man of undoubted understanding" (Hervey, *Memoirs*, p. 407) who could hardly be called a "Dunce". I regard the case for Henrietta as not proven.

72. Cf. "A teeming Widow, but a barren Wife", John Sheffield, Duke of Buckinghamshire, "An Essay on Satyre" (*Works*, 1723, I 122). The line is Sheffield's (see the early text in *The Fourth (and Last) Collection of Poems, Satyrs, Songs*, 1689), but in a passage much revised by Pope, who edited the posthumous collection of the Duke's writings. The reference in Sheffield is to Lady Dorset.

73. *fault*] Pope regularly rhymes "fault" with such words as "taught" (see l. 212), "brought" (*Dunciad*, I 226), "ought" (*Eloisa to Abelard*, 184). Clearly the *l* was not sounded. The pronunciation is not noticed, however, by H. C. Wyld, *A History of Modern Colloquial English*, 1920, though Mr Norman Ault tells me that the rhymes of Sheffield, Addison, Congreve, Prior, Gay, Broome, and Swift confirm its correctness in Pope's time.

78. *Tall-boy*] The booby young lover in Richard Brome's comedy *The Jovial*

As Helluo, late Dictator of the Feast,
The Nose of Hautgout, and the Tip of Taste,   80
Critick'd your wine, and analyz'd your meat,
Yet on plain Pudding deign'd at-home to eat;
So Philomedé, lect'ring all mankind
On the soft Passion, and the Taste refin'd,
Th' Address, the Delicacy—stoops at once,   85
And makes her hearty meal upon a Dunce.
    Flavia's a Wit, has too much sense to Pray,
To Toast our wants and wishes, is her way;
Nor asks of God, but of her Stars to give
The mighty blessing, "while we live, to live."   90
Then all for Death, that Opiate of the soul!
Lucretia's dagger, Rosamonda's bowl.
Say, what can cause such impotence of mind?
A Spark too fickle, or a Spouse too kind.
Wise Wretch! with Pleasures too refin'd to please,   95

95 Wretch] Fool *1735d–43* (*the return to* Wretch *was presumably neces-*
    stated by l. 124, which was only added in 1744).   with Pleasures]
    of Pleasures *1735*.

Crew (1641), which was still a stock piece in the eighteenth century. A particular
scandal is no doubt hinted at.
    Charles] Used generically for the typical footman, as "James" was in the nine-
teenth century.
    79. *Helluo*] Glutton, in Latin. There is another Helluo in *To Cobham*, 238.
    80. *Hautgout*] "Anything with a strong relish or strong scent, as overkept
venison or game" (Johnson).
    83. *Philomedé*] If not intended to suggest "lover of the Medes" perhaps the
name derives from the Homeric epithet for Aphrodite—"laughter-loving". See
p. xlvii, note 3 above.
    87–100. VI. Contrarieties in the *Witty* and *Refin'd*. [P. *1735c–51*.] Walpole
(Fraser marginalia, p. 31) thought Flavia was intended for Henrietta, Duchess
of Marlborough. See, however, note on 69–86. Lord Hailes, writing to Malone,
October 1791 (Sir J. Prior, *Life of Malone*, 1860, p. 253), took l. 92 to be an allu-
sion to the attempted suicide of Elizabeth, Lady Lechmere, in 1725 (see Lady
Mary's *Letters*, I 492). Flavia is probably a wholly ideal figure. If she has any basis
in reality she is more likely to have been modelled on the eccentric "intellectual"

With too much Spirit to be e'er at ease,
With too much Quickness ever to be taught,
With too much Thinking to have common Thought:
Who purchase Pain with all that Joy can give,
And die of nothing but a Rage to live.   100
    Turn then from Wits; and look on Simo's Mate,
No Ass so meek, no Ass so obstinate:
Or her, that owns her Faults, but never mends,
Because she's honest, and the best of Friends:
Or her, whose life the Church and Scandal share,   105
For ever in a Passion, or a Pray'r:
Or her, who laughs at Hell, but (like her Grace)
Cries, "Ah! how charming if there's no such place!"
Or who in sweet vicissitude appears
Of Mirth and Opium, Ratafie and Tears,   110
The daily Anodyne, and nightly Draught,

99 Who] You *1735–35c, 1744–51.*
107–8 *Add. 1735b, the irregular line-numbering there suggesting that this
was a last-minute insertion.*
108 Ah] oh *1735b–43.*

who was the younger Duchess of Marlborough, than on Lady Lechmere, who
was merely a gambler.

  98. *common Thought*] Common sense.

  107. *her Grace*] Warton asserts that the duchess intended was Mary Churchill,
Duchess of Montagu (1689–1751). Walpole (Fraser marginalia, p. 32) believed
it was the elder sister, Henrietta Churchill, Duchess of Marlborough, to whom
Pope was alluding. Pope had complimented all the four Churchill sisters in his
Epistle to Jervas (see vol. vi), 59, and in 1713 he had tried to copy the Duchess
of Montagu's portrait by Jervas (Pope to Caryll, 31 August 1713; Pope to Gay,
23 August 1713). He may have had no particular duchess in mind.

  108. *charming*] Feminine slang, like *odious* (l. 40). Cf. "that charming princess,
if I may use so familiar an expression" (*OED*, quoting Lady Mary's Letters,
I xix).

  110. *Ratafie*] A sort of cherry brandy made with peach and apricot stones.
Congreve's Lady Wishfort was a great drinker of ratafia (*The Way of the World*,
I i).

  111. *Draught*] Pronounced *drawt*; a good rhyme in the upper-class English of
Pope's time with *thought*. Cf. *To Burlington*, 103.

To kill those foes to Fair ones, Time and Thought.
Woman and Fool are two hard things to hit,
For true No-meaning puzzles more than Wit.
But what are these to great Atossa's mind?   115

115–50 *Add. 1744, printed separately 1746, and from a different text by William Oldys in* The Harleian Miscellany, VIII (*1746*) *212.*

114. One of Pope's "Thoughts on Various Subjects" (EC, x 558) runs: "Women, as they are like riddles in being unintelligible, so generally resemble them in this, that they please us no longer when once we know them."

115. *Atossa*] The name is well chosen. The historical Atossa was the daughter of Cyrus and the sister of Cambyses, the Duchess was a natural daughter of James II and a half-sister of the Old Pretender.

115–50. The character of Atossa was one of the suppressed passages (see Note on the Text, p. 40 above); and it is clear that it was suppressed because it was, at any rate in its origin, a caricature of a contemporary notability. The old view that Pope's victim was Sarah, Duchess of Marlborough, is discussed and dismissed in Appendix A (pp. 159–70 below). It is now virtually certain that his satire was directed solely against Katherine Darnley, Duchess of Buckinghamshire (1682?–1743), though a few of the lines may have come from the discarded character of the Duchess of Marlborough as "Orsini", which formed part of *To a Lady* in the poem's early stages (see Spence, p. 364). The Duke had been one of the earliest to salute Pope's genius (see *Epistle to Arbuthnot*, 139) and Pope edited his posthumous *Works* (1723). Pope would seem to have been on friendly terms with the Duchess until 1729, when his revision of a character she had written of herself (perhaps that published in 1746 as *The Character of Katharine, late Duchess of Buckinghamshire and Normanby. By the late Mr. Pope*, though its authenticity is not yet established) led to a quarrel "and we never saw each other in five or six years" (Pope to James Moyser, 11 July 1743; Sherburn, IV 460). The first draft of Atossa was probably written at this period. In 1735 there was a reconciliation and Pope wrote an epitaph on her "Booby Son" (*Dia.* II, 107) the second Duke (see vol. IV of this edition, pp. 362–3). They continued to meet until the Duchess's death in March 1743, but her will enraged Pope: "All her private papers and those of her correspondents, are left in the hands of Lord Hervey, so that it is not impossible another volume of my letters may come out . . . sure this is infamous conduct towards any common acquaintance. And yet this woman seemed once a woman of great honour, and many generous principles" (Pope to Hugh Bethel, 20 March 1743, as quoted in Owen Ruffhead's *Life of Pope*, 1769, pp. 407–8; Sherburn, IV 446). No doubt it was in this mood of righteous indignation that Pope put the final touches to the character of Atossa (see especially ll. 149–50). The Duchess was an arrogant, quarrelsome, eccentric woman, but was not without energy, intelligence, and public spirit.

Scarce once herself, by turns all Womankind!
Who, with herself, or others, from her birth
Finds all her life one warfare upon earth:
Shines, in exposing Knaves, and painting Fools,
Yet is, whate'er she hates and ridicules.   120
No Thought advances, but her Eddy Brain
Whisks it about, and down it goes again.
Full sixty years the World has been her Trade,
The wisest Fool much Time has ever made.
From loveless youth to unrespected age,   125

117 or] and *1746, Harl. Misc.*   120 and] or *1746, Harl. Misc.*
122 Whisks] Whirls *1746.*
124 much] that *Harl. Misc.*

116. Cf.   Not one, but all Mankind's Epitome.
                              Dryden, *Absalom and Achitophel,* 544.
The source is confirmed by the earlier version of the line in the Prince of Wales's
set (see p. 41, note 2 above):
                    That wild Epitome of Womankind!
118. The Duchess was engaged in constant law-suits with the Duke's natural
children. Pope spent 28 March 1737 "solliciting Lords to attend the Duchess of
Buckingham's Cause, which comes on to morrow" (Pope to Orrery, Sherburn,
IV 65). This case arose over some disputed property on the death of the second
Duke. The Duchess's will—dated 15 February and proved 15 March 1743—
bequeathes an annuity of £120 to Sophia Cox "for her respectfull behaviour to
my dear son . . . and to myself and for her not taking part with the other natural
Children of my late Husband . . . in their Suits against me and in the wrongs they
have done me". These phrases are repeated in the codicil which includes legacies
to other members of the Cox family.
119. One knave whom the Duchess exposed was John Ward (see *To Bathurst,*
20*n*, p. 87 below). Pope assisted her in his prosecution (see the letter from the
Duchess to Pope, Sherburn, II 286–7).
121–2. The Duchess, always eccentric, finally became insane. Pope wrote to
Bathurst, 9 July 1732: "She has dealt as mysteriously with you, as with me
formerly; both which are proofs that We are both less mad, than is requisite, for
her to think quite well of us" (Sherburn, III 296).
123. She was sixty-one when she died in 1743. The line may have been trans-
ferred from the "Orsini" character. It would have been more appropriately
applied to the Duchess of Marlborough. See p. 169 below.
125. Her first husband was James, third Earl of Anglesey. She obtained a
separation from him by an Act of Parliament in 1701 because of his brutality to

No Passion gratify'd except her Rage.
So much the Fury still out-ran the Wit,
The Pleasure miss'd her, and the Scandal hit.
Who breaks with her, provokes Revenge from Hell,
But he's a bolder man who dares be well: 130
Her ev'ry turn with Violence pursu'd,
Nor more a storm her Hate than Gratitude.
To that each Passion turns, or soon or late;
Love, if it makes her yield, must make her hate:
Superiors? death! and Equals? what a curse!   135
But an Inferior not dependant? worse.

134 makes] make *1746*.
135 and Equals?] an Equal, *1746*; if Equals? *Harl. Misc.*

her. In her old age she became one of the town's jokes. Horace Walpole has several allusions to "Princess Buckingham" in his early letters. "The Duchess of Buckingham," he writes to Mann, 24 December 1741, "who is more mad with pride than any mercer's wife in Bedlam, came the other night to the Opera *en princesse*, literally in robes, red velvet and ermine."

126. Pope later attributed her eventual insanity to the violence of her rages. "Her Fate has been hard upon her, but not so hard as herself, for her Passions have overturn'd Mind and Body" (Pope to Orrery, 9 February 1743; Sherburn, IV 441).

128. Her physician, Dr Hugh Chamberlain, was reputed, perhaps untruly, to have been her lover (Sherburn, *Early Career*, p. 295; Walpole, Huntington marginalia, p. 483).

129–32. That odd document *The Character of Katharine, late Duchess of Buckinghamshire and Normanby*, which was published in 1746 as "By the late Mr. Pope", puts it more eulogistically: "Her Love and Aversion, her Gratitude and Resentment, her Esteem and Neglect were equally open and strong, and alterable only from the Alteration of the Persons who created them" (p. 6, EC, v 443).

136. Her methods with "inferiors not dependent" are pleasantly illustrated in Walpole's letter to Mann, 24 December 1741: "last week she sent for Cori [the prompter], to pay him for her opera-ticket; he was not at home, but went in an hour afterwards. She said, 'Did he treat her like a tradeswoman? She would teach him to respect women of her birth'; said he was in league with Mr. Sheffield [one of the Duke's illegitimate children] to abuse her, and bade him come the next morning at nine. He came, and she made him wait till eight at night. . . At last she received him in all the form of a princess giving audience to an ambassador. 'Now', she said, 'she had punished him'."

Offend her, and she knows not to forgive;
Oblige her, and she'll hate you while you live:
But die, and she'll adore you—Then the Bust
And Temple rise—then fall again to dust.   140
Last night, her Lord was all that's good and great,
A Knave this morning, and his Will a Cheat.
Strange! by the Means defeated of the Ends,
By Spirit robb'd of Pow'r, by Warmth of Friends,
By Wealth of Follow'rs! without one distress   145
Sick of herself thro' very selfishness!
Atossa, curs'd with ev'ry granted pray'r,
Childless with all her Children, wants an Heir.
To Heirs unknown descends th' unguarded store
Or wanders, Heav'n-directed, to the Poor.   150
     Pictures like these, dear Madam, to design,
Asks no firm hand, and no unerring line;

140 rise] too *Harl. Misc.*   147 Atossa] *Atossa*'s *1746.*
149 unguarded] unnumber'd *1746.*

138. Pope had obliged her more than once, e.g. in editing the Duke's works and in the prosecution of Ward, but it was his attempt (made at her request) to revise the character she had written of herself that precipitated the explosion. After the quarrel the Duchess tried to liquidate her obligations to him by sending him a note for £100. Pope refused the money. (See Pope to Caryll, 12 February, 16 June 1730; Sherburn, III 91, 116.) Dilke has gone into the episode in great detail in *The Papers of a Critic*, 1875, I 271–7.

139–40. The Duchess erected elaborate and expensive monuments to her husband—as to which she consulted Pope (Sherburn, II 99)—and her son. But this was part of her megalomania. She also professed to love and revere her father James II. Walpole relates: "She always stopped at Paris, visited the church where lay the unburied body of James, and wept over it. A poor Benedictine of the convent, observing her filial piety, took notice to her grace that the pall that covered the coffin was become threadbare—and so it remained!" (*Works*, IV 316).

142. The disputes with the Duke's illegitimate children were over his will. This was printed in 1729 and is included in all editions of his *Works* issued after 1729.

148–50. Her five children by the Duke all predeceased her and at her death there was "a trial at bar to prove who was heir-at-law" to the Duke. Some distant Irish connections called Walsh were at last found to be his heirs. (See Dilke, *The Papers of a Critic*, 1875, I 286, quoting *The London Evening Post*, 5 May 1743.) Ll. 149–50 were presumably added after the Duchess's death in 1743.

Some wand'ring touch, or some reflected light,
Some flying stroke alone can hit 'em right:
For how should equal Colours do the knack?   155
Chameleons who can paint in white and black?
"Yet Cloe sure was form'd without a spot—"

---

153 touch, or] touches *1735, 1735b–51*.
154 'em] them *1735–43*.
157–98 *First add. 1744, though 157–80 had been printed separately as*
"*Cloe*: a character" *in the octavo Works, vol.* II, *part* ii (*1738*),
pp. 158–9. See vol. VI *of this edition, p. 377.*

---

155. *equal Colours*] Simple, unmixed.
do the knack] Ruffhead thought this "low, and unworthy the pen of so
great a genius" (*Life of Pope*, 1769, p. 284). The only other example of the phrase
quoted in the *OED* is from Thomas Jordan's *A Dialogue betwixt Tom and Dick*
(1660).
157–80. The character of Cloe was probably a last-minute addition (see Note
on the Text, p. 40 above). "This highly-finished portrait was intended for Lady
Suffolk" [Warton]. "Cloe, I suspect, from some touches & from its preceding the
Queen's character, to be meant for Lady Suffolk, the King's Mistress" (Walpole,
Fraser marginalia, p. 33). "The lady who counts the figures on an Indian Screen
—was Lady Suffolk—from Mr Cambridge, who knew Pope" (note by Malone
in Bodley MS. Malone 30; Malone's informant was no doubt Richard Owen
Cambridge, 1717–1802, the poet). Henrietta Hobart, later Mrs Howard, later
Countess of Suffolk (1681–1767), had been called Cloe by Lord Peterborough in
the lovely, and then widely known, song "I said to my Heart" (first printed in
The British Journal, 28 December 1723), and Warton's anecdote in explanation
of l. 178 has a convincing ring. But Cloe can hardly be a *portrait* of Mrs Howard.
She was the intimate friend of Martha Blount and it is impossible to believe that
Pope could have sanctioned the publication of the character if it had been
intended as a direct satire on Mrs Howard. His *Works*, vol. II, part ii (in which the
lines were originally printed), though dated 1738, was not published until 1 May
1739, and on 27 December [1739] Pope wrote to Martha Blount: "Pray tell my
Lady Suffolk in the first place that I think of her every night constantly, as the
greatest Comforter I have, under her Edder-down Quilt" (Sherburn, IV 212).
Could the intimate and affectionate relationship implied in this message—
which is typical of the many allusions to Mrs Howard in the letters and poems—
have survived the publication of the lines if they had really been directed at
Mrs Howard? But the consensus of eighteenth-century gossip implies that some
features in the character must derive from her. See also vol. VI of this edition,
p. 377, and N. Ault, *New Light on Pope*, 1949, ch. xvi.

Nature in her then err'd not, but forgot.
"With ev'ry pleasing, ev'ry prudent part,
"Say, what can Cloe want?"—she wants a Heart.   160
She speaks, behaves, and acts just as she ought;
But never, never, reach'd one gen'rous Thought.
Virtue she finds too painful an endeavour,
Content to dwell in Decencies for ever.
So very reasonable, so unmov'd,   165
As never yet to love, or to be lov'd.
She, while her Lover pants upon her breast,
Can mark the figures on an Indian chest;
And when she sees her Friend in deep despair,
Observes how much a Chintz exceeds Mohair.   170
Forbid it Heav'n, a Favour or a Debt
She e'er should cancel—but she may forget.
Safe is your Secret still in Cloe's ear;
But none of Cloe's shall you ever hear.
Of all her Dears she never slander'd one,   175
But cares not if a thousand are undone.
Would Cloe know if you're alive or dead?
She bids her Footman put it in her head.
Cloe is prudent—would you too be wise?
Then never break your heart when Cloe dies.   180
   One certain Portrait may (I grant) be seen,
Which Heav'n has varnish'd out, and made a *Queen:*

158 'Tis true, but something in her was forgot *1738.*
164 Decencies] Decency *1738.*

---

162. One of Pope's "Thoughts on Various Subjects (EC, x 555) runs: "Many
men have been capable of doing a wise thing, more a cunning thing, but very few
a generous thing."

170. Mohair was a fine material made from the hair of the Angora goat.

178. This "alludes to a particular circumstance: Pope, being at dinner with
her, heard her order her footman to put her in mind to send to know how Mrs.
Blount, who was ill, had passed the night" [Warton].

182. *varnish'd out*] A form not illustrated in *OED*, but presumably meaning

The same for ever! and describ'd by all
With Truth and Goodness, as with Crown and Ball:
Poets heap Virtues, Painters Gems at will, 185
And show their zeal, and hide their want of skill.
'Tis well—but, Artists! who can paint or write,
To draw the Naked is your true delight:
That Robe of Quality so struts and swells,
None see what Parts of Nature it conceals. 190
Th' exactest traits of Body or of Mind,
We owe to models of an humble kind.

---

that the painting has been completed and a coat of varnish is now applied to
preserve it.

a Queen] Queen Caroline (1683–1737). A firm supporter of Walpole, the Queen
used the ascendancy which she possessed over the King's mind to urge Walpole's
views, even when her own political sense prompted her to disagree with them.
Her religious opinions were latitudinarian; it was owing to her influence that
Butler and Berkeley were promoted to the episcopate. The worst that can be said
of such a sensible and tolerant woman is that she maintained an implacable
hatred of her eldest son [JB].

Pope's antipathy to the Queen was political, though politics may have been
reinforced by his dislike of her Vice-Chamberlain and confidant Lord Hervey
and his affection for the King's mistress, and Caroline's quasi-rival, Mrs Howard.
Hervey attributed Mrs Howard's disgrace in 1734 partly to "her intimacy with
Mr. Pope, who had published several satires, with his name to them, in which the
King and all his family were rather more than obligingly sneered at" (*Memoirs*,
p. 382). Dr Johnson reports (*Lives of the Poets*, III 171) that when the Court was at
Richmond, the Queen had declared her intention of visiting Pope. To avoid the
embarrassments of this honour Pope left Twickenham for some time. This is no
doubt the episode Swift refers to in "A Libel on D[r] D[elany]" (1730) (*Poems*,
ed. H. Williams, 1937, II 482):

> Hail! happy *Pope*, whose gen'rous Mind,
> Detesting all the Statesman Kind,
> Contemning *Courts*, at *Courts* unseen,
> Refus'd the Visits of a [Queen].

185–6. Cf. *E. on Criticism*, 293–6:

> Poets like painters, thus, unskill'd to trace
> The naked nature and the living grace,
> With gold and jewels cover ev'ry part,
> And hide with ornaments their want of art.

187. *write*] sketch, paint.

> If QUEENSBERRY to strip there's no compelling,
> 'Tis from a Handmaid we must take a Helen.
> From Peer or Bishop 'tis no easy thing   195
> To draw the man who loves his God, or King:
> Alas! I copy (or my draught would fail)
> From honest Mah'met, or plain Parson Hale.
> But grant, in Public Men sometimes are shown,

199 But . . . Public] In publick Stations *1735–43*.

193. Catherine Hyde, Duchess of Queensberry (1700–77), the "Female Phaeton" of Prior (?) and the friend and protectress of Gay, was one of the most beautiful women of the eighteenth century. In February 1741, when the Duchess was already over forty, Elizabeth Robinson (later Mrs Montagu, the bluestocking) wrote to her sister Sarah: "she in herself was so far beyond the masterpiece of art, that one could hardly look at her cloaths; allowing for her age I never saw so beautiful a creature" (*Correspondence*, ed. E. J. Climenson, 1906, 1 63). Young uses her as a *ne plus ultra* of beauty in *Love of Fame*, Satire IV, 104, and Lord Hervey speaks of her as "proverbially beautiful" (*Memoirs*, p. 98).

197. *draught*] Drawing, sketch or picture.

198. *Mah'met*] Servant to the late king, said to be the son of a Turkish Bassa, whom he took at the siege of Buda, and constantly kept about his person. [P. *1744–51*.] Possibly Mahomet is "Ulrick, the little Turk" referred to in "The Court Ballad" (see vol. VI of this edition, p. 184). Walpole (Huntington marginalia, p. 478) describes Ulrick as "belonging to George 1st".

Parson Hale] Dr Stephen Hales (1677–1761), the perpetual curate of Teddington and a famous physiologist, witnessed Pope's will. His vivisections distressed Pope. "Yes, he is a very good man; only I'm sorry he has his hands so much imbrued in blood.—'What, he cuts up rats?'—Ay, and dogs too!—[With what emphasis and concern he spoke it.]" (Spence, p. 293).

199. In the former Editions [*om. 1735c–43*], between this and the foregoing [former *1735c*] lines [and also in some following Parts *1734c–43*], a want of Connection might be perceived, occasioned by the omission of certain *Examples* and *Illustrations* to the Maxims laid down; and tho' some of these have since been found, viz., the Characters of *Philomedé*, *Atossa*, *Cloe*, and some verses following, others are still wanting, nor can we answer that these are exactly inserted. [P. *1735c–51*. *Instead of* and tho' . . . inserted *1735c–43 read*: which may put the Reader i n mind of what the Author has said in his Imitation of *Horace*.

> *Publish the present Age, but where the Text*
> *Is Vice too high, reserve it for the next.*]

This note is discussed in Note on the Text (p. 41 above). The quotation is from *Imit. Hor., Sat.*, II i, 59–60.

A Woman's seen in Private life alone: 200
Our bolder Talents in full light display'd,
Your Virtues open fairest in the shade.
Bred to disguise, in Public 'tis you hide;
There, none distinguish 'twixt your Shame or Pride,
Weakness or Delicacy; all so nice, 205
That each may seem a Virtue, or a Vice.
　　In Men, we various Ruling Passions find,
In Women, two almost divide the kind;
Those, only fix'd, they first or last obey,
The Love of Pleasure, and the Love of Sway. 210
　　That, Nature gives; and where the lesson taught
Is still to please, can Pleasure seem a fault?
Experience, this; by Man's oppression curst,
They seek the second not to lose the first.
　　Men, some to Bus'ness, some to Pleasure take; 215

201 light] view *1735–43.*
204 There,] Where *1735–43.*　or] and *1735.*
206 That ... Vice] Each is a sort of *Virtue,* and of *Vice 1735–43.*
207 In Men ... Ruling] In sev'ral Men we sev'ral *1735–35b.*
210 Pleasure] Pleasures *1735–43.*
212 Is still] Is but *1735–35c, 1744–51.*

207. The former part having shewn, that the *particular Characters* of Women are more various than those of Men, it is nevertheless observ'd, that the *general* Characteristic of the sex, as to the *ruling Passion,* is more uniform. [P. *1735c–51.*] The textual change (see textual note) was part of the attempt to make this Epistle a formal pendant to *To Cobham.* For Pope's theory of the Ruling Passion see notes to *E. on Man,* II 123*ff,* and the Introduction, pp. xxxvi*ff,* in vol. III i of this edition.
　211. This is occasioned partly by their *Nature,* partly by their *Education,* and in some degree by *Necessity.* [P. *1735c–51.*]
　212. *fault*] For the rhyme see note to l. 73.
　215–16. This couplet, like the characters of Calypso and Narcissa, derives from Pope's "Sylvia, a Fragment", ll. 15–16 (see vol. VI of this edition, pp. 286–8):
　　　　Men, some to Business, some to Pleasure take,
　　　　But ev'ry Woman's in her Soul a Rake.
William Ayre (*Memoirs of the Life and Writings of Alexander Pope,* 1745, II 52–3) records a complaint made to Pope about these lines by a "Lady whose Name for

But ev'ry Woman is at heart a Rake:
Men, some to Quiet, some to public Strife;
But ev'ry Lady would be Queen for life.
    Yet mark the fate of a whole Sex of Queens!
Pow'r all their end, but Beauty all the means.   220
In Youth they conquer, with so wild a rage,
As leaves them scarce a Subject in their Age:
For foreign glory, foreign joy, they roam;
No thought of Peace or Happiness at home.
But Wisdom's Triumph is well-tim'd Retreat,   225
As hard a science to the Fair as Great!
Beauties, like Tyrants, old and friendless grown,
Yet hate to rest, and dread to be alone,
Worn out in public, weary ev'ry eye,
Nor leave one sigh behind them when they die.   230
    Pleasures the sex, as children Birds, pursue,
Still out of reach, yet never out of view,

228 to rest] Repose *1735, 1735b–51.*

Virtue . . . has been conspicuous . . . and who in her Youth was thought one of
the handsomest Women of Quality". Pope replied, "Madam, I must intreat of
you to observe, that I only say:
                  But every WOMAN is at Heart a Rake.
This no Way affects your Ladyship, who was an Angel, when you were young,
and now advancing into Life, are almost already become a Saint." The com-
plainant "was Woman enough to be pleas'd with the Compliment".
   219. What are the *Aims* and the *Fate* of this Sex?—I. As to *Power.* [P. *1735c–51.*]
   229. Warton suggests that this line derives from Young's description of "Bri-
tannia's Daughters" (*Love of Fame*, Satire v, 17–18):
           Worn in the publick eye, give cheap delight
           To throngs, and tarnish to the sated sight.
   231. II. As to *Pleasure* [P. *1735c–51.*]
   231–2. This couplet derives from "Stanzas. From the french of Malherbe",
ll. 5–6 (*Poems on Several Occasions*, 1717, ed. N. Ault, 1935, p. 155, and vol. VI of this
edition, pp. 71–2):
           As children birds, so men their bliss pursue,
           Still out of reach, tho' ever in their view.
Mr Ault has shown that the earlier poem was probably also by Pope, though it
was never acknowledged by him.

Sure, if they catch, to spoil the Toy at most,
To covet flying, and regret when lost:
At last, to follies Youth could scarce defend,   235
'Tis half their Age's prudence to pretend;
Asham'd to own they gave delight before,
Reduc'd to feign it, when they give no more:
As Hags hold Sabbaths, less for joy than spight,
So these their merry, miserable Night;   240
Still round and round the Ghosts of Beauty glide,
And haunt the places where their Honour dy'd.
See how the World its Veterans rewards!

236 'Tis half] It grows *1735*, *1735^b–51*.

---

240. *Night*] Visiting night.
241–2. These two lines derive from Pope's quatrain, first published anonymously as "Epigram" in *Miscellaneous Poems by Several Hands. Publish'd by D. Lewis*, 1730, p. 32:

> When other Ladies to the Shades go down,
> Still *Flavia, Chloris, Celia* stay in Town;
> Those Ghosts of Beauty ling'ring there abide,
> And haunt the Places where their Honour dy'd.

Lewis's miscellany was published on 5 May. Pope sent a slightly different version of the lines to John Knight on 30 July 1730 (see vol. VI of this edition, pp. 316–17, and Sherburn, III 123).
243–8. These lines had already appeared as 5–10 of the version of "To Mrs. M.B. Sent on Her Birth-Day" printed in *Miscellanies. The Last Volume*, 1727, pp. 164–5. The text is identical except for the first line, which reads,

> Not as the World its pretty Slaves rewards.

This volume of *Miscellanies* was published on 8 March 1727/8 and represents the first authorized text of the lines. They had, however, already been included in Act II of James Moore Smythe's comedy *The Rival Modes* (acted 27 January 1727/8, pp. 24–5 of the first edition):

> 'Tis thus that Vanity Coquettes rewards,
> A Youth of Frolick, an Old Age of Cards;
> Fair to no purpose, Artful to no end,
> Young without Lovers, Old without a Friend.
> A Fool their Aim, their Prize some worn-out Sot;
> Alive ridiculous, when dead, forgot.

The lines are put by Smythe into the mouth of Sagely as a reflection upon the coquettish Amoret, but it is clear from their being in italics that Sagely is only

A Youth of frolicks, an old Age of Cards,
Fair to no purpose, artful to no end,   245
Young without Lovers, old without a Friend,
A Fop their Passion, but their Prize a Sot,
Alive, ridiculous, and dead, forgot!
  Ah Friend! to dazzle let the Vain design,
To raise the Thought and touch the Heart, be thine!   250
That Charm shall grow, while what fatigues the Ring
Flaunts and goes down, an unregarded thing.
So when the Sun's broad beam has tir'd the sight,
All mild ascends the Moon's more sober light,
Serene in Virgin Modesty she shines,   255
And unobserv'd the glaring Orb declines.

---

supposed to be quoting. (A moment later two other characters, Melissa and
Bellamine, also quote Pope:

  Bell. Nay, fly to Altars there I'll talk you dead.
  Mel. For Fools rush in where Angels fear to tread.)

Pope, however, chose to look upon the insertion of his lines as a plagiarism and
a quarrel developed. Details will be found in vol. VI of this edition, pp. 244–7.

  249. Advice for their true Interest. [P. *1735c–51.*]

  251. *the Ring*] This was a clump of trees in Hyde Park, round which the car-
riages of the fashionable world used to drive. "The Ring in Hyde Park is shaded
by fine lofty trees, and the dust laid by water-carts, when the dryness of the season
requires it; and here we frequently see four or five lines of noblemen's and
gentlemen's coaches rolling gently round the Ring, in all their gayest equipage,
some moving this way, others that, which makes a very splendid show" (EC,
quoting *History of the Present State of the British Islands*, 1730, II 339). The creation
of the Serpentine in 1733 involved the partial disappearance of the Ring.
Further details will be found in vol. II of this edition, pp. 375.*f.* "That phrase
'*fatigues* the ring' is derived from 'silvas *fatigant*', and similar expressions in
Virgil; that is, harass, and weary out, as it were, by long continuance" [Wake-
field].

  253–6. Transferred from the lines to "Erinna" (Judith Cowper) that Pope had
written in 1722 (see letter to Judith Cowper, 18 October 1722, Sherburn, II 138–9,
and vol. VI of this edition, p. 306):

  So while the sun's broad beam yet strikes the sight,
  All mild appears the moon's more sober light,
  Serene, in virgin majesty, she shines;
  And, un-observed, the glaring sun declines.

Oh! blest with Temper, whose unclouded ray
Can make to morrow chearful as to day;
She, who can love a Sister's charms, or hear
Sighs for a Daughter with unwounded ear;　　　260
She, who ne'er answers till a Husband cools,
Or, if she rules him, never shows she rules;
Charms by accepting, by submitting sways,
Yet has her humour most, when she obeys;
Lets Fops or Fortune fly which way they will;　　265
Disdains all loss of Tickets, or Codille;

259 She . . . hear] That pleas'd can see a younger charm, or hear
　　1735–35b; She, who can own a Sister's charms, or hears *1735c*;
　　She, who can own a Sister's charms, or hear *1735d–36*.
260 Daughter with unwounded ear] Sister with unwounded ear
　　1735–35b; Daughter with unwounded ears *1735c*.
261 She . . . cools] That ne'er shall answer till a Husband cool
　　1735–35b; That never answers till a Husband cools *1735cd*;
　　Who never answers till a Husband cools *1736–43*.
262 Or . . . rules] Or, if you rule him, never show you rule *1735–35b*.
263 Please by receiving, by submitting sway *1735–35b*.
264 Yet have your humour most, when you obey *1735–35b*.
265 Lets] Let *1735–35b*, *1744–51 (a misprint?)*.
266 Disdains] Despise *1735–35b*.

257. *Temper*] Equanimity. The pejorative sense is a nineteenth-century development.

260. *Sighs for a Daughter*] In the earlier editions (see textual note) the reading had been "Sister" with an obvious reference to Martha's more striking-looking sister Teresa Blount. No doubt the reference had been too obvious and had started gossips talking (see note to l. 289).

266. *Tickets*] Lottery tickets. Many years before, Pope had written to Martha Blount to wish her success in a lottery: "God give you good fortune (the best thing he can give in this world to those who can be happy). You know I have no palate to taste it, and therefore am in no concern or haste to hear whether I gain or lose. But I will not release you from your engagement of sending me word of the tickets" (30 Oct. 1719(?); Sherburn, II 17).

Codille] A term in the fashionable card game *ombre* (three players), with its variant *quadrille* (four players). The principal player or *Ombre* set out, with trumps of his own choosing, to make more tricks than either of the other players.

Spleen, Vapours, or Small-pox, above them all,
And Mistress of herself, tho' China fall.
    And yet, believe me, good as well as ill,
Woman's at best a Contradiction still.   270
Heav'n, when it strives to polish all it can
Its last best work, but forms a softer Man;
Picks from each sex, to make its Fav'rite blest,
Your love of Pleasure, our desire of Rest,
Blends, in exception to all gen'ral rules,   275
Your Taste of Follies, with our Scorn of Fools,
Reserve with Frankness, Art with Truth ally'd,
Courage with Softness, Modesty with Pride,
Fix'd Principles, with Fancy ever new;

268 herself] yourself *1735–35b*.
272 but forms a] creates this *1735a*; *corrected in Errata 1735ab to* It
       forms a
273 its Fav'rite] the Fav'rite *1735, 1735b–51*.

If he failed to do so, his opponents were said to give Codille to the Ombre.
Belinda was the Ombre in *The Rape of the Lock*, and after exhausting her trumps,
            She sees, and trembles at th' approaching Ill,
            Just in the Jaws of Ruin and *Codille*. (III 91–2)
There is an appendix on ombre in vol. II of this edition, pp. 361–8.
    267. *Small-pox*] Martha Blount had had small-pox in 1714. While she was still
ill, Pope wrote to Teresa: "whatever Ravages a merciless Distemper may com-
mit, I dare promise her boldly what few (if any) of her Makers of Visits &
Complements, dare to do; she shall have one man as much her Admirer as ever"
(late October 1714; Sherburn, I 265).
    268. *tho' China fall*] Addison was of the opinion that none of his "fair Readers"
were "Philosophers enough to keep their Temper at the fall of a Tea Pot or a
China Cup" (*The Lover*, 18 March 1714). Cf. *Rape of the Lock*, III 157–60:
            Not louder Shrieks to pitying Heav'n are cast,
            When Husbands or when Lap-dogs breathe their last,
            Or when rich *China* Vessels, fal'n from high,
            In glittring Dust and painted Fragments lie!
    269. The Picture of an estimable Woman, with the best kinds of contrarieties.
[P. *1735c–44*.] Warburton maliciously adds (1751), "created out of the poet's
imagination; who therefore feigned those circumstances of a *Husband*, a *Daughter*,
and love for a *Sister*, to prevent her being mistaken for any of his acquaintance".
See note on Heading (p. 46 above).

Shakes all together, and produces—You.   280
    Be this a Woman's Fame: with this unblest,
Toasts live a scorn, and Queens may die a jest.
This Phœbus promis'd (I forget the year)
When those blue eyes first open'd on the sphere;
Ascendant Phœbus watch'd that hour with care,   285
Averted half your Parents simple Pray'r,
And gave you Beauty, but deny'd the Pelf
Which buys your sex a Tyrant o'er itself.
The gen'rous God, who Wit and Gold refines,

---

281 Be this a] Ev'n such is *1735–43*.
288 Which buys] That buys *1735–35a, 1735c–51*.
289 The gen'rous] That gen'rous *1735, 1735b*.

---

280. Perhaps a reminiscence of Swift's lines on "Mrs Biddy Floyd" (*Poems*, ed. H. Williams, 1937, I 118):
    Jove mix'd up all, and his best Clay imploy'd;
    Then call'd the happy Composition, *Floyd*.

283. Martha Blount was forty-four when the Epistle was published in 1735. The poet's amnesia was no doubt suggested by Swift's
    Stella this Day is thirty four,
    (We won't dispute a Year or more),
                      Poems, ed. H. Williams, 1932, II 721.

285. Horace Walpole, writing to the Countess of Upper Ossory, 27 January 1786, reflects how posterity will envy him the historic figures he had associated with. "I remember many years ago making the same kind of reflection. I was standing at my window after dinner, in summer, in Arlington Street, and saw *Patty Blount* (after Pope's death), with nothing remaining of her immortal charms but her *blue eyes*, trudging on foot with her petticoats pinned up, for it rained, to visit *blameless Bethel* [*E. on Man*, IV 126], who was sick at the end of the street." Pope had extolled Martha Blount's eyes as early as 1711 (letter to Henry Cromwell, 21 December 1711; Sherburn, I 137).

286. *half your Parents simple Pray'r*] An allusion to *Aeneid*, II 794*f*—which Dryden had translated,
    Apollo heard, and granting half his Pray'r,
    Shuffled in Winds the rest, and toss'd in empty Air.
The conceit had already been used in *Rape of Lock*, II 45–6,
    The Pow'rs gave Ear, and granted half his Pray'r,
    The rest, the Winds dispers'd in empty Air.

289. *Wit and Gold refines*] Phoebus refined wit as god of poetry, gold as the god

And ripens Spirits as he ripens Mines,   290
Kept Dross for Duchesses, the world shall know it,
To you gave Sense, Good-humour, and a Poet.

---

of the sun—in accordance with the vulgar error that it was created by the sun's rays. The conceit reappears in *To Bathurst*, 12, and *To Cobham*, 93.

291. *Duchesses*] The plural here may be a survival from the original version of the poem, which included characters of both the Duchess of Buckinghamshire and Sarah, Duchess of Marlborough. See Appendix A below.

292. Pope wrote to Caryll, 18 February 1734/5 (Sherburn, III 45), "about intending marriage made me laugh: for if that line meant any such thing, it must be over. 'Tis in the preterperfect tense, *Gave a Poet.*" Pope had sent Caryll the first edition of the Epistle ten days before. There was a series of rumours that Pope and Martha Blount were getting married (see Sherburn, *Early Career*, pp. 291–7), and it was no doubt to avoid such jumping-to-conclusions as Caryll's that the revision of ll. 260–1 was undertaken.

Good-humour] Martha's sunny disposition particularly endeared her to Pope. In an early letter he confessed to her, "this Good humor and Tenderness for me has a charm that cannot be resisted" (Sherburn, I 268). Twenty-five years later he was still on the same theme, "I think we have both of us the Ingredients about us to make us happy; Your natural Moderation is greater than mine. . . Your Temper is much more chearful" (7 July 1739; Sherburn, IV 187). Pope had already sung the praises of good humour in *Rape of Lock*, V 29–32:

> What then remains, but well our Pow'r to use,
> And keep good Humour still whate'er we lose?
> And trust me, Dear! good Humour can prevail,
> When Airs, and Flights, and Screams, and Scolding fail.

See also the note on these lines in vol. II of this edition, p. 197.

EPISTLE III

To ALLEN *Lord* BATHURST

NOTE ON THE TEXT

The first edition is a twenty-four-page folio with the title *Of The Use of Riches, an Epistle to the Right Honorable Allen Lord Bathurst*, and is dated 1732, though it was not actually published until 15 January 1732/3. An octavo edition, textually identical with the first and also dated 1732, followed a few weeks later. Two other editions of the poem, neither apparently pirated, are both described on their title-pages as "The Second Edition". They are both folios, both are dated 1733, and both contain one new reading (in l. 117) for which Pope must be responsible. There were also three Dublin editions in 1733, including one by George Faulkner.

The textual problems raised by Pope's extensive revisions in the four editions (*1735 abcd*) of his *Works*, vol. II—in which the poem becomes Epistle III of the second Book of "Ethic Epistles" (the *Essay on Man* being the first Book)—and the relationship of these collections and their four successors (*1736, 1739, 1740, 1743*) to the "death-bed" edition (*1744*), have been summarized in the General Note on the Text. As in the case of *To a Lady* (and *To Burlington*) *1744* was unquestionably printed from partly corrected sheets of *1735c*, which in its turn derives from *1735a* or *1735b* (which are textually identical for this Epistle except for the addition in *1735b* of a penultimate couplet). Overlooked Revisions need therefore only be expected from variants in *1735d* (which is in fact a close reprint of *1735c*), *1736* (which has only two readings that can be ascribed to Pope), and *1739* (which has three Popian readings). None of them is of much interest, though I have adopted two (ll. 147 and 265) in pursuance of the principle laid down in the General Note on the Text that such revisions must be considered as authoritative as any later revision, each case being then decided on its stylistic merits.

To Bathurst was the first of the Epistles to come under Warburton's heavy hand in the preparation of *1744*, and many of its readings are more properly ascribable to him than to Pope. The twenty verbal changes seem to be Pope's work, but the omission of ll. 27–8 and the resurrection of a couplet from the original draft to follow l. 202 are probably Warburton's responsibility. Two drastic transpositions of paragraphs in the earlier part of the poem, into which he also coaxed Pope, were intended to improve the logic of its evolution in the same way as the similar reshufflings in the first half of *To Cobham*. "The introduction of the epistle on Riches," Warburton boasted in a note added to the Commentary on *To Cobham* after Pope's death, "was in the same condition, and underwent the same reform."[1]

Warburton's transpositions have been excluded from this edition. It is true they are to be found in *1744* and must therefore be assumed to have received Pope's sanction. They may well be the "Method" to which he refers in a letter to Warburton postmarked 15 November 1743 that takes up a number of suggestions about *To Bathurst*. "Upon the whole," Pope writes there, "I will follow your Method, & therefore return the paper that you may accordingly refer the notes. [The mark N which I've put upon the margin is only to direct the Printer to such Notes as are in the Copies already printed.] and the beginnings of verses crost over again, only to shew you how once they did stand.]"[2] Pope has got his brackets muddled in this letter, but a slightly reluctant acquiescence ("Upon the whole") is clearly intended. He may have had second thoughts later—a letter to Warburton written in March 1743/4[3] makes it clear that the Commentary on *To Bathurst* had still not received its final form. But the important thing is that the changes are all decidedly for the worse. The omission of ll. 27–8 and the insertion of a couplet after l. 202 are discussed in the notes on those passages. The question of Warburton's two transpositions will be best treated here.

Warburton's first transposition was of ll. 37–8 to follow l. 34 and so conclude the third paragraph of the poem. At a first glance the change would not seem to do very much harm. It is objectionable, however, if not disastrous, on two grounds: (i) ll. 29–34 are a series of one-line *pros* and *cons* on the general question of the utility of gold, and Warburton by adding two lines to the last *con* has upset the balance of the comparisons; (ii) the antithesis in ll. 33–4 is between the honest soldiers and the corrupt politicians, and Warbur-

---

1. Warburton, III 163. See also pp. 6–12 above.

2. Sherburn, IV 480. See also an earlier letter to Warburton (7 October 1743), which may refer to these or the *To Cobham* transpositions (Sherburn, IV 474).

3. Sherburn, IV 505–6.

ton spoils the antithesis by introducing uncorrupt politicians in the
"Patriots" of l. 37. The attraction of the transposition to Warbur-
ton must have been that in both ll. 33–4 and 37–8 you have soldiers
contrasted with politicians; the fact that the two couplets make the
contrasts on different grounds makes the change unnecessary and
unjustifiable.

The second transposition consisted in inserting the sixth para-
graph of the poem (ll. 65–78) after the third paragraph. The attrac-
tion here to Warburton must have been to juxtapose the bribed
senate of l. 34 and the bribed senator "Old Cato" of ll. 65–8. But
once again his ingenuity has done more harm than good. Pope's
original paragraphs 4 and 5 were a whimsical picture of what Eng-
land would be like if money was abandoned and exchange in kind
took its place. The story of Cato made a natural pendant to them.
Cato's burst bag of guineas was the *solitary* modern instance
("Once, we confess") of gold serving the same purpose as oxen or
casks of wine of the sort of bribe that betrays itself. Another objec-
tion to Warburton's transposition is that the transition from his l. 76
to his l. 77 becomes awkward in the extreme. In Warburton's text
ll. 49–76 portray an ideal England saved from corruption by ex-
change in kind, and the reader is disconcerted to find them followed
by the cynical

> Since then, my Lord, on such a World we fall,
> What say you? "Say? Why take it, Gold and all."

In this transposed form of the text "such a World" must refer to
the Utopia of the preceding paragraph; and there, of course, there
was no "Gold" to "take". Warburton has made Pope talk non-
sense.

Warburton's final text is in *The Works*, vol. III, 1751. His com-
mentary and notes are here expanded or rewritten, Pope's notes are
for the first time signed, and a number of readings from Pope's
MSS. are recorded under the heading "Variations". The text of
the poem, however, is verbally identical with that of the "death-
bed" edition. The one new reading—it is in l. 38—is probably a
printer's error. But there is one remarkable difference between
1751 and the earlier texts in the breaking up of the poem into a
dialogue between Pope and Bathurst. As in the case of the *Epistle
to Arbuthnot* (see vol. IV of this edition, pp. 93–4) the change to

dialogue, though occasionally effective,[1] has been made unsyste-
matically and rather perfunctorily. Editors have generally agreed
that the change is for the worse, and Lord Bathurst himself was
furious about it. "That very lively and amiable old nobleman, the
Lord BATHURST, told me," Warton reports,[2] " 'that he was
much surprised to see what he had with repeated pleasure so often
read as an *epistle* addressed to himself, in this edition converted into
a *dialogue*; in which', said he, 'I perceive I really make but a shabby
and indifferent figure, and contribute very little to the spirit of the
dialogue, if it *must be* a *dialogue*; and I hope I had generally more to
say for myself in the many charming conversations I used to hold
with POPE and Swift, and my old poetical friends.' " Bathurst's in-
dignation is comprehensible. Out of the 402 lines in the poem only
21 are assigned to him!

It is most unlikely that Pope was responsible for the dialogue
form. He only completed the "death-bed" edition a few weeks be-
fore he died (see Introduction, p. ix above), and he was far too ill to
have had either the time or the inclination for recasting a poem
which he had already thoroughly revised several times. A curious
feature, too, about the change to dialogue in the poem is that it is
made without the alteration of a single word. If the alteration was
Pope's it is difficult to believe that he would not have introduced at
least a few minor changes to make the dialogue more effective. The
culprit is almost certainly Warburton. Warburton, it will be re-
membered, obtained under Pope's will the copyright in those
poems that "he shall publish without future alterations". No doubt
to the legalistic Warburton the imposition of dialogue did not con-
stitute an "alteration". The text after all *was* unchanged. Not a
word had been displaced. And there is this to be said for War-
burton, that from the beginning Pope certainly intended the poem
to be partly in dialogue. An interlocutor, who may or may not be
Bathurst, is clearly required in all the editions in ll. 276–80 and
285–6, and in the "death-bed" edition Bathurst himself speaks in
ll. 80 and 340. Warburton was only carrying to its logical conclu-
sion a process that Pope had himself begun. But unfortunately
Warburton is very clumsy over it. One instance only need be cited.
The opening paragraphs make it clear that Bathurst's rôle in the

---

1. e.g. l. 82.   2. *Essay*, II 153. See also note to l. 338.

K

poem is to be that of the cynical man of the world, while Pope's is that of the optimistic philosopher. But in the dialogue of ll. 21–34, as it is arranged in Warburton's editions (and all the modern editions descending from them), all the cynicisms come from Pope and the optimistic phrases from Bathurst.

Verbally, then, with the minor exceptions noted above, the text adopted in this edition is that of the "death-bed" edition. The order of its paragraphs, however, is that of the earlier editions, and the dialogue form introduced by Warburton after Pope's death is totally rejected.

KEY TO THE CRITICAL APPARATUS

1732 = First edition, Griffith 280–283 (three folio and one octavo, but with identical texts).

1733 = Second edition, Griffith 323, 324 (two folio editions with identical texts).

1735a = Works, vol. II, large and small folio, Griffith 370, 371.

1735b = Works, vol. II, quarto, Griffith 372.

1735c = Works, vol. II, octavo, Griffith 388.

1735d = Works, vol. II, octavo, Griffith 389.

1736 = Works, vol. II, octavo, Griffith 430.

1739 = Works, vol. II, octavo, Griffith 505.

1740 = Works, vol. II, part i, octavo, Griffith 523.

1743 = Works, vol. II, part i, octavo, Griffith 583.

1744 = Epistles to Several Persons, Griffith 591.

1751 = Works, ed. Warburton, vol. III, large octavo, Griffith 645.

ARGUMENT[1]
Of the Use *of* RICHES

THAT *it is known to few, most falling into one of the extremes,* Avarice *or* Profusion, v. 1, &c. *The Point discuss'd, whether the invention of Money has been more commodious, or pernicious to* Mankind, v. 21 to 78. *That Riches, either to the* Avaricious *or the* Prodigal, *cannot afford Happiness, scarcely Necessaries,* v. 81 to 108. *That*   5
Avarice is an absolute Frenzy, without an End or Purpose, v. 109 &c. *Conjectures about the Motives of Avaricious men,* v. 113 to 152. *That the conduct of men, with respect to Riches, can only be accounted for by the* ORDER OF PROVIDENCE, *which works the general Good out of Extremes, and brings all to its great End by perpetual Revolutions,* v. 161 to 178. *How a*   10
Miser *acts upon Principles which appear to him reasonable,* v. 179. *How a* Prodigal *does the same,* v. 199. *The due Medium, and true use of Riches,* v. 219. *The* Man *of* Ross, v. 250. *The fate of the* Profuse *and the*

Argument] Add. 1735a and reprinted in all the later editions except 1739; 1735c–43 also break up, with some minor changes, as footnotes to the separate paragraphs of the poem. Errors and changes in the line numbers are not recorded here.

1   *That it] The true Use of Riches 1735ab.*

3   *has been] was 1735ab.*

4–5   *That Riches . . . Necessaries] Riches can scarce afford Necessaries either to the Avaritious or Prodigal, much less any happiness 1735a–36, 1740–43.*

5–6   *That Avarice . . . Frenzy,] It is never for their own Families, or for the Poor, that Misers covet Wealth, but a direct Phrensy 1735a–36, 1740–43.*

7–8   *the conduct . . . Riches] it 1735a–36, 1740–43.*

10–11   *How . . . acts] A Picture of . . . acting 1735a–36, 1740–43.*

11–12   *How . . . does the same] Another of . . . acting on the contrary Principles which seem to him equally right 1735a–36, 1740–43.*

13   *The Man] The Character and Praises of the Man 1735a–36, 1740–43.*

13–14   *Profuse . . . Covetous] Covetous . . . Profuse 1735a–36, 1740–43.*

---

[1] Perhaps not by Pope, but by the younger Jonathan Richardson (see p. 4, note 2 above).

Covetous, *in two examples; both miserable in Life and in Death*, v. 291, &c. *The Story of Sir* Balaam, v. 339 to the end.

---

1 *both miserable*] *That both are miserable 1735a–36, 1740–43.*
2 *Story of Sir* Balaam] *Tale of Sir* Balaam, *the Degrees of Corruption by Riches, and the Consequences 1735a–36, 1740–43.*

EPISTLE III
To ALLEN *Lord* BATHURST

WHO shall decide, when Doctors disagree,
    And soundest Casuists doubt, like you and me?
    You hold the word, from Jove to Momus giv'n,
That Man was made the standing jest of Heav'n;
And Gold but sent to keep the fools in play,   5
For some to heap, and some to throw away.
    But I, who think more highly of our kind,
(And surely, Heav'n and I are of a mind)
Opine, that Nature, as in duty bound,

Heading] An Epistle To the Right Honorable *Allen* Lord Bathurst
1732; Epistle III. To the Rt. Honourable Allen Lord Bathurst
1736–43.
1–20 *1751, which arranges the poem as a dialogue between Pope and
Bathurst, prefixes* P.
6 some . . . some] half . . . half *1732–43.*

The line numbers in brackets are those of Warburton's editions and the
reprints descending from them, including EC.

Heading] Allen Bathurst (1685–1775), Tory M.P. for Cirencester from 1705
till he was raised to the peerage as Baron Bathurst (1712). He was created an
Earl in 1772. In *Sober Advice from Horace*, 158, Bathurst is described as "Philo-
sopher and Rake". His easy morals were notorious, but the philosophy does not
seem to have amounted to much more than worldly wisdom. Bathurst was a life-
long friend of Congreve, Prior, and Swift as well as Pope, and in his old age he
befriended Sterne. He was an enthusiastic landscape gardener at both his country
houses (Cirencester and Riskins, *recte* Richings, near Slough, where "Pope's
Walk" is still preserved). He was also one of the three noblemen to whom Pope
assigned the copyright of the *Dunciad Variorum*, the other two being the Earl of
Oxford (see l. 243*n*) and the Earl of Burlington (see p. 134 below). Pope told
Warburton about 1740 that he had loved Bathurst "on twenty years Experience"
(Brit. Mus. Egerton MS. 1946, f. 17ʳ, and Sherburn, IV 236). In fact they were on
intimate terms by 1718, if not earlier.

    3. *Momus*] Derisive blame; personified as a god in the *Theogony* of Hesiod.
    9–12. Wakefield compares Cowley, *Davideis*, I 74–7:
        Beneath the silent chambers of the earth,

Deep hid the shining mischief under ground: 10
But when by Man's audacious labour won,
Flam'd forth this rival to, its Sire, the Sun,
Then careful Heav'n supply'd two sorts of Men,
To squander these, and those to hide agen.
    Like Doctors thus, when much dispute has past,   15
We find our tenets just the same at last.
Both fairly owning, Riches in effect
No grace of Heav'n or token of th' Elect;

13 careful . . . supply'd], in plain prose, were made *1732–43*.
14 these . . . those] some . . . some *1732–43*.

> Where the Suns fruitful beams give *metals* birth,
> Where he the growth of *fatal Gold* does see,
> *Gold* which above more *Influence* has than *He*.

Cf. too Ben Jonson, *Volpone*, I i 10*f*:

> O, thou sonne of SOL,
> (But brighter than thy father).

The vulgar error that gold is created by the sun's rays is also exploited by Pope in *To Cobham*, 93, *To a Lady*, 289, and *Windsor Forest*, 396.

    10. *shining mischief*] Pope had already used this phrase to describe Helen in his translation of the *Iliad*, bk xix (1720), 61:

> And shot the shining Mischief to the Heart!

    13–14. These lines adumbrate the doctrine preached more fully in ll. 161–70 and *E. on Man*, II 231–48. Although Savage's statement to Spence that "L[d] Bolingbroke has sent M[r] P a long letter on these heads" (see Introduction, p. xxi above) suggests that its immediate source was Bolingbroke, it is difficult to resist the impression that Pope owed some of its details to Mandeville. Cf. (1) "Was it not for Avarice, Spendthrifts would soon want Materials. . . Was it not for Prodigality, nothing could make us amends for the Rapine and Extortion of Avarice in Power. When a Covetous Statesman is gone . . . it ought to fill every good Member of the Society with Joy to behold the uncommon Profuseness of his Son" (*The Fable of the Bees*, ed. F. B. Kaye, 1924, I 101, 103–4). (2) "I look upon Avarice and Prodigality in the Society as I do upon two contrary Poisons in Physick, of which it is certain that the noxious Qualities being by mutual Mischief corrected in both, they may assist each other, and often make a good Medicine between them" (*ibid.*, I 106). Pope's attitude to the cynical and realistic philosophy of Mandeville seems to resemble his attitude to La Rochefoucauld. Theoretically he disapproves of Mandeville, who was the *enfant terrible* of early eighteenth-century thought, but there is at least a superficial sympathy between his mind and that of Mandeville.

Giv'n to the Fool, the Mad, the Vain, the Evil,
To Ward, to Waters, Chartres, and the Devil.   20
What Nature wants, commodious Gold bestows,
'Tis thus we eat the bread another sows:

20 Ward ... Chartres] W—d, to W—t—rs, Ch—rs *1732–33*.
21–2 *1751 prefixes* B. (*for Bathurst*).

20. JOHN WARD, of Hackney, Esq.; Member of Parliament, being pro-
secuted by the Duchess of Buckingham, and convicted of Forgery, was first
expelled the House, and then stood in the Pillory on the 17th of March 1727.
He [join'd *1735ab*] was suspected of joining in a conveyance with Sir John Blunt,
to secrete fifty thousand pounds of that Director's Estate, forfeited to the South
Sea Company by Act of Parliament [which afterwards detaining from his
Friend, Sir John informed the Company of the Fraud, on promise of a Pardon
for himself *1735ab*]. The Company recovered the fifty thousand pounds against
Ward; but he set up prior conveyances of his real estate to his brother and son,
and conceal'd all his personal [Estate *1735ab*], which was computed to be one
hundred and fifty thousand pounds: These conveyances being also set aside by a
bill in Chancery, Ward was imprisoned, and hazarded the forfeiture of his life,
by not giving in his effects till the last day, which was that of his examination.
During his confinement, his amusement was to give poison to dogs and cats, and
see them expire by slower or quicker torments. To sum up the *worth* of this
gentleman, at the several æra's of his life; at his standing in the Pillory he was
worth above two hundred thousand pounds; at his commitment to Prison [Newgate
1735ab], he was *worth one hundred and fifty thousand,* but has been since so far
diminished in his reputation, as to be thought a *worse man* by *fifty or sixty
thousand.*

FR. CHARTRES, a man infamous for all manner of vices. When he was an
ensign in the army, he was drumm'd out of the regiment for a cheat; he was
next banish'd Brussels, and drumm'd out of Ghent on the same account. After
a hundred tricks at the gaming-tables, he took to lending of money at exorbitant
interest and on great penalties, accumulating premium, interest, and capital
into a new capital, and seizing to a minute when the payments became due; in
a word, by a constant attention to the vices, wants, and follies of mankind, he
acquired an immense fortune. His house was a perpetual bawdy-house. He was
twice condemn'd for rapes, and pardoned: but the last time not without im-
prisonment in Newgate, and large confiscations. He died in Scotland in 1731,
aged 62. The populace at his funeral rais'd a great riot, almost tore the body out
of the coffin, and cast dead dogs, &c. into the grave along [*1735ab omit* along]
with it. The following Epitaph contains his character very justly drawn by Dr
Arbuthnot:

HERE continueth to rot

The Body of FRANCIS CHARTRES,

Who with an INFLEXIBLE CONSTANCY,
and INIMITABLE UNIFORMITY of Life,
PERSISTED,
In spite of AGE snd INFIRMITIES,
In the Practice of EVERY HUMAN VICE;
Excepting PRODIGALITY and HYPOCRISY:
His insatiable AVARICE exempted him from the
first,
His matchless IMPUDENCE from the second.
Nor was he more singular
in the undeviating *Pravity* of his *Manners*
Than successful
in *Accumulating* WEALTH.
For, without TRADE or PROFESSION,
Without TRUST of PUBLIC MONEY,
And without BRIBE-WORTHY Service,
He acquired, or more properly created,
A MINISTERIAL ESTATE.
He was the only Person of his Time,
Who cou'd CHEAT without the Mask of HONESTY,
Retain his Primeval MEANNESS
When possess'd of TEN THOUSAND a YEAR,
And having daily deserved the GIBBET for what
he *did*,
Was at last condemn'd to it for what he *could*
not *do*.
Oh Indignant Reader!
Think not his Life useless to Mankind!
PROVIDENCE conniv'd at his execrable Designs,
To give to After-ages
A conspicuous PROOF and EXAMPLE,
Of how small Estimation is EXORBITANT WEALTH
in the Sight of GOD,
By his bestowing it on the most UNWORTHY of
ALL MORTALS.

This Gentleman was *worth seven thousand pounds a year* estate in Land, and about *one hundred thousand in Money*. P.

Mr WATERS, the third of these worthies, was a man no way resembling the former in his military, but extremely so in his civil capacity; his great fortune having been rais'd by the like diligent attendance on the necessities of others. But this gentleman's history must be deferred till his death, when his *worth* may be known more certainly. [P. *1735a–51*.]

John Ward (d. 1755) was M.P. for Weymouth, 1722–6. He had been the agent of the Duke of Buckinghamshire and had forged the contracts under which he held certain estates from the Duke. He was expelled from the House of Commons on 16 May 1726. "After this, the House took into Consideration the Copy of the Record of the Proceding upon the Information in the Court of King's Bench, against *John Ward*, Esq; a Member of this House, and the said Mr. *Ward* not attending in his Place, pursuant to the Order of the House for that Purpose, *Thomas Hollingshead*, one of the Messengers belonging to the Serjeant at Arms, was call'd in, and being examin'd, gave the House an Account of his leaving Copies of the said Orders at Mr. *Ward's* Houses in *London* and at *Hackney*, and that, upon Inquiry after the said Mr. *Ward* he was inform'd, that Mr. *Ward* was gone from his said Houses: And it appearing by the said Record, that *John Ward*, Esq; upon an Information in the Court of King's Bench exhibited against him, had this present *Easter* Term, been convicted of the Crime of Forgery, it was resolv'd, *nemine contradicente*, that the said *John Ward*, Esq; be expell'd this House" (*Historical Register*, 1726, p. 178). Ward was prosecuted by the Duchess of Buckinghamshire, and Pope had helped her in the case. There are further references to Ward in *Dunciad* A, III 26 and *Epilogue to Satires*, I 119. Pope's note on Ward was modified in *1735c* and the "Errata" in *1735ab* had previously required the deletion of the second sentence, "the Fact not being exactly stated by the Annotator". Francis Chartres, or Charteris (1675–1732) was a notorious debauchee who amassed a fortune by gambling and usury. To Pope's account of his military career one or two details can be added. After his expulsion from a Dutch regiment of foot, "his father purchased for him a pair of colours in the 3rd regiment of foot guards, then commanded by Major-general Ramsay, but the officers refused to enrol him. While in command of a company in the 1st regiment of foot guards a charge was brought against him in 1711 of receiving large sums of money from tradesmen for enlisting them in his company to save them from arrest, and the charge having been investigated by a committee of the House of Commons, he was on 20 May reported guilty, whereupon he received a severe reprimand on his knees at the bar of the house by the speaker" (*DNB*). Details of his seamy career will be found in E. B. Chancellor, *The Lives of the Rakes*, 1925, vol. III, which fully substantiates Pope's note. But political bias may have reinforced Pope's indignation. Chartres "was one of the Runners of Sir Robert Walpole, and defended him in all places of resort, which drew the wrath of the Tories upon him" (A. Carlyle, *Autobiography*, 1860, ch. 1). Arbuthnot's epitaph was first published in the April 1732 numbers of both *The London Magazine* and *The Gentleman's Magazine*, and the Pope–Swift *Miscellanies* (October 1732), III 61. (See L. M. Beattie, *John Arbuthnot*, 1935, pp. 301–3.)

For Peter Waters, or Walter, see note to l. 125.

21–6. This passage may perhaps derive from Mandeville's discussion of luxury. "If everything is to be Luxury (as in strictness it ought) that is not immediately necessary to make Man subsist as he is a living Creature, there is nothing else to be found in the World" (*The Fable of the Bees*, "Remark (L)", ed. Kaye, I 107).

But how unequal it bestows, observe,
'Tis thus we riot, while who sow it, starve.
What Nature wants (a phrase I much distrust)   25
Extends to Luxury, extends to Lust:
And if we count among the Needs of life
Another's Toil, why not another's Wife?
Useful, I grant, it serves what life requires,   (27)
But dreadful too, the dark Assassin hires: 30
Trade it may help, Society extend;
But lures the Pyrate, and corrupts the Friend: (30)
It raises Armies in a Nation's aid,
But bribes a Senate, and the Land's betray'd.
  Oh! that such bulky Bribes as all might see,   35 (49)
Still, as of old, incumber'd Villainy!
In vain may Heroes fight, and Patriots rave;   (33)
If secret Gold saps on from knave to knave.

23–30 *1751 prefixes* P. 27–8 *1744–51 om. (see note).*
29 I] we *1732–43.*   31 *1751 prefixes* B.
32 *1751 prefixes* P.   33 *1751 prefixes* B.
34–80 *1751 prefixes* P.; *after l. 34 1744–51 insert ll. 37–8.*
38 saps] sap *1751.* to knave] *1744–51 follow on with ll. 65–78.*

27–8. Warburton's note in *1744* refers to these lines as "in all the former editions". In *1751* the note is expanded to "but, for their bad reasoning, omitted". Warburton was, no doubt, responsible for their suppression, but the "bad reasoning" is his rather than Pope's. The lines merely expand the preceding couplet, "Another's Toil" defining "Luxury", and "another's Wife" illustrating "Lust". Their omission makes the transition unpleasantly abrupt, and the lines are accordingly restored in this edition.

37. *Patriots*] "The character of modern Patriots was, in the opinion of our poet, very equivocal; as the name was undistinguishingly bestowed on every one in opposition to the court; of whose virtues he gives a hint in v. 139 [=141] of this Epistle" [Warburton]. Pope certainly uses the word in this specialized sense in his later poems (e.g. *Epilogue to Satires*, I 24) as well as in ll. 141, 150 below, but I doubt if either here or in l. 65 so specific an allusion is intended. Warburton's note is primarily an incident in the protracted war that he carried on against Bolingbroke.

38. *saps*] A military metaphor; "undermines the position".

Could France or Rome divert our brave designs,   (51)
With all their brandies or with all their wines?   40
What could they more than Knights and Squires confound,
Or water all the Quorum ten miles round?
A Statesman's slumbers how this speech would spoil!   (55)
"Sir, Spain has sent a thousand jars of oil;
"Huge bales of British cloth blockade the door;   45
"A hundred oxen at your levee roar."

---

39. *Rome*] The Pretender's headquarters.

42. *OED* quotes a letter, 15 December 1742, from Philip Yorke (later second Earl of Hardwicke), "Charles is watring the Quorum of Bennet, ten miles round; or, to speak less quaintly, is treating away at Cambridge" (G. Harris, *The Life of Lord Chancellor Hardwicke*, 1847, II 43). Cf. Thomas May, *The Old Couple* (1658), III i 76–80:

> So usurers, so dying Aldermen
> Pour out at once upon their sive-like heirs,
> Whole gusts of envy'd wealth; which they together
> Through many holes let out again in showers,
> And with their ruine water a whole country.

Pope may also have had this passage in mind in ll. 175–7. May's play was reprinted in 1744 by Pope's protégé Robert Dodsley (*A Select Collection of Old Plays*, vol. VII).

Quorum] Justices of the Peace.

44–5. "Spain" and "British" because the original reading had not been "Statesman's" but "Fl**ry's" (it survives in the earlier of the two Huntington drafts). But Pope was an admirer of "honest" Cardinal Fleury (see vol. IV of this edition, pp. 301–2) and no doubt realized on reflection that the sneer was not fair to Louis XV's minister. Moreover Fleury had recently earned his gratitude by installing his friend Father Thomas Southcote into a French abbey (see vol. IV, p. xx). The change has led to a loss of satiric point.

46. Cf. John Sheffield, Duke of Buckinghamshire, *Works*, 1723, I 172 ("The Rapture"):

> Oh, happy Times, when no such thing as Coin
> E'er tempted Friends to part, or Foes to join!
> Cattle, or Corn, among those harmless Men,
> Was all their Wealth, the Gold and Silver then:
> Corn was too bulky to corrupt a Tribe,
> And bellowing Herds would have betray'd the Bribe.

Pope's familiarity with Sheffield's indifferent verse (see also *To a Lady*, 72, and *Imit. Hor.*, *Sat.*, II ii 115) is explained by the fact that he had edited, and partly re-written, the Duke's posthumous *Works* (1723). This passage, however, was not one of those revised by Pope.

> Poor Avarice one torment more would find;
> Nor could Profusion squander all in kind.   (60)
> Astride his cheese Sir Morgan might we meet,
> And Worldly crying coals from street to street,   50
> (Whom with a wig so wild, and mien so maz'd,
> Pity mistakes for some poor tradesman craz'd).
> Had Colepepper's whole wealth been hops and hogs, (65)
> Could he himself have sent it to the dogs?

53 Colepepper's . . . been] H–wl–y's fortune layn in *1732–33.*
54 Could . . . have] Scarce H–wl–y's self had *1732–33.*

---

49. Cf. John Philips, "The Splendid Shilling" (1701), 21–2, 24–6:
    Not blacker Tube, nor of a shorter Size
    Smoaks *Cambro-Britain* . . . when he
    O'er many a craggy Hill and barren cliff,
    Upon a Cargo of fam'd *Cestrian* Cheese,
    High over-shadowing rides. [Wakefield.]
Pope wrote to Caryll, 8 March 1732/3: "I . . . can assure [you] Morgan is a fictitious name" (Sherburn, III 353).

50. Some Misers of great wealth, proprietors of the coal-mines, had enter'd at this time into an association to keep up coals to an extravagant price, whereby the poor were reduced almost to starve, till one of them taking the advantage of underselling the rest, defeated the design. One of these Misers was *worth ten thousand*, another *seven thousand* a year. [P. *1735a–51.*]
    Worldly is Lady Mary's penurious husband Edward Wortley Montagu (1681–1761). Gray wrote to Wharton, 31 January 1761: "You see, old Wortley-Montagu is dead at last at 83. it was not mere avarice, & its companion, abstinence, that kept him alive so long. he every day drank (I think, it was) half a pint of Tokay, wch he imported himself from Hungary in greater quantity than he could use, & sold the Overplus for any price he chose to set upon it. he has left better than half a million of money." Pope also satirizes Wortley Montagu's avarice in *Imit. Hor., Sat.,* II ii, 49 and *Ep.,* II ii, 234.

53. Sir WILLIAM COLEPEPPER, Bart. [1668–1740] a person of an ancient family, and ample fortune, without one other quality of a Gentleman, who, after ruining himself at the Gaming-table, past the rest of his days in sitting there to see the ruin of others; preferring to subsist upon borrowing and begging, rather than to enter into any reputable method of life, and refusing a post in the army which was offer'd him. [P. *1735a–51.*] The H–wl–y of the first edition (see textual note) is perhaps Francis, second Baron Hawley of Duncannon (1663?–1743), whose poverty is referred to in *Suffolk Letters,* I 61–2, rather than the eccentric Lieutenant-General Henry Hawley (1679–1759).

His Grace will game: to White's a Bull be led,   55
With spurning heels and with a butting head.
To White's be carried, as to ancient games,
Fair Coursers, Vases, and alluring Dames.   (70)
Shall then Uxorio, if the stakes he sweep,
Bear home six Whores, and make his Lady weep?   60
Or soft Adonis, so perfum'd and fine,

55. *His Grace*] The allusion is no doubt to Wriothesley Russell, third Duke of Bedford (1708–32), who on 27 November 1731 lost £3,800 at White's to Henry Jansen. The episode is commemorated in *Imit. Donne*, II, 88 (q.v. and note).

White's] A chocolate-house established in St James's Street about 1699 and converted into a club about 1730. White's was already notorious for the high play there in Queen Anne's reign: "I have heard, that the late Earl of Oxford, in the time of his ministry, never passed by White's chocolatehouse (the common rendezvous of infamous sharpers and noble cullies) without bestowing a curse upon that famous academy, as the bane of half the English nobility" (Swift, "Essay on Modern Education", *Prose Works*, ed. Temple Scott, XI 53). The chocolate-house was transformed into a club to exclude the professional sharpers. Among the early members were two of Pope's *bêtes noires*—Colley Cibber and Bubb Doddington. See also *Dunciad* B, I 203, *Imit. Donne*, II, 88, J. Timbs, *Club Life of London*, 1866, I 108–21, and R. J. Allen, *The Clubs of Augustan London*, 1933, pp. 145–51.

56. Cf. Dryden's Virgil, *Ecl.*, III 134–5:

> My *Pollio* writes himself; a Bull be bred,
> With spurning Heels, and with a butting Head. [Wakefield.]

Pope's own copy of the third edition of Dryden's translation (3 vols., 1709)—inscribed "Ex Libris A. Pope. 1710"—is now in the British Museum. The lines he particularly admired are marked, as in the edition of Shakespeare, with marginal commas. This passage, however, is not marked. In 1731 Pope's copy came into the possession of Thomas Gray.

59. *Uxorio*] A cancelled reading in the Huntington drafts is "good B**". Uxorio is therefore presumably John Hervey, first Earl of Bristol (1665–1751), who was certainly nothing if not uxorious: "the whole correspondence between Lord and Lady Bristol . . . from their marriage in 1695 to 1737, has been preserved, and it exhibits a series of *love letters*, by almost every post, of a passionate fondness that would seem excessive after a few months' matrimony" (Lord Hervey's *Memoirs*, ed. J. W. Croker, 1848, I xxii). And Lord Bristol's sporting proclivities were notorious. Macky describes him as "a great sportsman, lover of Horse-matches and play" (*Memoirs*, 1733, p. 108).

61. *Adonis*] Apparently Lord Bristol's son John, Baron Hervey (1696–1743), who as Vice-Chamberlain had official apartments in St James's Palace, and whose effeminate appearance was continually satirized by Pope. Details of Pope's

Drive to St. James's a whole herd of swine?
Oh filthy check on all industrious skill,   (75)
To spoil the nation's last great trade, Quadrille!
   Once, we confess, beneath the Patriot's cloak,   65 (35)
From the crack'd bag the dropping Guinea spoke,

---

quarrel with Hervey will be found in vol. IV of this edition, pp. xv, xix*f*, 365*f*, and Robert W. Rogers, *The Major Satires of Alexander Pope*, 1955, Appendix D ("Pope's Quarrel with Lady Mary and Lord Hervey").

63. *filthy*] Feminine slang. Cf. Millamant, *The Way of the World* (IV ii "filthy Verses", IV v "filthy strong Waters", IV ix "filthy Creature").

64. Quadrille was the fashionable card-game. Its complicated rules will be found in Edmond Hoyle's *A Short Treatise On the Game of Quadrille*, 1745. See also *To a Lady*, 266*n*.

65–8. This is a true story, which happened in the reign of William III [King William *1732–3*], to an [*1732–3 add* eminent] unsuspected old Patriot, who coming out at the back-door from having been closeted by the King, where he had received a large bag of Guineas, the bursting of the bag discovered his business there. [P. *1732–51*.] The episode is also alluded to by Sir Charles Hanbury Williams in "To the Earl of Bath (1743)" (*Works*, 1822, I 198):

> More safe, less open ways pursue,
>   Nor tread in Musgrave's path.
>
> He once, my lord, his party sold,
> Unluckily for too much gold,
>   You know the story well;
> And therefore be not such a fool,
> To cram your money-bag too full,
>   Lest it should break and tell.

Details are supplied by Arthur Onslow (1691–1768) in a note to Burnet (*History of his Own Time*, 1833, IV 196). Sir Christopher Musgrave (1632?–1704) was a leader of the Tory opposition to William III, and one of the bribes—totalling £12,000 according to Burnet—was in connection with the settling of the Civil List in 1698. "Somebody for the court was to propose a million, upon which Musgrave was to rise up, and exclaim against the extravagancy of the demand, and the danger of it, and after many severe reflections upon the court, he was to conclude with saying, 'he dared venture to answer for country gentlemen, that if the demand had been for a modest and reasonable sum, it would not have met with any opposition; that they were not unwilling to support the greatness and dignity of the crown, and that he thought for all good purposes of government 700,000 l. would be sufficient, and he hoped no larger sum would be given in to.'"

And gingling down the back-stairs, told the crew,
"Old Cato is as great a Rogue as you."
Blest paper-credit! last and best supply!
That lends Corruption lighter wings to fly!   70 (40)
Gold imp'd by thee, can compass hardest things,
Can pocket States, can fetch or carry Kings;
A single leaf shall waft an Army o'er,
Or ship off Senates to a distant Shore;
A leaf, like Sibyl's, scatter to and fro   75 (45)
Our fates and fortunes, as the winds shall blow:
Pregnant with thousands flits the Scrap unseen,
And silent sells a King, or buys a Queen.

69 last . . . supply] that advanc'd so high *1732–43*.
70 That lends] Shall lend *1732–33*; Now lends *1735a–43*.
71 by thee] with this *1732–43*. can] may *1732–3*.
72 Can pocket] May pocket *1732–33*. can fetch] or fetch *1732–43*.
73 shall] may *1732–33*; can *1735a–43*.
74 to a] to some *1732–43 and note (but not text) in 1744–51*.
75 scatter] scatters *1735a–40*.
77–8 *Add. 1735a.*

71. *imp'd*] A term of falconry, meaning to insert a feather into a hawk's damaged wing, so as to increase its power of flight.

72. In our author's time, many Princes had been sent about the world, and great changes of Kings projected in Europe. The partition-treaty [1700] had dispos'd of Spain; France had set up a King of England [1701], who was sent to Scotland, and back again [1715]; King Stanislaus was sent to Poland [1704 and 1733], and back again [1709 and 1733]; the Duke of Anjou was sent to Spain [1700], and Don Carlos to Italy [1731]. [P. *1735c–51*.]

74. Alludes to [*1735ab add* the Fate of] several Ministers, Counsellors, and Patriots banished in our times to Siberia, and to that MORE GLORIOUS FATE [ONE *1735b*] of the PARLIAMENT OF PARIS, banished to Pontoise in the year 1720. [P. *1735a–51*.] The Parliament of Paris was banished by the Regent because of its opposition to the schemes of Law.

75. *A Leaf like Sybils.*—Virg. Aen. 6. [P. *1735a–43*.] The passage Pope had in mind was ll. 74–5 of Book VI—in Dryden's version (ll. 116–17):
> But, oh! commit not thy prophetick Mind
> To flitting Leaves, the sport of ev'ry Wind. [Wakefield.]

78. *buys a Queen*] An allusion to the rumour that Queen Caroline had accepted

Since then, my Lord, on such a World we fall,   (77)
What say you? "Say? Why take it, Gold and all."   80
    What Riches give us let us then enquire:
Meat, Fire, and Cloaths. What more? Meat, Cloaths, and Fire.
Is this too little? would you more than live?   (81)
Alas! 'tis more than Turner finds they give.
Alas! 'tis more than (all his Visions past)   85
Unhappy Wharton, waking, found at last!

79 Since . . . we] Well then, since with the world we stand or *1732–
    43.*
80 What . . . take] Come take it as we find *1732–43*; What say you?
    B. Say? Why take *1751.*
81 *1751 prefixes* P.   then] first *1732–43.*
82 What] *1751 prefixes* B.   Meat, Cloaths] *1751 prefixes* P.
84 Turner] Tu**r *1732–33.*   86 Wharton] Wh**n *1732–33.*

a large present from Robert Knight, the cashier of the South Sea Company.
Pope's letter to Swift, 28 November 1729 (Sherburn, III 80), suggests that Pope
at any rate credited the report.
    82. EC compares Juvenal, xiv 36–8:
                         Mensura tamen quae
            Sufficiat census, si quis me consulat, edam:
            In quantum sitis atque fames et frigora possunt.
Leslie Stephen suggested the influence of William Law: "Like Pope, he delights
in exhibiting the logical inconsistency embodied in the ordinary ideals of con-
duct; and coincidences in language suggest that Law was amongst the various
authors from whom Pope borrowed. 'Meat, drink, and clothing are the only
things necessary in life,' says Law, for example" (*History of English Thought in the
Eighteenth Century*, 1876, II 399).
    84. *Turner*] One, who, being possessed of three hundred thousand pounds,
laid down his Coach, because Interest was reduced from five to four *per cent.* and
then put seventy thousand into the Charitable Corporation for better interest;
which sum having lost, he took it so much to heart, that he kept his chamber ever
after. It is thought he would not have outliv'd it, but that he was heir to another
considerable estate, which he daily expected, and that by this course of life he
sav'd both cloaths and all other expences. [P. *1735a–51.*] Richard Turner,
known as "Plum" Turner, was a Turkey merchant who died 8 February 1733.
The *Historical Register* in reporting his death describes him as "*of Gray's Inn,*
Esq", but his name does not occur in any of the Gray's Inn lists.
    86. *Wharton*] A Nobleman of great qualities, but as unfortunate in the appli-
cation of them, as if they had been vices and follies. See his Character in the first

What can they give? to dying Hopkins Heirs; (85)
To Chartres, Vigour; Japhet, Nose and Ears?

87 Hopkins] H*p*s *1732–33*.

Epistle [*1735abcd add* of the second book]. [P. *1735a–51*.] For the career of Philip
Duke of Wharton see the notes to *To Cobham*, 179–209.

87. *Hopkins*] A Citizen, whose rapacity obtained him the name of *Vultur
Hopkins* [*1732–3 om.* Hopkins]. He lived worthless, but [lived ... but *om.* *1732–3*]
died *worth three hundred thousand pounds*, which he would give [and left it *1732–3*]
to no person living, but left it so as not to be inherited till after the second genera-
tion. His counsel representing to him how many years it must be, before this
could take effect, and that his money could only lie at interest all that time, he
exprest great joy thereat, and said, "They would then be as long in spending,
as he had been in getting it." But the Chancery afterwards set aside the will, and
gave it to the heir at law. [P. *1732–51, but after* person living *1732–3 read:* but to
the first Son that should be born of the first Daughter of his next Relation. Being
told by his Lawyer, that it would probably be thirty Years before his Money could
be inherited, and it must all that time lie at Interest, he answer'd. He liked it the
better, and so died.] The note in its first form was incorrect. Hopkins's will is
summarized in *Gent. Mag.*, 1732, II 832. His cousin John Hopkins—who, accord-
ing to "E." (William Seward?) (*Gent. Mag.*, 1788, LVIII 511), was then "in the
humble situation of a farmer's servant"—received £100 a year and £1,000 down;
John's only son Samuel was to inherit all Hopkins's estates in London, Middle-
sex, Surrey, Kent, Wilts, Northants, etc. for life, with remainders to his first and
other sons in tail male, and in default of issue to him to such other sons as John
Hopkins might have, or failing sons to the sons of his daughters. But the young
Samuel died before Hopkins himself, and as no one was then alive who was
entitled to an estate for life the Master of the Rolls decided in October 1732 that
John Hopkins should for the time being receive the rents of the estate. Hopkins's
meanness had already been satirized by Gay ("A Panegyrical Epistle to Mr
Thomas Snow", 1721, 30–31):

> Let Vulture *H—ns* stretch his rusty Throat,
> Who ruins Thousands for a single Groat.

Hopkins was "so generally distinguished by the appellation of *Vulture* Hopkins,
that several persons, of whom, from their knowledge of the world, I should not
have expected it, were fully persuaded that it was his Christian name" (*Gent.
Mag.*, 1788, LVIII 510). The inscription on his grave, in the south-west corner of
Wimbledon churchyard, bears this out: "In a vault under this stone lies interred
the body of John Hopkins, Esq., familiarly known as 'Vulture Hopkins', who
departed this life the 25th April, 1732, Aged 69" (see *Notes and Queries*, 10 Sep-
tember 1859, p. 208).

88. *Chartres*] See l. 20*n*.

Japhet, Nose and Ears] JAPHET CROOK [1662–1734], alias Sir *Peter Stranger*,

L

Can they, in gems bid pallid Hippia glow,
In Fulvia's buckle ease the throbs below,   90

was punished with the loss of those parts, for having forged a conveyance of an Estate to himself, upon which he took up several thousand pounds. He was at the same time sued in Chancery [on suggestion of *1732*] for having fraudulently obtain'd a Will by which he possess'd another [*1732 adds* very] considerable Estate, in wrong of the brother of the deceas'd. By these means he was *worth* a great sum, which (in reward for the small loss of his ears) he enjoy'd in prison till his death, and quietly left to his executor. [P. *1732–51, but 1732–3 om. final sentence.*] Crook's courage in the pillory is described in *The London Journal*, 12 June 1731: "Japhet Crook, alias Sir Peter Stranger, who was sometime since found guilty of forging certain Deeds of Conveyance of two Thousand Acres of Land, and Mortgaging the same for four Thousand five Hundred Pounds, was on Thursday at Twelve o'Clock brought to the Pillory at Charing Cross, and stood thereon till One; then a Chair was set on the Pillory, and Crook put therein, when Jack Ketch with a sort of Pruning (or Incision) Knife, cut off both his Ears, and when that was done, a Surgeon clapt a Styptick thereon; then Jack Ketch with a Pair of Scissors, cut his left Nostril twice before it was quite through, and then at once cut quite through his right Nostril; all which Crook bore with great Patience; but at the Searing (with a hot Iron) his right Nostril, the Pain was so violent, that he was in great Torture and Agony, and got up from his Chair; his left Nostril was not sear'd, so he went from the Pillory bleeding." Crook's chequered career—it has been suggested that he is the ultimate original of Sir Walter Scott's Dousterswivel—is recounted in James Moore's *The Unparalled'd Impostor: Or, The Whole Life, Artifices and Forgeries of Japhet Crook . . . containing, I, An Account of the several Employments he followed in Hertfordshire (under the Profession of a Quaker) as Brewer. . . II. Of his Rambles to Ireland, Scotland, and the North of England, the various Pranks he play'd in all these Places, and of his being taken up during the Preston Rebellion, and defrauding the King's Messenger of a considerable Sum of Money. . . III. Of his twice becoming a Bankrupt. His artifices, to inform Mr. Hawkins. Copies of his Wife's Last Will and Testament to Him; and his own Will to Mr. Hawkins; in order (as he did) to draw in that Gentleman to leave him his Estate. Also Mr. Hawkins's Will. . . London. . .* (1731).

89. *Hippia*] Hippia's name and complexion both derive from the "hyp", a fashionable early eighteenth-century abbreviation of *hypochondria*, a variant of the universal *spleen* (see *To Cobham*, 121n). The earlier Huntington draft reads "Beauty" here, and I doubt if Hippia had a specific identifiable original.

90. *Fulvia's buckle*] "This article of female dress, which appears to have had it's position at the top of the stomacher, is mentioned in the Rape of the Lock, V. 91. where the parody is the most humourous imaginable:

—which after, melted down,
Form'd a vast *buckle* for his *widow's gown*." [Wakefield.]

There were two notorious Fulvias in Roman history, (i) the immoral aristocrat

Or heal, old Narses, thy obscener ail,
With all th' embroid'ry plaister'd at thy tail?   (90)
They might (were Harpax not too wise to spend)
Give Harpax self the blessing of a Friend;
Or find some Doctor that would save the life   95
Of wretched Shylock, spite of Shylock's Wife:
But thousands die, without or this or that,   (95)
Die, and endow a College, or a Cat:

who betrayed Catiline's conspiracy to Cicero, (ii) the brutal and haughty wife of Clodius who later married Mark Antony. Pope had introduced another Fulvia into the first version of *To a Lady*, but the passage (which followed l. 198) was cancelled. The Fulvia of *To a Lady* was apparently Queen Caroline, but as the earlier Huntington draft reads "Diamond Buckle" here a living original is unlikely to have been intended in this passage.

91. *old Narses*] Among the cancelled readings in the Huntington drafts are "C***n" and "old Gen'ral". Narses is therefore William, first Earl Cadogan (1675–1726), a distinguished soldier who is often, but wrongly (see GEC) said to have become Commander-in-Chief in 1722. Cadogan is commemorated in the fine lines by Thomas Tickell which begin,

> Of Marlb'rough's captains and Eugenio's friends,
> The last, Cadogan, to the grave descends.

Pope refers to Cadogan's death in a letter to Hugh Bethel, 9 August 1726 (Sherburn, II 386): "Esteem I never had for him, but concern and humanity I had: the latter was due to the infirmity of his last period." Cadogan's vindictive attitude to Atterbury was never forgiven by Pope (Spence, p. 156). Cadogan is called Narses (Justinian's general, who was of humble origin) because he was of comparatively low birth. His father was a Dublin lawyer. There is also presumably a punning allusion to the *fistula ani* from which Cadogan must be presumed to have suffered.

93–4. Harpax (Greek for "robber") is perhaps an ideal figure, like Molière's Harpagon. This is certainly implied in *Imit. Hor., Sat.*, II i, 43–4,

> The fewer still you name, you wound the more;
> *Bond* is but one, but *Harpax* is a Score.

But the earlier Huntington draft corrects "Harpax" to "Gu–" (Guise?) and then "S–k"; the later draft has only "S***", i.e. Charles Douglas, Earl of Selkirk (see *To Cobham*, 114*n*).

96. *Shylock*] The final reading in the later Huntington draft is "Worldly", though "Shylock" had been the original reading of the earlier draft. A further reference is therefore probably intended to Wortley Montagu (see l. 50*n*). The Shylock in l. 117 and *To Cobham*, 114, was apparently Charles Douglas, Earl of Selkirk.

98. A famous Dutchess of R. [*1732–3 om.* of R.] in her last will left consider-

To some, indeed, Heav'n grants the happier fate,
T' enrich a Bastard, or a Son they hate.   100
      Perhaps you think the Poor might have their part?
Bond damns the Poor, and hates them from his heart: (100)

102 Bond] B*nd *1732–33, 1735c.*

---

able legacies and annuities to her Cats. [P. *1732–51.*] "This benefactress was no other than La Belle Stuart [Frances Theresa Stuart, Duchess of Richmond (1647–1702)] of the Comte de Grammont; and her endowment was not a proper object of satire. The real truth was, that she left annuities to certain female friends, with the burden of maintaining some of her cats; a delicate way of providing for poor, and probably, proud, gentlewomen, without making them feel that they owed their livelihood to her mere liberality" [Warton]. Warton's note derives from a footnote by Lord Hailes (*The Opinions of Sarah Duchess-Dowager of Marlborough,* 1788, p. 44), who knew members of the Duchess of Richmond's family. But her will in Somerset House—proved 21 October 1702—includes no mention of cats. It does, however, contain a large number of small legacies and annuities to feminine relations, acquaintances, and servants, and it is possible some of the annuitants were expected to look after the cats. The line's alliteration has been the subject of much critical comment. ". . . the reader having encountered the two spaced *d*s expects the first *c* of the second half of the line to be followed by a second. But being schooled in Pope's effects he expects a contrast as well as an agreement. *Cat,* when it comes, produces therefore two simultaneous effects" (G. Tillotson, *On the Poetry of Pope,* 1938, p. 142). See also Shenstone, *Works,* 1764, II 179.

      102. This epistle was written [This . . . written *om. 1735a–43*] in the year 1730, when a corporation was established to lend money to the poor upon pledges, by the name of the *Charitable Corporation*; [*1735a–43 insert here* It was under the direction of the Right Honourable Sir R. S., Sir Arch. Grant, Mr. Denis Bond, Mr. Burroughs, &c]. but the whole was turned only to an iniquitous method of enriching particular people, to the ruin of such numbers, that it became a parliamentary concern to endeavour the relief of those unhappy sufferers, and three of the managers, who were members of the house, were expelled. [*1751 inserts here* By the report of the committee, appointed to enquire into that iniquitous affair, it appears, that when it was objected to the intended removal of the office, that the Poor, for whose use it was erected, would be hurt by it, Bond, one of the Directors, replied, Damn the Poor.] That "God hates the poor," and, "That every man in want is knave or fool," &c. were the genuine apothegms of some of the persons here mentioned. [P. *1735a–51.*] The suppression of the second sentence of the original note was due to Warburton's anxiety to spare the feelings of Sir Robert Sutton. See l. 107*n.* A summary of the report to the House of Commons by the committee appointed to investigate the affairs of the Charitable Corporation will be found in *Historical Register,* 1732, XVII 220–32, 255–81. "The

The grave Sir Gilbert holds it for a rule,
That "every man in want is knave or fool:"
"God cannot love (says Blunt, with tearless eyes)   105

---

103 Gilbert] G**t *1732–33.*
105 Blunt] Bl*t *1732–33.*   tearless] lifted *1732–43 (see note).*

Charitable Corporation, for Relief of Industrious Poor, by assisting them with small Sums upon Pledges at legal Interest" was incorporated in 1707, but only became active in 1725. By 1732 its subscribed capital amounted to £353,817. A large proportion of the capital found its way into the pockets of John Thomson, the chief warehouse-keeper, and his tools, but Thomson's depredations were only made possible by the active connivance of most of the eight directors of the company. Three of the directors were M.P.s and Pope's statement that they were all expelled the House of Commons is correct. Sir Robert Sutton and Sir Archibald Grant were expelled 10 May 1732; Denis Bond (d. 1747), the third director Pope had in mind, had already been expelled the previous March because of a swindle perpetuated as a Commissioner for the sale of the Earl of Derwentwater's estates (forfeited in the 1715 rebellion). Bond's part in the Charitable Corporation swindle appears to have been small. Some of the directors "were for keeping to the Intent of their Charter, in lending Money in small Sums to the Poor, but the Majority were for lending Money in the City in large Sums; and Mr Bond, who was of the Majority, said, Damn the Poor, let us go into the City, where we may get Money" (*ibid.*, p. 268). Bond owned Creech Grange, Dorset, and had been M.P. 1709–10, 1715–27, 1727–32 for various Dorset constituencies. His misfortunes in 1732 did not prevent his being appointed a churchwarden of St George's, Hanover Square, in 1735, and he died a very wealthy man. Pope has another contemptuous fling at Bond in *Epilogue to Satires,* I 121.

103. *Sir Gilbert*] Sir Gilbert Heathcote (1652–1733), one of the founders of the Bank of England, of which he was appointed Governor, 1709; Lord Mayor, 1710–11, and the prototype, it is believed, of Sir Andrew Freeport in *The Spectator.* He was reputed to be the richest commoner in England, and died worth £700,000. He seems to have owed his reputation for meanness to a dispute (1712) with the parson of his parish over his brother's funeral fees; his objection, however, was for paying fees for the same corpse in two places (see E. D. Heathcote, *Account of the Families of Heathcote,* 1899, pp. 85, 242). Heathcote bought the estate of Normanton in Lincolnshire about the year 1729 [JB]. Pope has another reference to Heathcote's parsimony in "A Master Key to Popery" (see p. 182 below).

105. *Blunt*] Sir John Blunt. See l. 135*n.*

tearless] The change from "lifted" to "tearless" is perhaps to be explained by the wish to avoid an echo of *To a Lady,* 12,

In Magdalen's loose hair and lifted eye.

"The wretch he starves"—and piously denies:
But the good Bishop, with a meeker air,   (105)
Admits, and leaves them, Providence's care.
    Yet, to be just to these poor men of pelf,
Each does but hate his Neighbour as himself: 110
Damn'd to the Mines, an equal fate betides

---

107 the good Bishop] rev'rend S**n *1732–36*; rev'rend S—on
1739–43 (*see note*).   meeker] softer *1732–43*.

---

107. *the good Bishop*] The change from "rev'rend S**n" (see textual note) was
due to Warburton's interposition. Sir Robert Sutton (1672–1746) had been suc-
cessively ambassador at Constantinople, the Hague, and Paris, and he was M.P.
for Notts, 1722–32, and for Great Grimsby, 1734–6. As a director of the Chari-
table Corporation (see l. 102*n*) he had been expelled from the House of Com-
mons, but he does not seem to have been directly concerned in the embezzle-
ments. Warburton received from Sutton the valuable living of Brant Broughton.
His explanation (*Works*, III 230) that Sutton "was unwarily drawn in by a pack
of infamous Cheats, to his great loss of fortune as well as reputation" is borne
out by the report of the House of Commons committee (1732) and by Lord
Hardwicke's judgment (1742) in a Chancery case which the Corporation brought
against the directors (*Reports of Cases argued and determined in the High Court of
Chancery, in the time of Lord Chancellor Hardwicke*, ed. J. C. Atkyns, 1781, II 400–7).
Sutton was probably guilty of nothing worse than gross negligence. One of the
innocent directors told the parliamentary committee that he "often persuaded
Sir *Robert Sutton* to exert himself, and not to be governed by *Burroughs* and *Squire
&c.* but [he] took little Notice; and when he was at the Committee, frequently
took the News Papers and perused them, neglecting the Business for which they
met" (*Historical Register*, 1732, XVII 277). Warburton's letter to Pope pleading for
the suppression of the allusions to Sutton here and in *Epilogue to Satires*, I 16 is
printed in Hurd's *A Discourse by way of General Preface to Bishop Warburton's Works*,
1794, pp. 143–6, and in Sherburn, IV 492. Pope calls Sutton "rev'rend" because,
according to Croker (EC, III 140), "He was at first intended for the Church,
and actually took Deacon's orders, and accompanied his relation Lord Lexington
on his embassy to Vienna." This is confirmed by William Cole's MS. note in his
copy of Pope's *Works*, vol. II (1736), now in the Bodleian Library, "Sir Robt.
Sutton, in Deacon's Orders"; a MS. note in an eighteenth-century hand in the
Huntington Library copy of *1735a* to the same effect ("Sir Robt. Sutton, who
was in Deacon's Orders . . .") suggests that many of Pope's original readers will
have caught the allusion. The "good Bishop" who takes Sutton's place in the line
is stated by Warburton in the revised *Works*, 1757, III 253–4, to have been
"imaginary".

The Slave that digs it, and the Slave that hides.   (110)
Who suffer thus, mere Charity should own,
Must act on motives pow'rful, tho' unknown:
Some War, some Plague, or Famine they foresee,   115
Some Revelation hid from you and me.
Why Shylock wants a meal, the cause is found,   (115)
He thinks a Loaf will rise to fifty pound.
What made Directors cheat in South-sea year?
To live on Ven'son when it sold so dear.   120
Ask you why Phryne the whole Auction buys?
Phryne foresees a general Excise.   (120)

113–14 *1751 prefixes* B.   114 motives] Reasons *1732–33*.
115 or] some *1732–43*.   117 Shylock] S–l–k *1732*.

111–12. "The witty allusion to the punishment of avarice in the Epistle on Riches ... is plainly taken from 'The Causes of the Decay of Christian Piety', where that excellent and neglected writer says, 'It has always been held the severest treatment of slaves and malefactors', damnare ad metalla, 'to force them to dig in the mines: now this is the covetous man's lot, from which he is never to expect a release'. Cowley has also used the same allusion" (Z, i.e. Joseph Warton, *The Adventurer*, no. 63, 12 June 1753). *The Causes of the Decay of Christian Piety* (1667) is by Richard Allestree.

117. *Shylock*] See l. 96n. The "S–l–k" of the first edition (see textual note) must be Charles Douglas, Earl of Selkirk (*see To Cobham*, 114n).

120. In the extravagance and luxury of the South-sea year, the price of a haunch of Venison was from three to five pounds. [P. *1732–51*.]

121–2. Many people about the year 1733, had a conceit that such a thing was intended, of which it is not improbable this lady might have some intimation. [P. *1735a–51*.] Walpole's Excise Bill of 1733 was a warehousing scheme designed to make England a storehouse for the temporary deposit of goods, and London a free port. The Opposition interpreted it as a general excise, which so much alarmed the public that Walpole decided to withdraw the measure. Warburton told Spence (p. 371) that Phryne was "Miss Skirret". This is very probable. Maria Skerret (1702?–38), who is alternatively described as the daughter of an Irish gentleman, "a sort of beau" (Lady Mary's *Letters*, I 74) and as "daughter to a merchant", who left her £14,000 (Hervey, I 86), was Walpole's mistress for many years and finally, on the death of Lady Walpole, his second wife. According to the Duchess of Marlborough (Lady Mary's *Letters*, I 497), Maria was a constant patron of the auction-rooms. The historical Phryne was an Athenian hetaira of humble origin, but of great beauty and wealth.

Why she and Sappho raise that monstrous sum?
Alas! they fear a man will cost a plum.
Wise Peter sees the World's respect for Gold,   125
And therefore hopes this Nation may be sold:
Glorious Ambition! Peter, swell thy store,   (125)
And be what Rome's great Didius was before.

123 Sappho] Lesbia *1732–33 and uncancelled copies of 1735a* (*see Griffith, p. 281*).

123. The change of "Lesbia" to "Sappho" (see textual note) was part of Pope's campaign against Lady Mary Wortley Montagu, which is discussed in *To a Lady*, 24n. Lady Mary was an intimate friend of Maria Skerret. Writing to Lady Mar, January 1725, she boasted, "I see every body, but converse with nobody but *des amies choisies*; in the first rank of these are Lady Stafford, and dear Molly Skerritt, both of which have now the additional merit of being old acquaintances, and never having given me any reason to complain of either of 'em" (Lady Mary's *Letters*, 1 480).

124. *plum*] Eighteenth-century slang for £100,000. "A 'plum' is no temptation to [an honest man]. He likes and loves himself too well to change hearts with one of those corrupt miscreants, who amongst them gave that name to a round sum of money gained by rapine and plunder of the commonwealth" (Shaftesbury's *Characteristics*, ed. J. M. Robertson, 1 86) [JB].

125. PETER WALTER, a person not only eminent in the wisdom of his profession, as a dextrous attorney, but allow'd to be a good, if not a safe, conveyancer; extremely respected by the Nobility of this land, tho' free from all manner of luxury and ostentation: his Wealth was never seen, and his bounty never heard of, except to his own son, for whom he procured an employment of considerable profit, of which he gave him as much as was *necessary*. Therefore the taxing this gentleman with any Ambition, is certainly a great wrong to him. [P. *1735a–51*.] Peter Walter, or Waters (1664?–1746) was a "money scrivener", that is, "one who received money to place out at interest, and who supplied those who wanted to raise money on security." He was Clerk of the Peace for Middlesex and the Duke of Newcastle's Land Steward, and represented Bridport in Parliament from 1715 to 1727. At his death he is said to have been worth £300,000 (*Gent. Mag.*, XVI 45). He was the original of Fielding's Peter Pounce. His activities as money-lender-in-chief to the aristocracy brought him much notoriety and he is satirized by Swift ("To Mr. Gay" (1731)) and Sir Charles Hanbury Williams ("Peter and my Lord Quidam") as well as by Pope and Fielding. There are allusions to Walter in l. 20 as well as in *Imit. Hor., Sat.*, II i, 3, 40, II ii, 168, *Ep.*, II i, 197, *Imit. Donne*, II, 66f, *Epilogue to Satires*, I 121, II 58, and *1740*, 26(?) [JB].

128. A Roman Lawyer, so rich as to purchase the Empire when it was set to

The Crown of Poland, venal twice an age,
To just three millions stinted modest Gage. 130

130 Gage] —— *1732–33*; G* *1735ab*.

sale [*1732–3 insert* by the Prætorian Bands] upon the death of Pertinax. [P. *1732–
51*.] "The Prætorians, after the death of Pertinax, A.D. 193, put the Empire up
to sale, and Didius Salvius Julianus outbid Sulpicianus, father-in-law of Pertinax.
He only held the Empire for two months, at the end of which period he was
killed by Septimius Severus" [EC].

129. The Polish throne became vacant in 1696 with the death of John Sobieski,
in 1707 at the abdication of Augustus II, in 1709 at the abdication of Stanislas I,
and in 1733 on the death of Augustus II. The Polish nobility, who were the
electors to the crown, were unblushingly venal.

130–4. The two persons here mentioned were of Quality [*for* The ... Quality
1732–3 read Two persons of distinction], each of whom in the [*1732–3 insert* time
of the] Missisippi despis'd to realize above *three hundred thousand pounds*; the Gentle-
man with a view to the purchase of [*1732–3 om.* the purchase of] the Crown of
Poland, the Lady on a vision of the like royal [*1732–3 om.* royal] nature. They
since retired [*1732–3 add* together] into Spain, where they are still in search of
gold in the mines of the Asturies. [P. *1732–51*.] Joseph Gage (1678?–1753?) was
a member of an old Catholic family with which Pope was at one time in touch
(C. W. Dilke, *The Papers of a Critic*, 1875, I 134). (His sister Mrs Weston has been
supposed to be the original of Pope's "Unfortunate Lady".) In 1719 Gage "is
said to have acquired Missisippi stock representing the value of 13,000,000 l.
Intoxicated with his success, Gage ... sent a gentleman to Augustus, king of
Poland, to offer 3,000,000 l. for the crown, which was declined. He next sent an
agent to the king of Sardinia, to offer a vast sum for that island, which proposal
was likewise rejected" (*DNB*). In 1727 Gage obtained from the King of Spain a
grant for working and draining all the gold mines in Old Spain, and for fishing
for all wrecks on the coasts of Spain and the Indies. The Asturian gold-mines
were not very profitable, but in 1741 the King gave him a silver mine of great
value. He proved an able commander of the Spanish troops in Italy, 1743–6,
and was created a grandee of the first class. Gage's second wife was Lady Mary
Herbert (1700?–70?). Lord Oxford scribbled against this passage in his copy
of the first edition (now Bodley M. 3. 19. Art.): "Lady Mary Herbert in the
Missisippi time borrowed of Her Servant 10 Luidores for necessary expences
because she said she would not Break a million never paid the Servant". Horace
Walpole also annotated his copy of Pope (Fraser marginalia, p. 39): "Lady
Mary Herbert, sister of the last Marquis of Powis, had made a prodigious fortune
in the Missisipi, & refused the Duke of Bouillon, being determined to marry
nobody but a Sovereign Prince; but refusing to realise, lost the whole, & met
Gage in the Asturian mines. Some years after, the young Pretender being at
Madrid, she sent to desire to see him. He found her in a garret, so poor that she

But nobler scenes Maria's dreams unfold,
Hereditary Realms, and worlds of Gold.   (130)
Congenial souls! whose life one Av'rice joins,
And one fate buries in th' Asturian Mines.
  Much injur'd Blunt! why bears he Britain's hate? 135
A wizard told him in these words our fate:
"At length Corruption, like a gen'ral flood,   (135)
"(So long by watchful Ministers withstood)

135 Blunt] Bl—t *1732–33*.

could not rise for want of clothes; he gave her his greatcoat, & what money he
had about him. In 1766, when I was at Paris she and Gage were both alive at
Paris; he died in May that year. She was in a lodging given to her by the Prince
of Conti at the Temple, & in April of the same year recovered two annuities &
the arrears from the Earl of Powis, by a sentence of the House of Lords."

 132. *Hereditary Realms*] Lady Mary Herbert's mother is said by William
Bennet (Wakefield, p. 216) to have been the illegitimate daughter of James II.
GEC and Burke do not confirm this.

 135. Sir JOHN BLUNT, originally a scrivener, was one of the first projectors
of the South-sea company, and afterwards one of the directors [*1735 add* and
chief Managers] of the famous scheme in 1720. He was also one of those who
suffer'd most severely by the bill of pains and penalties on the said directors.
[*1735ab insert* The fraudulent Conveyance he made of part of his Estate, to the
value of fifty thousand pounds, to John Ward of Hackney being detected, thro'
a Misunderstanding between these two Friends, he not only lost that great Sum,
but had forfeited his Live, without a Pardon for the discovery.] He was a Dis-
senter of a most religious deportment, and profess'd to be a great believer.
Whether he did really credit the prophecy here mentioned is not certain, but it
was constantly in this very style he declaimed against the corruption and luxury
of the age, the partiality of Parliaments, and the misery of party-spirit. He was
particularly eloquent against *Avarice* in great and noble persons, of which he had
indeed liv'd to see many miserable examples. He died in the year 1732. [P.
1735–51.] Sir John Blunt (1665–1733) was the "chief Projector" (*Historical
Register*, 1734, XVIII, "Chronological Diary", under 24 January) and one of the
most unscrupulous of the Directors of the South-Sea Company. An account of
his examination by the House of Lords on 4 February 1721 will be found in
Historical Register, 1721, VI 278–80. Of his estate of £183,350 he was only allowed
to retain £1,000 (*ibid.*, p. 221). Further details of Blunt's conspiracy with John
Ward will be found in Pope's note to l. 20. Pope seems to have obtained some of
his information about Blunt from his friend Caryll (see Pope's letter, 8 March
1733; Sherburn, III 353).

"Shall deluge all; and Av'rice creeping on,
"Spread like a low-born mist, and blot the Sun;   140
"Statesman and Patriot ply alike the stocks,
"Peeress and Butler share alike the Box,   (140)
"And Judges job, and Bishops bite the town,
"And mighty Dukes pack cards for half a crown.
"See Britain sunk in lucre's sordid charms,   145
"And France reveng'd of ANNE's and EDWARD's arms!"
No mean Court-badge, great Scriv'ner! fir'd thy brain, (145)
Nor lordly Luxury, nor City Gain:
No, 'twas thy righteous end, asham'd to see
Senates degen'rate, Patriots disagree,   150

143 And Judges] The Judge shall *1732–43*.   and Bishops] the
     Bishop *1732–43*.
147 No mean] No poor *1732–33*; 'Twas no *1735abcd, 1744–51*; No
     gay *1736 (see note)*.
148 Nor ... nor] No ... no *1732–33*; No ... nor *1739–43 (see note)*.
149 No,] But *1732–33, uncancelled copies of 1735a (see Griffith, p. 281)*,
     1735b.

141. *Statesman and Patriot*] Members of the Government and of the Opposition.
    142. The point here is not only "the general confusion of ranks in consequence
of the fortunes made by speculation" [EC], but also perhaps the attendant
confusion of the sexes. Normally, although the practice was not by any means
universal, the women occupied the front-boxes in the London theatres and
the men the side-boxes. Thus in *The Theatre*, 5 January 1720, Steele selected
"Three of the Fair Sex" to "represent the Front-Boxes" on his committee of
"Auditors of the Drama" and "Two Gentlemen of Wit and Pleasure for the
Side-Boxes". Pope refers to this division of the sexes in *Rape of Lock*, v 13–18.
    147–8. I have preferred to read "No mean" rather than " 'Twas no" (as in
1744–51) because l. 149 begins "No, 'twas". In l. 148 "Nor ... nor" seems pre-
ferable to the Overlooked Revision "No ... nor" to avoid three consecutive lines
beginning "No" (especially as the "No" of l. 149 is not the same word syntacti-
cally). See also p. liv above for the textual principle involved.
    150. *Patriots disagree*] Walpole owed his long tenure of power at least in part
to the divisions within the Opposition. The Jacobite Tories led by Shippen, the
Hanoverian Tories led by Wyndham, and the discontented Whigs led by Car-
teret and Pulteney agreed in their detestation of Walpole, but in little else.
Bolingbroke made it his special task to organize the Opposition; his complaints
on its difficulty must often have been poured into Pope's sympathetic ears.

And nobly wishing Party-rage to cease,
To buy both sides, and give thy Country peace.   (150)
  "All this is madness," cries a sober sage:
But who, my friend, has reason in his rage?
  "The ruling Passion, be it what it will,   155
"The ruling Passion conquers Reason still."
Less mad the wildest whimsey we can frame,   (155)
Than ev'n that Passion, if it has no Aim;
For tho' such motives Folly you may call,
The Folly's greater to have none at all.   160
  Hear then the truth: "'Tis Heav'n each Passion sends,
"And diff'rent men directs to diff'rent ends.   (160)
"Extremes in Nature equal good produce,

---

152. EC interprets this to refer to the South Sea Company's offer (22 January 1720) to take over the National Debt for £3,500,000 (increased 1 February to £7,567,500). (See *Historical Register*, 1720, v 25*f*.) As, when Parliament agreed to this (the Act received the Royal Assent 7 April), members of every political complexion rushed to buy stock, Blunt might be said to have bought both sides.

153–60. Warburton seems to have tried to get Pope to revise this passage. Pope's reply has survived (Brit. Mus. Egerton MS., 1946, f. 68^r, and Sherburn, IV 480): "As for the other part, concerning the Extravagant Motives of Avarice, I meant to show those wch were Real were yet as mad or madder than those wch are Imaginary [vid. vers.

> For tho' Such Motives Folly y^u may call,
> The folly's greater to have none at all.

So I w^d let that remain as it is.—. . ." The note is not dated, but the postmark is 15 November; the year is almost certainly 1743.

155–6. Pope's theory of the Ruling Passion receives an extended exposition in *To Cobham* (especially ll. 174*f*) and *E. on Man*, II 123–44. He is not quoting himself here. Quotation marks were regularly used in the eighteenth century and earlier to call attention to some striking aphorism or generalization.

160. "Qui vit sans folie n'est pas si sage qu'il croit" (La Rochefoucauld, *Maximes*, no. CCIX). Pope professed to disapprove of La Rochefoucauld's realistic ethics, but he had certainly read him with care and admiration. See Audra, pp. 504–28.

163–4. This couplet is also in *E. on Man*, II 205–6:

> Extremes in Nature equal ends produce,
> In Man they join to some mysterious use.

Though *An Essay on Man. Epistle II* was published more than two months later than *Of the Use of Riches*, the *E. on Man* couplet was written earlier, as the auto-

"Extremes in Man concur to gen'ral use."
Ask we what makes one keep, and one bestow?   165
That Pow'r who bids the Ocean ebb and flow,
Bids seed-time, harvest, equal course maintain,   (165)
Thro' reconcil'd extremes of drought and rain,
Builds Life on Death, on Change Duration founds,
And gives th' eternal wheels to know their rounds.   170
    Riches, like insects, when conceal'd they lie,
Wait but for wings, and in their season, fly.   (170)
Who sees pale Mammon pine amidst his store,
Sees but a backward steward for the Poor;
This year a Reservoir, to keep and spare,   175
The next a Fountain, spouting thro' his Heir,

---

graph MSS. in the Huntington Library demonstrate conclusively. The earlier
of the two drafts has the couplet in the margin and verbatim as in *E. on Man*; it
was then corrected to its present form, which is more appropriate to the context
of Pope's argument. The point is not quite the same in the two passages. In
E. on Man the emphasis is apparently on man the individual, and the paradox is
the co-operation between vice and virtue in a particular person. Here, however,
Pope is thinking in terms of society, e.g. that the spendthrift is balanced by the
miser. Pope's optimistic ethics, taught him in the first place by Bolingbroke, may
perhaps partly derive from Mandeville's paradox of private vices being public
benefits, though Swift (in "The Foolish Methods of Education among the
Nobility", 1728) also gives the sequence of avaricious father and spendthrift son
as an example of the "continual Circulation of human Things for [God's] own
unsearchable Ends". See note to ll. 13–14 above, and for a detailed discussion
of the whole matter the Introduction to vol. III i of this edition, and the notes on
E. on Man, II 205–6.

167–8. "While the earth remaineth, seedtime and harvest, and cold and
heat, and summer and winter, and day and night shall not cease", Genesis,
VIII 22 [Dilke].

171–2. "Wilt thou set thine eyes upon that which is not? for riches certainly
make themselves wings; they fly away as an eagle toward heaven", Proverbs,
XXIII 5 [Dilke].

175. Young, *Love of Fame*, VI 319–21:
    All *hoarded* treasure they repute a load,
    Nor think their wealth *their own*, till well bestow'd.
    Grand *reservoirs* of publick happiness . . .
The conceit is also to be found in Thomas May's *The Old Couple*, III i 76–80
(see l. 42*n*).

In lavish streams to quench a Country's thirst,   (175)
And men and dogs shall drink him 'till they burst.
Old Cotta sham'd his fortune and his birth,

---

179. *Old Cotta*] Almost the only clue to the identification of Cotta is the cancelled passage which (according to a "Variation" supplied by Warburton) originally followed l. 218:

> Where one lean herring furnish'd Cotta's board,
> And nettles grew, fit porridge for their Lord;
> Where mad good-nature, bounty misapply'd,
> In lavish Curio blaz'd awhile and dy'd;
> There Providence once more shall shift the scene,
> And shewing H—y, teach the golden mean.

An early draft in the Huntington Library has "Harley" instead of "H—y". The successor to the younger Cotta is therefore Edward Harley, second Earl of Oxford, whose country seat was at Wimpole in Cambridgeshire. His predecessors at Wimpole were his father-in-law John Holles, Duke of Newcastle (1662–1711), and Sir John Cutler (see l. 315*n*). Some of Pope's contemporaries seem to have believed that Cotta was this Duke of Newcastle and the son his nephew and heir Thomas Pelham-Holles (1693–1758). The latter was the well-known politician, and it is true that he died some £300,000 poorer for his services to the Whig cause. When Spence questioned Pope about the identification (p. 300) "Mr. Pope did not confirm it outright . . . but spoke of their characters in a manner that seemed not at all to disown it." On the other hand the elder Duke was not, as far as is known, a miser, and the younger Duke never owned Wimpole. Cotta's character fits Sir John Cutler far better. (i) Cutler was the most notorious miser of his generation; he is the hero, for example, of Wycherley's "Praise of Avarice". (ii) The description of Cotta's hall is closely paralleled by an episode in Cutler's career. "In 1657, when Lord Strafford was obliged to part with his estate and manor of Harewood and Gawthorpe in Yorkshire, Cutler, along with Sir John Lewys, bart., became a joint purchaser, and soon afterwards the sole possessor. He chose to reside for a while at Gawthorpe Hall, where, tradition says, he lived in miserly seclusion" (*DNB*). (iii) After l. 198 the later Huntington draft inserts in the margin a version of ll. 291–6—a passage which derives from the account of Cutler's own funeral (see note to ll. 291–2). (iv) The name Cotta seems to be pointless except in application to Cutler (cf. Worldly for Wortley, Bubo for Bubb Dodington, Atticus for Addison, etc.). At least, though there were several distinguished Romans of the name, I have not been able to discover one that was especially avaricious. But if Cutler is Cotta, who is Cotta's son? Cutler had no sons, the baronetcy was extinguished by his death, and Wimpole passed to his son-in-law the Earl of Radnor, who sold it in 1710 to the Duke of Newcastle. As l. 199 originally began "Not so his Heir" (corrected in the same Huntington draft to "Not Curio so"), the younger Cotta may well have been drawn from this son-in-law. Charles Bodvile Robartes, second Earl of Radnor

Yet was not Cotta void of wit or worth: 180
What tho' (the use of barb'rous spits forgot)
His kitchen vy'd in coolness with his grot?   (180)
His court with nettles, moats with cresses stor'd,
With soups unbought and sallads blest his board.
If Cotta liv'd on pulse, it was no more   185
Than Bramins, Saints, and Sages did before;
To cram the Rich was prodigal expence,   (185)
And who would take the Poor from Providence?
Like some lone Chartreux stands the good old Hall,
Silence without, and Fasts within the wall;   190
No rafter'd roofs with dance and tabor sound,
No noontide-bell invites the country round;   (190)
Tenants with sighs the smoakless tow'rs survey,
And turn th' unwilling steeds another way:
Benighted wanderers, the forest o'er,   195
Curse the sav'd candle, and unop'ning door;
While the gaunt mastiff growling at the gate,   (195)
Affrights the beggar whom he longs to eat.
   Not so his Son, he mark'd this oversight,

---

183 moats] Moat *1735a–43*.   194 steeds] Steed *1735c–43*.

(1660–1723), was certainly as keen a Whig as young Cotta. In 1688 he was one
of the nobility who took up arms to support William III. He was also very
extravagant. In a letter dated 26 September 1713 to the Earl of Oxford his
brother Russell Robartes refers to Radnor's bad management of his affairs, and
to the £20,000 that he had spent at Wimpole (Hist. MSS. Comm. Portland
MSS., p. 341). Unfortunately very little else appears to be discoverable about
this Lord Radnor, except that Swift, who tried hard to persuade him to join the
Tories, told Stella that he was never "abroad till three in the afternoon" (*Journal
to Stella*, ed. H. Williams, pp. 13, 131, 451–2, 454). The Lord Radnor in whose
garden at Twickenham Warburton first met Pope, and who was one of the
witnesses of Pope's will, was the fourth Earl and a nephew of young Cotta.
  181–2. Cf. Dryden, *Absalom and Achitophel*, 620–1:
     His Cooks, with long disuse, their Trade forgot;
     Cool was his Kitchin, though his Brains were hot.
  184. —dapibus mensas onerabat inemptis. VIRG. [P. *1735c–51*.] *Georg.*, IV
133.

And then mistook reverse of wrong for right.   200
(For what to shun will no great knowledge need,
But what to follow, is a task indeed.)   (200)
What slaughter'd hecatombs, what floods of wine,
Fill the capacious Squire, and deep Divine!
Yet no mean motive this profusion draws,   205
His oxen perish in his country's cause;
'Tis GEORGE and LIBERTY that crowns the cup,
And Zeal for that great House which eats him up.
The woods recede around the naked seat,
The Sylvans groan—no matter—for the Fleet: 210
Next goes his Wool—to clothe our valiant bands,
Last, for his Country's love, he sells his Lands.
To town he comes, completes the nation's hope,
And heads the bold Train-bands, and burns a Pope.
And shall not Britain now reward his toils,   215

202 indeed.)] *1744–51 (see note) add*
              Yet sure, of qualities deserving praise,
              More go to ruin Fortunes, than to raise.
203 What . . . what] Whole . . . and *1735c–43.*
205 Yet no mean] No selfish *1735ab.*
207 'Tis . . . the] 'Tis the dear Prince (Sir John) that crowns thy
        1732–33 (see note).
208 that . . . him] his . . . thee *1732–33.*
213–16 *Add. 1735a.*

202. This line is followed in the later editions by a further couplet (see textual note). Warburton's note in the revised edition (1754) runs: "I found these two lines in the Poet's MS. . . . which, as they seemed to be necessary to do justice to the general Character going to be described, I advised him to insert in their place." Pope was wrong in taking Warburton's advice, if he did. The couplet —an interlineated addition in the earlier Huntington draft and cancelled in the later one—is clearly a rejected *alternative* to ll. 201–2. As a sort of parenthetic aside to the reader either couplet would have been adequate, but to have both is to interrupt the main sequence of thought. The result is an unnecessary clumsiness.

214. *Train-bands*] "A trained company of citizen soldiery, organized in London and other parts in the 16th, 17th and 18th centuries" (*OED*).

Britain, that pays her Patriots with her Spoils?
In vain at Court the Bankrupt pleads his cause,
His thankless Country leaves him to her Laws.
   The Sense to value Riches, with the Art
T'enjoy them, and the Virtue to impart,   220
Not meanly, nor ambitiously pursu'd,
Not sunk by sloth, nor rais'd by servitude;
To balance Fortune by a just expence,
Join with Oeconomy, Magnificence;
With Splendor, Charity; with Plenty, Health;   225
Oh teach us, BATHURST! yet unspoil'd by wealth!
That secret rare, between th' extremes to move
Of mad Good-nature, and of mean Self-love.
   To Want or Worth well-weigh'd, be Bounty giv'n,
And ease, or emulate, the care of Heav'n.   230
Whose measure full o'erflows on human race
Mend Fortune's fault, and justify her grace.
Wealth in the gross is death, but life diffus'd,
As Poison heals, in just proportion us'd:
In heaps, like Ambergrise, a stink it lies,   235
But well-dispers'd, is Incense to the Skies.

---

217 In vain . . . Bankrupt] Bankrupt, at Court in vain he *1732–33*;
    Alas! at Court he vainly *1735ab*.
229 *1751 prefixes* B.
232 Mend . . . justify] Mends . . . justifies *1732–43*.

---

226. BATHURST] See Heading *n* (p. 83 above).

231. i.e. Such of the Rich whose full measure overflows on the human race,
repair the wrongs of Fortune done to the indigent; and, at the same time, justify
the favours she had bestow'd upon themselves [Warburton, *1744–51*].

233. A favourite sentiment of Mandeville's (e.g. *The Fable of the Bees*, ed.
Kaye, 1 103, "as the Avaricious does no good to himself, and is injurious to all
the World besides, except his Heir, so the Prodigal is a Blessing to the whole
Society, and injures no body but himself").

235. Perhaps a reminiscence of Bacon's dictum "money is like muck, not good
except it be spread" (*Essays*, xv). Cf. too Pope's own aphorism, "Praise is like
ambergris; a little whiff of it is very agreeable" ("Thoughts on Various Subjects",
EC, x 558) (G. K. Hunter).

M

Who starves by Nobles, or with Nobles eats?
The Wretch that trusts them, and the Rogue that cheats.
Is there a Lord, who knows a cheerful noon
Without a Fiddler, Flatt'rer, or Buffoon?   240
Whose table, Wit, or modest Merit share,
Un-elbow'd by a Gamester, Pimp, or Play'r?
Who copies Your's, or OXFORD's better part,

---

237 *1751 prefixes* P.

---

240. No doubt an unconscious reminiscence of Dryden (*Absalom and Achitophel*,
1 550),

> Was Chymist, Fidler, Statesman, and Buffoon.   (G. K. Hunter.)

242. *or Play'r*] Pope's apparent animus against the stage has not been satis-
factorily explained. The orthodox explanation is that it all derives from Cibber's
jocular reference to *Three Hours after Marriage* in a "gag" in *The Rehearsal* in
1717. But this seems unlikely. The social status of "players", then as now, varied
with the individual. Wilks, Booth, Cibber, Estcourt, Quin, Mrs Bracegirdle,
and Mrs Oldfield were "accepted" by society almost as fully as Pope himself.

243. *Oxford's*] Edward Harley, Earl of Oxford [1689-1741]. The son of
Robert, created Earl of Oxford and Earl Mortimer by Queen Anne. This
Nobleman died regretted by all men of letters, great numbers of whom had
experienc'd his benefits. He left behind him one of the most noble Libraries in
Europe. [P. *1735-51. First sentence only 1734-43.*] The Earl was a personal friend
of Prior and Swift as well as of Pope. Among the scholars and antiquaries whom
he financed or assisted were George Vertue, Zachary Grey, William Oldys,
and Joseph Ames. His library contained some 50,000 printed books, 41,000
prints, and 350,000 pamphlets—all bought by Thomas Osborne, the bookseller
—as well as 7,639 volumes of MSS. and 14,236 rolls, charters, and legal docu-
ments. The MSS. were bought by the nation in 1753 and are now in the British
Museum. In a letter of 7 November 1731 Pope told Lord Oxford that he had
"taken the Liberty to call at Your Door, in my way to Moral Virtue", though the
reference may not be to this passage but to the rejected lines that originally
followed l. 218 (see l. 179*n*) in the earlier Huntington draft. In a letter of 22 Janu-
ary 1731-2 Pope informs Oxford that the poem at that time complimented the
Duke of Chandos as well as Bathurst and Oxford. When publication was be-
coming imminent, Pope sent the whole of this passage to Oxford (22 September
1732) and asked his permission to print it. Chandos's name was still in the
passage then, but by 29 October, when Pope had obtained the required per-
mission, he had decided to omit the allusion to Chandos, in order "not to joyn
with your Name any other's for whom I have less affection" (Sherburn, III 241,
267, 325).

To ease th' oppress'd, and raise the sinking heart?
Where-e'er he shines, oh Fortune, gild the scene,   245
And Angels guard him in the golden Mean!
There, English Bounty yet a-while may stand,
And Honour linger ere it leaves the land.
　　But all our praises why should Lords engross?
Rise, honest Muse! and sing the MAN of Ross: 250

---

248. A reference, no doubt, to Virgil, *Georg.*, II 473–4,
　　　　　　　　　　extrema per illos
　　　　Justitia excedens terris vestigia fecit.
250. MAN of Ross] The person here celebrated, who with a small [*1732–35b read* This Person who with no greater] Estate actually [actually *added 1735a*] performed all these good works, and whose true name was almost lost (partly by [*1732–3 insert* having] the title of the *Man of Ross* given him by way of eminence, and partly by being buried without so much as an [any *1732–35b*] inscription) was called Mr. John Kyrle. He died in the year 1724, aged [*1732–3 insert* near] 90, and lies interr'd [buried *1732*] in the chancel of the church of Ross in Herefordshire. [P. *1732–51*.] A tradition survives that Pope wrote the lines on the Man of Ross while staying with Lady Scudamore (the sister of his friend Digby) at Holm Lacy in Herefordshire (note by James Dallaway in Walpole's *Anecdotes of Painters*, ed. R. N. Wornum, 1888, p. 654). Much of his information, however, about Kyrle was derived from the elder Jacob Tonson, the publisher, who had bought an estate at Ledbury. On 14 November 1731 Pope wrote to Tonson for "Exact information of the *Man of Ross*. what was his Xtian and Surname? what year he dyed, and about what age? and to transcribe his Epitaph, if he has one . . ." (Sherburn, III 244). Tonson's letters have not survived, but on 7 June 1732 Pope wrote to thank him for the details he had collected. "You know, few of these particulars can be made to shine in verse, but I have selected the most affecting, and have added 2 or 3 which I learnd fro' other hands. A small exaggeration you must allow me as a poet; yet I was determined the ground work at least should be *Truth*, which made me so scrupulous in my enquiries. . . I was not sorry he had no monument, and will put that circumstance into a note, perhaps into the body of the poem itself" (Sherburn, III 290–1). What was the extent of the "small exaggeration" Pope admitted to? A Herefordshire friend, to whom Hearne put this question in 1734, considered the truth was not "strained in any particulars of the character", except in three details—(i) Kyrle was not "Founder of the Church and Spire of Ross", (ii) nor was he "Founder of any Hospital", (iii) "his knowledge in Medicine extended no farther than Kitchin Physick, of which he was very liberal, and might thereby preserve many lives" (*Remarks and Collections*, XI, Ox. Hist. Soc., 1921, p. 326). After Pope's death Spence began to collect what information he could about Kyrle (pp. 423–6, letter from R. Wheeler, 25 February 1748; pp.

Pleas'd Vaga echoes thro' her winding bounds,
And rapid Severn hoarse applause resounds.
Who hung with woods yon mountain's sultry brow?
From the dry rock who bade the waters flow?
Not to the skies in useless columns tost,   255
Or in proud falls magnificently lost,
But clear and artless, pouring thro' the plain
Health to the sick, and solace to the swain.
Whose Cause-way parts the vale with shady rows?
Whose Seats the weary Traveller repose?   260
Who taught that heav'n-directed spire to rise?

437–8, letter from Stephen Duck, 1 January 1751), and later accounts are by
"Viator" (*The Gentleman's Magazine*, 1786, LVI ii 1026), and a certain Thomas
Hutcheson, who was a connection of Kyrle's (EC, III 150–1).

251. *Vaga*] The Wye.

253. "There was and still is a very long shady walk, of nearly a mile and a
half in length, called Kyrle's Walks . . . on the summit of an eminence com-
manding a beautiful prospect of the Wye and the country to a great extent"
(Hutcheson, p. 150). "He had a singular taste for Prospects: and by a vast
plantation of Elms, which he has dispos'd of in a fine manner, he has made one
of the most entertaining Scenes the County of Hereford affords—His point of
View is on an Emenence which he has wall'd in and dispos'd of into walks"
(Wheeler, p. 424). The Prospect is now a public park.

254. "He inclosed within a stone-wall, ornamented with two elegant en-
trances, a space of ground of near half an acre, in the centre of which he sunk
a bason as a reservoir of water, for the use of the inhabitants of Ross" ("Viator").
I suspect this is also the Prospect, which still has Kyrle's two original stone gate-
ways. "The Man of Ross promoted and partly assisted, by his own pecuniary
aid, the erection of a small waterwork near the river Wye, which supplied the
town of Ross with water, in which article it was very deficient before" (Hutche-
son, p. 150).

257. "artless" in contrast to the ostentatious use of water by formal-gardening
(l. 255) and landscape-gardening (l. 256) peers.

259. "He made a causeway on the Monmouth road, for the use of foot-
passengers" ("Viator"). "He was a considerable contributor to a long handsome
Causeway which leads to the Town; which with the stately Avenue of Elms
planted by it, gives the Traveller a very favourable prejudice to the place"
(Wheeler, pp. 424–5).

261. "He raised the spire of Ross upwards of one hundred feet" ("Viator").
Royal Comm. on Hist. Mon., *Herefordshire*, 1932, II 158, partly confirms this:

The MAN of Ross, each lisping babe replies.
Behold the Market-place with poor o'erspread!
The MAN of Ross divides the weekly bread:
Behold yon Alms-house, neat, but void of state,   265
Where Age and Want sit smiling at the gate:
Him portion'd maids, apprentic'd orphans blest,
The young who labour, and the old who rest. *He*
Is any sick? the MAN of Ross relieves,
Prescribes, attends, the med'cine makes, and gives.   270
Is there a variance? enter but his door,
Balk'd are the Courts, and contest is no more.
Despairing Quacks with curses fled the place,

265–6 Behold . . . gate] Who feeds . . . gate *1732–35b and inserted
after l. 260*; He feeds . . . gate *1735cd, 1744–51 (see note).*

"In 1721 the greater part of the spire was rebuilt with the old materials and the pinnacles added to the tower."

263–4. "He kept two public Days in a Week; the Market Day, and Sunday. . . On Sunday he feasted the poor people of the Parish at his House; and not only so, but would often send them home loaded with broken meat and jugs of beer" (Duck, p. 438). Kyrle's house was opposite the south-east corner of the market-place. It is still in existence.

265. The reading adopted is an Overlooked Revision (see p. liii above). "Behold" seems preferable to "He feeds" not only because it maintains the rhetorical elevation better but also because it concentrates the reader's attention on the alms-house. Kirle as dispenser of food to the poor has exhausted his interest in the preceding line.

265–6. "He founded a small alms-house in Ross, and left an annual sum charged on his estate towards its assistance" (Hutcheson, p. 151). *DNB* suggests this may be Rudhall's Hospital, a medieval foundation near Kyrle's house, to which he often sent food (W. H. Cooke, *Herefordshire*, III 116).

268–70. "He distributed medicines to the poor *gratis*, and when the advice of a physician was necessary, he sent for one at his own expence" (note to "Viator").

271–4. ". . . there was one set of men, he tried to ruin, the Attorneys in his neighbourhood. It was very rare that any difference terminated in a Lawsuit. He was general Referee" (Wheeler, p. 424). On market days "the Neighbouring Gentlemen and Farmers dined with him; and if they had any differences or disputes with one another, instead of going to Law, they appealed to the Man of Ross to decide and settle them, And his Decision was generally final" (Duck, p. 438).

And vile Attornies, now an useless race.
  "Thrice happy man! enabled to pursue   275
"What all so wish, but want the pow'r to do!
"Oh say, what sums that gen'rous hand supply?
"What mines, to swell that boundless charity?"
      Of Debts, and Taxes, Wife and Children clear,
This man possest—five hundred pounds a year.   280
Blush, Grandeur, blush! proud Courts, withdraw your
Ye little Stars! hide your diminish'd rays.   [blaze!
"And what? no monument, inscription, stone?
"His race, his form, his name almost unknown?"
Who builds a Church to God, and not to Fame,   285
Will never mark the marble with his Name:
Go, search it there, where to be born and die,
Of rich and poor makes all the history;
Enough, that Virtue fill'd the space between;
Prov'd, by the ends of being, to have been.   290
When Hopkins dies, a thousand lights attend

275 *1751 prefixes* B.   279 *1751 prefixes* P.
283 *1751 prefixes* B.   285 *1751 prefixes* P.
291 Hopkins] H*p*s *1732–33.*

---

279. Kyrle was really a bachelor.

280. Wheeler confirms this: "his income was no more than 600£ a year" (p. 425). Warburton adds, "We must understand what is here said, of *actually performing*, to mean by the contributions which the *Man of Ross*, by his assiduity and interest, collected in his neighbourhood." Benjamin Victor was also told this by "the minister of the place" (Johnson, *Lives of the Poets*, III 172–3).

282. Cf. *Par. Lost*, IV 34–5,

> at whose sight all the Starrs
> Hide their diminisht heads.

287. The Parish-register. [P. *1732–51.*]

291–2. See l. 87*n*. The statement—originally made by B. (i.e. William Bennet, bishop of Cloyne) in Wakefield's *Observations*, p. 220, and repeated by Bowles, Carruthers, EC, and Ward—that Hopkins's executor Edmund Boulter spent £7,666 on his funeral—is an error. Boulter was Sir John Cutler's nephew and joint-executor, and it was Cutler's funeral that cost £7,666. However the information is relevant because, as one of the Huntington MSS. shows, the pas-

The wretch, who living sav'd a candle's end:
Should'ring God's altar a vile image stands,
Belies his features, nay extends his hands;
That live-long wig which Gorgon's self might own,   295
Eternal buckle takes in Parian stone.
Behold what blessings Wealth to life can lend!
And see, what comfort it affords our end.
   In the worst inn's worst room, with mat half-hung,

---

sage originally came earlier in the poem and then referred to Cotta, a character almost certainly based upon Cutler (see l. 179*n*). An anecdote about Hopkins and his crazy candle-economy will be found in *Notes and Queries*, 10 September 1859, p. 208. Compare, too, Young, *Love of Fame*, IV 228–30,

   the veriest hunks in Lombard-street,
From rescued candles' ends, who rais'd a sum,
And starves, to join a *penny* to a *plumb*.

293–6. The poet ridicules the wretched taste of carving large perriwigs on Busto's, of which there are several vile examples in the tombs at Westminster and elsewhere. [P. *1735c–51*.] Hopkins, however, was innocent of this offence. A plain slab covers his vault in Wimbledon churchyard. See l. 87*n*. Cutler was buried at St Margaret's, Westminster, but Royal Comm. on Hist. Mon., *Westminster* (1925), has not noted his tomb there.

299–314. This Lord, yet more famous for his vices than his misfortunes, after having been possess'd of about 50,000 pound a year, and past thro' many of the highest posts in the kingdom, died in the year 1687, in a remote inn in Yorkshire, reduc'd to the utmost misery. [P. *1744–51*. *1735c–43 read* George Villiers, Duke of Buckingham, who died in this manner.] Though poetically effective Pope's lines and note are historically inaccurate. Buckingham did die in Yorkshire in 1687, but not in an inn or in poverty. "As it fell to my share", writes an eye-witness of his death, "to know as much of the last moments of the Duke of Buckingham as any there about him, so at your instance I shall readily give answer to satisfy any that he died in the best house in Kirby Moorside, which neither is nor ever was an ale house" (John Gibson to Brian Fairfax, 27 February 1707, Hist. MSS. Comm., Rep. VI, App., p. 467). Pope was only reproducing a legend already in existence a few days after Buckingham died. A friend wrote to John Ellis, 23 April 1687, "The duke of Bucks, who hath some time supported himself with artificial spirits, on Friday fell to a more manifest decay, and on Sunday yielded up the ghost at Helmesley in Yorkshire, in a little ale-house (where these eight months he hath been without meat or money, deserted of all his servants almost)" (*The Ellis Correspondence*, 1829, I 275–6). See A. Mizener, *Mod. Lang. Notes*, 1938, LIII 368–9.

299. *mat*] "Plaited of woven rushes, straw, etc." (*OED*).

> The floors of plaister, and the walls of dung,   300
> On once a flock-bed, but repair'd with straw,
> With tape-typ'd curtains, never meant to draw,
> The George and Garter dangling from that bed
> Where tawdry yellow strove with dirty red,
> Great Villers lies—alas! how chang'd from him,   305
> That life of pleasure, and that soul of whim!
> Gallant and gay, in Cliveden's proud alcove,

300. *The floors of plaister*] A correspondent signing himself W. C. wrote to *The St James's Chronicle*, 7–9 March 1786, from Kirby-Moorside, giving some details about Buckingham's death. The house he died in was next to W. C.'s and "the same Floor still remains; not indeed of Plaister; (for it is a Chamber)."

the walls of dung] "I remember the first time I read Pope's lines, being profoundly impressed by those walls of dung. Indeed, they still disturb my imagination. They express, for me, the Essential Horror. A floor of dung would have seemed almost normal, acceptable. But *walls*—Ah, no, no!" (Aldous Huxley, *Texts and Pretexts*, 1932, pp. 214–15).

301. Flock-beds were only used by the middle classes; the aristocracy had feather-beds.

304. Cf. Dryden, *Works of Virgil*, *Aeneid*, v 326,
> Where Gold and Purple strive in equal Rows   [EC]

305. Cf. Virgil, *Aeneid*, II 274, "quantum mutatus ab illo
> Hectore."
Par. Lost, I 84–5, "But O how fall'n! how chang'd
> From him."

306. *soul of whim*] Pope no doubt intended a half-allusion to Dryden's character of Zimri (*Absalom and Achitophel*, I 544–68).

307. A delightful palace, on the banks of the Thames, built by the Duke of Buckingham. [P. *1744–51.*] Evelyn visited it in July 1679. "I went to *Clifden* that stupendious natural Rock, Wood, and Prospect of the Duke of *Buckinghams*, and building of extraordinary Expense: The Grotts in the Chalky rock are pretty, 'tis a romantic object, and the place alltogether answers the most poetical description that can be made of a solitude, precipice, prospects and whatever can contribute to a thing so very like their imaginations: The [house] stands somewhat like *Frascati* as to its front, and on the platforme is a circular View to the uttmost verge of the Horison, which with the serpenting of the Thames is admirably surprising" (*Diary*, ed. E. S. de Beer, 1955, IV 176–7). At the time of Evelyn's visit the Duke of Buckingham had only recently acquired Cliveden (Hist. MSS. Comm. Rep. XI, App. II, p. 305), and Pope is almost certainly wrong in making it the scene of his liaison with the Countess of Shrewsbury, which came to an end in January 1674. According to John Hookham Frere, "*Clifden's proud Alcove* has not at present, and probably never had, any existence" (*The Microcosm*, 29 January

The bow'r of wanton Shrewsbury and love;
Or just as gay, at Council, in a ring
Of mimick'd Statesmen, and their merry King.   310
No Wit to flatter, left of all his store!
No Fool to laugh at, which he valu'd more.
There, Victor of his health, of fortune, friends,
And fame; this lord of useless thousands ends.

His Grace's fate sage Cutler could foresee,   315
And well (he thought) advis'd him, "Live like me."
As well his Grace reply'd, "Like you, Sir John?

308 Shrewsbury] Sh***y *1732–35b*.
310 their] the *1732–35b*.

1787). In Pope's time Cliveden was occupied by "poor Fred", the Prince of
Wales. The house was burnt down in 1795.

308. The Countess of Shrewsbury, a woman abandon'd to gallantries. The
Earl her husband was kill'd by the Duke of Buckingham in a duel; and it has
been said, that during the combat she held the Duke's horses in the habit of a
page. [P. *1744–51*.] Pope gave Spence a slightly different account of the episode:
"The witty Duke of Buckingham was an extreme bad man. His duel with Lord
Shrewsbury was concerted between him and Lady Shrewsbury. All that morn-
ing she was trembling for her gallant, and wishing the death of her husband;
and, after his fall, 'tis said the duke slept with her in his bloody shirt" (p. 164).
Anthony Hamilton's *Mémoires de la Vie du Comte de Grammont* (1713), ch. XI,
which had been translated into English in 1714, deals with the duel, but the
details Pope must have learned from gossip. The duel took place on 16 January
1667/8.

315. *Cutler*] Sir John Cutler (1608?–1693) was a rich London merchant, who
promoted the subscriptions raised by the City for Charles II. He received both
a knighthood and a baronetcy in 1660. Although he was a generous benefactor
of the Grocers' Company, Gresham's College, the College of Physicians, and
the parish of St Margaret's, Westminster, his personal parsimony earned for
him an undeserved notoriety, which by Pope's time had become legendary.
Further details about Cutler will be found in ll. 179*n* and 291–2*n*. Pope's account
is quite unhistorical. A grain of fact can perhaps be detected in Pope's comment
on Cutler's daughter (ll. 325–6). Cutler had two daughters, one by each of his
wives and both called Elizabeth. The elder Elizabeth married without Cutler's
consent and so without a dower, although he forgave her and her husband two
days before he died and left them property. The younger daughter, who had
married with Cutler's consent, received a dower of £30,000.

"That I can do, when all I have is gone."
Resolve me, Reason, which of these is worse,
Want with a full, or with an empty purse?   320
Thy life more wretched, Cutler, was confess'd,
Arise, and tell me, was thy death more bless'd?
Cutler saw tenants break, and houses fall,
For very want; he could not build a wall.
His only daughter in a stranger's pow'r,   325
For very want; he could not pay a dow'r.
A few grey hairs his rev'rend temples crown'd,
'Twas very want that sold them for two pound.
What ev'n deny'd a cordial at his end,
Banish'd the doctor, and expell'd the friend?   330
What but a want, which you perhaps think mad,
Yet numbers feel, the want of what he had.
Cutler and Brutus, dying both exclaim,
"Virtue! and Wealth! what are ye but a name!"
        Say, for such worth are other worlds prepar'd?   335
Or are they both, in this their own reward?
A knotty point! to which we now proceed.
But you are tir'd—I'll tell a tale. Agreed.

337–8 That knotty point, my Lord, shall I discuss,
        Or tell a Tale?—A Tale—it follows thus.   *1732–43*;
        A knotty point! to which we now proceed.
        But you are tir'd—I'll tell a tale.—B. Agreed.   *1751.*

333–4. "Brutus made an effort to force his way from the strong position, whither he had retreated, into the camp; but, finding this impossible, and learning that some of his soldiers had submitted to the conquerors, he abandoned himself to despair; but, disdaining captivity, he resolved on death: and desired some of his attendants to dispatch him, after he had repeated with a loud voice that exclamation of Hercules, in the tragedy:

Ah! hapless Virtue! deem'd a truth by me;
But Fortune's slave thou wert, and a mere empty name."

(Wakefield, quoting Dion Cassius, XLVII 49). The allusion was a favourite of Bolingbroke's, e.g. "The second BRUTUS exclaimed, that virtue was an empty name" (*Philosophical Works*, 1754, V 10).

338. "I never saw [Lord Bathurst], but he repeatedly expressed his disgust,

Where London's column, pointing at the skies
Like a tall bully, lifts the head, and lyes;   340
There dwelt a Citizen of sober fame,
A plain good man, and Balaam was his name;

339 *1751 prefixes* P.

---

and his surprise, at finding, in later editions, this *Epistle* awkwardly converted
into a *Dialogue*, in which he has but little to say. And I remember he once
remarked, 'that this line,

P. But you are tir'd. I'll tell a tale. B. Agreed;—

was insupportably insipid and flat' " [Warton]. See textual note.

339. The Monument, built in memory of the fire of London, with a inscrip-
tion, importing that city to have been burnt by the Papists. [P. *1732–51.*] The
inscription—which accused "the Popish faction" of setting fire to London as
part of a plot to extirpate "the Protestant religion and old English liberty"—
was erased in James II's reign, restored in William III's, and finally erased in
1831.

342. *Balaam*] Carruthers, Dilke ("I agree that Sir Balaam is a fancy"), and
EC have dismissed Balaam and his career as *fictions*. And *Imit. Hor., Sat.,* II i, 42,

A hundred smart in *Timon* and in *Balaam*,

appears to show that Pope intended a generalized portrait—like Addison's
nouveau riche Sir John Anvil, who also married into the nobility with disastrous
results (*Spectator*, no. 299). But, though admittedly not an exact portrait, a good
case has been made in *Notes and Queries*, 18 September 1869, p. 236—apparently
by the editor W. J. Thoms—for identifying Balaam with Thomas Pitt (1653–
1726). Pitt was "said to have been the son of a person concerned in trade at
Brentford", had made a great deal of money in underhand ways, was remark-
ably pious, owned an estate in Cornwall, and bought and represented the rotten
borough of Old Sarum. Moreover Sir Charles Hanbury Williams alludes to
William Pitt (Thomas's grandson) as "the true son of Sir Balaam" in "The
Unembarrassed Countenance" (*Works*, II 158). These facts can hardly all be
coincidences. And an allusion to the Pitt diamond in l. 364 is confirmed by the
reading of the Huntington MSS.,

So robb'd the Robber, and was rich as P—t.

The earlier of the two drafts also has this note by Pope: "†P-tt, once Governour
of Fort St. George, who there became Master of a Diamond wch he afterw^ds
sold to the K. of France for one hundred & twenty thous^d pounds." I suspect
Sir Balaam was modelled on Pitt in the first instance and was later generalized
—but not to such a degree that the original lineaments do not occasionally
show through. Lady [Anne] Irwin, one of the poem's first readers, was more
confident that a real person was being satirized. She sent a copy to her father,
Lord Carlisle, on 18 January 1732/3 in which she had "marked the characters

Religious, punctual, frugal, and so forth;
His word would pass for more than he was worth.
One solid dish his week-day meal affords,   345
An added pudding solemniz'd the Lord's:
Constant at Church, and Change; his gains were sure,
His givings rare, save farthings to the poor.
     The Dev'l was piqu'd such saintship to behold,
And long'd to tempt him like good Job of old: 350
But Satan now is wiser than of yore,
And tempts by making rich, not making poor.
     Rouz'd by the Prince of Air, the whirlwinds sweep
The surge, and plunge his Father in the deep;
Then full against his Cornish lands they roar,   355
And two rich ship-wrecks bless the lucky shore.
     Sir Balaam now, he lives like other folks,

according to my interpretation". She added in the covering letter (which has
alone survived), "The last character does not hit in every particular, but I think
where 'tis disguised, 'tis with a design it mayn't be fixed" (Hist. MSS. Comm.,
15th Report, App., Part 6, p. 97).
     355. The author has placed the scene of these shipwrecks in Cornwall, not
only from their frequency on that coast, but from the inhumanity of the inhabi-
tants to those to whom that misfortune arrives: When a ship happens to be
stranded there, they have been known to bore holes in it, to prevent its getting
off; to plunder, and sometimes even to massacre the people: Nor has the Parlia-
ment of England been yet able wholly to suppress these barbarities. [P. *1735c–
51*.] Thomas Pitt had bought from the devisees of Lord Mohun (killed in the
duel with the Duke of Hamilton) the estate of Boconnor, near Lostwithiel. Corn-
wall's sinister reputation is referred to in Lillo's *Fatal Curiosity* (1737), I iii 1–9,

Y. Wilm.   Welcome, my friend! to *Penryn*: Here we're safe.
Eust.   Then we're deliver'd twice; first from the sea,
            And then from savage men, who, more remorseless,
            Prey on shipwreck'd wretches, and spoil, and murder those
            Whom fatal tempests and devouring waves,
            In all their fury, spar'd.
Y. Wilm.   It is a scandal,
            Tho' malice must acquit the better sort,
            The rude unpolisht people here in *Cornwall*
            Have long laid under, and with too much justice ...
The evil was ultimately extirpated by the Wesleyan preachers.

He takes his chirping pint, and cracks his jokes:
"Live like yourself," was soon my Lady's word;
And lo! two puddings smoak'd upon the board.   360
    Asleep and naked as an Indian lay,
An honest factor stole a Gem away:
He pledg'd it to the knight; the knight had wit,
So kept the Diamond, and the rogue was bit.
Some scruple rose, but thus he eas'd his thought,   365
"I'll now give six-pence where I gave a groat,
"Where once I went to church, I'll now go twice—
"And am so clear too of all other vice."
    The Tempter saw his time; the work he ply'd;
Stocks and Subscriptions pour on ev'ry side,   370
'Till all the Dæmon makes his full descent,
In one abundant show'r of Cent. per Cent.,
Sinks deep within him, and possesses whole,
Then dubs Director, and secures his soul.
    Behold Sir Balaam, now a man of spirit,   375
Ascribes his gettings to his parts and merit,
What late he call'd a Blessing, now was Wit,
And God's good Providence, a lucky Hit.
Things change their titles, as our manners turn:

358 and] he *1732–43*.   371 'Till] And *1732–35b*.

361–4. Thomas Pitt bought the celebrated Pitt diamond for £20,400 when he was Governor of Fort St George, Madras. Later he sold it for over six times as much to the Duke of Orleans. His conduct was so generally criticized that he found it necessary to publish a "Vindication" in the London papers towards the close of July 1710. See *Notes and Queries*, 26 July 1851, p. 71, 18 September 1869, p. 236. Gray's allusion in a letter to Mason, October 1761, to "the *naked Indian* that found Pitt's diamond" (*Letters*, ed. Toynbee and Whibley, II 758) shows that these lines must have been generally taken in the eighteenth century to refer to Thomas Pitt.

377–8. Addison's Sir Andrew Freeport, in a moral mood, "reckoned up to me abundance of those lucky Hits, which at another time he would have called pieces of good Fortune; but in the Temper of Mind he was then, he termed them Mercies, Favours of Providence, and Blessings upon an honest Industry" (*Spectator*, no. 549).

His Compting-house employ'd the Sunday-morn;   380
Seldom at Church ('twas such a busy life)
But duly sent his family and wife.
There (so the Dev'l ordain'd) one Christmas-tide
My good old Lady catch'd a cold, and dy'd.
        A Nymph of Quality admires our Knight;   385
He marries, bows at Court, and grows polite:
Leaves the dull Cits, and joins (to please the fair)
The well-bred cuckolds in St. James's air:
First, for his Son a gay Commission buys,
Who drinks, whores, fights, and in a duel dies: 390
His daughter flaunts a Viscount's tawdry wife;
She bears a Coronet and P–x for life.
In Britain's Senate he a seat obtains,
And one more Pensioner St. Stephen gains.
My Lady falls to play; so bad her chance,   395
He must repair it; takes a bribe from France;
The House impeach him; Coningsby harangues;
The Court forsake him, and Sir Balaam hangs:
Wife, son, and daughter, Satan, are thy own,
His wealth, yet dearer, forfeit to the Crown: 400

397 Coningsby] Co**by *1732–35b*.
398 forsake] forsakes *1732–33*.
399 own] prize *1732–35a*.   400–1 *Add. 1735b*.

388. *St. James's air*] The City with its solid brick citizens' houses had become almost wholly mercantile. "The cleavage between the City and St James's— 'the polite end of the town'—was profound, fostered by social, political, and commercial jealousies" (*Johnson's England*, ed. A. S. Turberville, 1933, I 163).

394. —atque unum civem donare *Sibyllæ*. Juv. [P. *1735c–51*.] Juvenal, III 3. The medieval St Stephen's Chapel, Westminster, was still being used as the House of Commons until burnt down in 1834.

397. *Coningsby*] Thomas, Earl Coningsby (1645?–1729) was a strong Whig who was appointed in 1715 a commissioner to investigate the intrigue leading up to the Peace of Utrecht, and to impeach Harley. Pope's satirical epitaph on Coningsby is in vol. VI of this edition, p. 297.

400–1. These lines are in the earlier Huntington draft, but with a deletion mark against them in the margin, and "the King" is so thoroughly erased as to

The Devil and the King divide the prize,
And sad Sir Balaam curses God and dies.

be almost illegible. They are not in the second draft or the early editions. Pope, realizing that the lines were technically treasonable, may have preferred to reserve them for an edition less likely to be scrutinized by his enemies. Cf. the comment to Warburton quoted in the note on p. 43.

EPISTLE IV

To RICHARD BOYLE
Earl of BURLINGTON

NOTE ON THE TEXT

The first edition is a sixteen-page folio which was published on 13 December 1731. As in the case of *To Cobham* the poem has two titles. The title-page's is *An Epistle To The Right Honourable Richard Earl of Burlington. Occasion'd by his Publishing Palladio's Designs of the Baths, Arches, Theatres, &c. of Ancient Rome.*[1] The half-title, on the other hand, reads *Of Taste, An Epistle To the Right Honourable Richard Earl of Burlington.* An octavo reprint dated 1732, which is probably a piracy,[2] may have preceded the authorized second edition—a folio textually identical with the first edition, except that the half-title begins *Of False Taste,*[3] which was published on 4–6 January 1731/2 (though it is dated 1731). The authorized third edition, a folio with the title-page now reading *Of False Taste. An Epistle* [etc.] and with an open letter prefixed from Pope to Burlington on the Timon gossip, is also dated 1731,[4] though it was actually published on 15 January 1731/2. As far as the poem itself is concerned the third edition has exactly the same text, except for a few misprints, as the earlier editions. Two Dublin editions by Faulkner followed in 1732, and a third in 1733 with the Pope-Swift *Miscellanies*. An interesting unauthorized early edition is the reprint in *A Miscellany On Taste* (published 15 January 1731/2), which has a "Clavis" identifying the persons Pope had alluded to as well as some jeering critical notes—written "by Concanen and Welsted, as was supposed" (Warton, *Works*, III, p. 289). Matthew Concanen and Leo-

---

1. Burlington's *Fabriche antiche disegnate da Andrea Palladio Vicentino* had been published in 1730, but this only included Palladio's drawings of the Roman baths. It seems certain that Pope is referring to a projected second volume, which was not, as far as is known, ever issued. See the Introduction, p. xxv above.

2. This is perhaps the edition referred to by Aaron Hill in his letter to Pope, 17 December 1731: "We have printers, too, of better *taste* than *morals*, who *like* you so well, that they cannot endure, you should be made a monopoly.—The *hawker's* wind is upon you, already; and your last incense, to the muses, is blown about the streets, in thinner, and less fragrant expansions" (Sherburn, III 257–8).

3. This title had been suggested by Hill as "properer" in the same letter.

4. The letter to Burlington is printed on different paper from the poem. No doubt it was a last-minute addition. The title page, which is conjugate with the letter, carries an epigraph from Horace (*Epist.*, I xvi 39–40) on scandalmonger-ing.

nard Welsted were two of the "dunces" and the character of Timon would have given them an obvious opportunity, if they were indeed the authors of the notes, to get their own back on Pope. *A Miscellany On Taste* also has as a frontispiece a re-engraving (by an unidentified engraver) of Hogarth's print showing a hunch-backed Pope daubing Burlington House with whitewash and incidentally bespattering the Duke of Chandos who is passing by in his coach. (The frontispiece of this edition is a reproduction of Hogarth's engraving.)

In 1735 Pope collected his later poems in *The Works Of Mr. Alexander Pope. Volume II*. In this *To Burlington* is grouped with *To Cobham*, *To a Lady*, and *To Bathurst* as "Epistle IV" of "Ethic Epistles, the Second Book", and it now becomes "Of the Use of Riches"—complementing *To Bathurst*, the defective use of wealth, with its examples of the excessive use. The textual problems raised by the four editions of this collection (*1735 abcd*) and the reprints of it in 1736 and 1739, and the question of their relationship to the "death-bed" text (*1744*) are discussed in the General Note on the Text. *1735a* adds an "Argument", and the text is drastically revised. In all Pope added two passages, transposed two paragraphs, and emended some twenty phrases. The general effect of these alterations was to improve the structure of the poem. In its original form it had been too much the mere catalogue of offences against taste in the Georgian garden and house; as emended the poem has a more logical evolution. *1735b* is a close reprint of *1735a*, but *1735c* has further revisions by Pope—six new lines, many new notes, and four new readings. There are no changes in *1735d* or *1736* (except in the notes) but *1739* has alterations in three passages of the poem as well as in the notes. This text reappears in *The Works*, vol. II, part i, of *1740* and *1743*. *1744*, the text normally followed in this edition, added a libellous couplet (ll. 77–8) and Warburton's commentary and notes, and six passages in the poem were emended. *1744* was set up from a copy of *1735c*, as the punctuation and typography demonstrate, and *1735c* descends, on similar evidence, from *1735a* or *1735b*.[1] Overlooked Revisions can therefore only be anticipated from *1739*. Its three variants (ll. 35, 59, and 83) have been

1. The punctuation and typography of *1735a* and *1735b* appear to be identical until the last couplet, where *1735a* (and *1735c*) changes to italics and *1735b* is in roman.

adopted in pursuance of the policy laid down in the General Note on the Text. Warburton's edition of Pope's *Works* (*1751*) deletes one of Warburton's notes and adds others, but the poem itself, and Pope's notes, are left as in *1744*.

With the three exceptions just noted, the text presented in this edition is that of the "death-bed" edition (*1744*).

KEY TO THE CRITICAL APPARATUS

1731*a* = First edition, Griffith 259.
1731*b* = Second edition, Griffith 265.
1731*c* = Third edition, Griffith 267.
1735*a* = Works, vol. II, large and small folio, Griffith 370, 371.
1735*b* = Works, vol. II, quarto, Griffith 372.
1735*c* = Works, vol. II, octavo, Griffith 388.
1735*d* = Works, vol. II, octavo, Griffith 389.
1736   = Works, vol. II, octavo, Griffith 430.
1739   = Works, vol. II, octavo, Griffith 505.
1740   = Works, vol. II, part i, octavo, Griffith 523.
1743   = Works, vol. II, part i, octavo, Griffith 583.
1744   = Epistles to Several Persons, Griffith 591.
1751   = Works, ed. Warburton, vol. III, large octavo, Griffith 645.

ARGUMENT[1]
Of the Use *of* RICHES

T HE *Vanity of Expence in People of Wealth and Quality. The abuse
of the word* Taste, v. 13. *That the first principle and foundation, in
this as in every thing else, is* Good Sense, v. 40. *The chief proof of
it is to follow* Nature, *even in works of mere Luxury and Elegance. In-*

Argument] *Add. 1735a, but until 1744 grouped with arguments of* To Cob-
ham, To Bathurst, *and* To a Lady *before text of* To Cobham *and headed*
Epistle IV. Of the same [i.e. the Use of Riches *as in* To Bathurst], To
the Earl of Burlington. *1735c–36, 1740–43 also break up and, with
minor changes, insert the separate sentences as footnotes to the passages sum-
marized. Errors and changes in the line numbers are not recorded here. 1731c
alone prefixes the following open letter:*[2]

MY LORD,
The Clamour rais'd about this Epistle could not give me so much pain, as I

---

[1] Perhaps contributed by the younger Richardson (see p. 4 above).

[2] According to Johnson (*Lives of the Poets*, III 152), Burlington "privately
said" that Pope had meant Timon for the Duke of Chandos. This is most un-
likely. See G. Sherburn, *Huntington Library Bulletin*, no. 8, 1935, pp. 149–50.
Some of the phrases in the letter echo other statements by Pope on the Timon
scandal. Cf. especially Pope to Hill, 5 February 1732, "It will be a Pleasure felt
by you, to tell you, his Grace has written to me the strongest Assurance imagin-
able of the Rectitude of his Opinion, and of his Resentment of that Report, which
to *Him* is an Impertinence, to *me* a *Villany*" (Sherburn, III 268), and *Imit. Hor.*,
Sat., II i, 41–3,

> A hundred smart in *Timon* and in *Balaam*:
> The fewer still you name, you wound the more;
> *Bond* is but one, but *Harpax* is a score.

Pope wrote to Oxford, 22 January 1731–2, "I have been much blamed by the
Formalists of the Town for subscribing my Letter in print to Lord Burlington,
with *your Faithful, Affectionate Servant*'" (Sherburn, III 267). It is possible a few
copies of the letter were issued separately, though none have survived. According
to Pope's letter to Caryll, 29 March [1732] (Sherburn, III 279), Martha Blount
had privately sent Caryll "the prose letter prefixed to the last edition". Further
discussions of the letter will be found in the Introduction (p. xxviii above) and in
l. 90*n*.

receiv'd pleasure in seeing the general Zeal of the World in the cause of a Great Man who is Beneficent, and the particular Warmth of your Lordship in that of a private Man who is innocent.

It was not the Poem *that deserv'd this from you ; for as I had the Honour to be your Friend, I cou'd not treat you quite like a Poet : but sure the* Writer *deserv'd more Candor even from those who knew him not, than to promote a Report which in regard to that Noble Person, was* Impertinent; *in regard to me,* Villainous. *Yet I had no great Cause to wonder, that a Character belonging to* twenty *shou'd be applied to* one; *since, by that means,* nineteen *wou'd escape the Ridicule.*

I was too well content with my Knowledge of that Noble Person's Opinion in this Affair, to trouble the publick about it. But since Malice and Mistake are so long a dying, I take the opportunity of this third Edition to declare His Belief, *not only of* My Innocence, *but of* Their Malignity, *of the former of which my own Heart is as conscious, as I fear some of theirs must be of the latter. His Humanity feels a Concern for the Injury done to* Me, *while His Greatness of Mind can bear with Indifference the Insult offer'd to* Himself.

However, my Lord, *I own, that Critics of* this Sort *can intimidate me, nay half incline me to write no more : It wou'd be making the* Town *a Compliment which I think it deserves, and which some, I am sure, wou'd take very kindly. This way of Satire is dangerous, as long as Slander rais'd by Fools of the lowest Rank, can find any Countenance from those of a Higher. Even from the Conduct shewn on this occasion, I have learnt there are some who wou'd rather be* wicked *than* ridiculous; *and therefore it may be safer to attack* Vices *than* Follies. *I will leave my Betters in the quiet Possession of their* Idols, *their* Groves, *and their* High-Places; *and change my Subject from their* Pride *to their* Meanness, *from their* Vanities *to their* Miseries : *And as the only certain way to avoid Misconstruction, to lessen Offence, and not to multiply ill-natur'd Applications, I may probably in my next make use of* Real *Names and not of Fictitious Ones.* I am,

My Lord,

Your Faithful,

Affectionate Servant,

A. POPE.

---

1   *The Vanity*] *1735a–36, 1740–43 read* The Extremes of *Avarice* and *Profusion* being treated of in the foregoing Epistle, this takes up one particular Branch of the latter; the *Vanity.*

stanced in Architecture *and* Gardening, *where all must be adapted to the* Genius *and* Use *of the Place, and the Beauties not forced into it, but resulting from it,* v. 50. *How men are disappointed in their most expensive undertakings, for want of this true Foundation, without which nothing can please* long, *if* at all; *and the best* Examples *and* Rules *will but be perverted into something* burdensome *or ridiculous,* v. 65, &c. to 98. *A description of the* false Taste *of* Magnificence; *the first grand Error of which is to imagine that* Greatness *consists in the* Size *and* Dimension, *instead of the* Proportion *and* Harmony *of the* whole, v. 99, *and the second, either in joining together* Parts incoherent, *or too* minutely resembling, *or in the* Repetition *of the* same *too frequently,* v. 115, &c. *A word or two of false* Taste *in* Books, *in* Music, *in* Painting, *even in* Preaching *and* Prayer, *and lastly in* Entertainments, v. 133, &c. *Yet* PROVIDENCE *is justified in giving* Wealth *to be squandered in this manner, since it is dispersed to the* Poor *and* Laborious *part of mankind,* v. 169. [*Recurring to what is laid down in the first book, Ep.* ii.[1] *and in the Epistle preceding this,* v. 161, &c.] *What are the* proper Objects *of Magnificence, and a proper field for the* Expence *of* Great Men, v. 177, *&c., and finally, the Great and Public* Works *which become a* Prince, v. 191, *to the end.*

---

[1] *E. on Man,* II 238*ff.*

EPISTLE IV

To RICHARD BOYLE,
Earl of BURLINGTON

'TIS strange, the Miser should his Cares employ,
To gain those Riches he can ne'er enjoy:
Is it less strange, the Prodigal should waste
His wealth, to purchase what he ne'er can taste?
Not for himself he sees, or hears, or eats;   5
Artists must chuse his Pictures, Music, Meats:
He buys for Topham, Drawings and Designs,
For Pembroke Statues, dirty Gods, and Coins;

Heading] An Epistle To the Right Honourable *Richard* Earl of *Bur-lington 1731abc*; Epistle IV. To Richard *Earl of* Burlington *1735a–43*.
8 For Pembroke . . . Coins] For *Fountain* Statues, and for *Curio* Coins *1731abc*; For Fountain Statues, and for Pembroke Coins *1735a–43*.

Heading] Richard Boyle, third Earl of Burlington and fourth Earl of Cork (1695–1753); succeeded to his father's title and estates in 1704; spent several years in Italy prior to 1714 studying architecture; Privy Councillor October 1714; Knight of the Garter 1730. Burlington was an enthusiastic Palladian and was largely responsible for the exclusion of baroque and rococo influences from Georgian architecture. He reconstructed Burlington House, Piccadilly, on classical lines *c.* 1716, and added to his country house at Chiswick a villa (1727–36) modelled on one of Palladio's own. A considerable part of his large fortune was spent in the erection of public buildings (often to his own designs), and he was eventually compelled to sell some of his Irish estates. He married Lady Dorothy Savile, a first cousin of Chesterfield's, who was a great patroness of music and a talented caricaturist in crayons. Pope was on friendly terms with the Burlingtons by 1716 or earlier.

6. *Artists*] Experts, connoisseurs.

7. *Topham*] A Gentleman famous for a judicious collection of Drawings. [P. *1735c–51*.] Richard Topham (d. 1735) was Keeper of the Records in the Tower, and had an estate near Windsor which he left to Lord Sidney Beauclerc. His valuable collection of drawings, portraits, and engravings was bequeathed with his books to Eton College Library. Dr Mead (see l. 10) was one of his executors.

Rare monkish Manuscripts for Hearne alone,

8. Thomas Herbert, eighth Earl of Pembroke (1656–1733) was a Whig politician who devoted his leisure to collecting statues, pictures, and coins. Pope intended to look in at Wilton in 1722 (EC, IX 305), when he may have inspected Pembroke's collections. They were catalogued by George Richardson as *Aedes Pembrochianae* (1774), and included a high proportion of Renaissance pseudo-antiques ("dirty Gods"). Pembroke's coins were utilized by Sir Andrew Fountaine (1676–1753), a more discriminating collector, in his *Numismata Anglo-Saxonica & Anglo-Danica* (1705), which is dedicated to Pembroke. Sir Andrew is the "Fountain" of the early editions (see textual note); he was a close friend of Pembroke's, to whom he sold his own collection of coins and the two are grouped together by Young (*Love of Fame*, I 177–8) as notoriously enthusiastic collectors of "antique statues":

> Not Fountaine's self more Parian charms has known;
> Nor is good Pembroke more in love with stone.

Fountaine is possibly the "Annius" of *Dunciad*, IV 347–94. He was Queen Caroline's vice-chamberlain for many years. The "Curio" of the early editions was identified by *A Miscellany on Taste* as "*Dr. A—tt*", i.e. no doubt Arbuthnot, who had published in 1727 *Tables of Ancient Coins, Weights and Measures*. There is another "Curio", also a collector of coins, in "To Mr. Addison" (1721), 43–4:

> And Curio, restless by the Fair-one's side,
> Sighs for an Otho, and neglects his bride.

The couplet follows a jeer at "Vadius", who was Arbuthnot's *bête noire* Dr Woodward, and makes it certain that that Curio is not Arbuthnot. The Curio of "To Mr. Addison" is probably (see vol. VI of this edition) Pembroke again, who re-married in 1708. And in this passage too it seems likely that Pembroke was intended from the first. The abbreviation *curio* for *curiosity* is a nineteenth-century form; Pope must have intended a suggestion of *curioso*, "one curious in matters of science and art, a connoisseur, virtuoso". Curio was also the name of a distinguished Roman family.

9. Thomas Hearne (1678–1735) was the most eminent medievalist of Pope's generation. Between 1716 and 1735 he issued small editions of no less than twenty-three medieval English chronicles. He is apparently the "Wormius" of *Dunciad* A, III 181–90, in spite of Pope's denial in the note on "Wormius"—"Let not this name, purely fictitious, be conceited to mean . . . our own Antiquary Mr. Thomas Herne, who had no way aggrieved our Poet, but on the contrary published many curious tracts which he hath to his great contentment perused." Hearne's opinion of Pope, based on hearsay, was more unequivocal: "This Alexander Pope, tho' he be an English Poet, yet he is but an indifferent scholar, mean at Latin & can hardly read Greek. He is a very ill-natured man, and covetous and excessively proud" (*Remarks and Collections*, 18 July 1729, x 158). See also vol. v of this edition, p. 443.

And Books for Mead, and Butterflies for Sloane.   10
Think we all these are for himself? no more
Than his fine Wife, alas! or finer Whore.

10 Butterflies] Rarities *1731a–43*.
12 Wife, alas!] Wife (my Lord) *1731abc*.

10. *Mead . . . Sloane*] Two eminent Physicians; the one had an excellent Library, the other the finest collection in Europe of natural curiosities; both men of great learning and humanity. [P. *1735c–51*.] Richard Mead (1673–1754) was Physician in Ordinary to George II and Queen Caroline, and Pope was under his care in 1743. Mead was proud of Pope's friendship. "He was the friend of *Pope*, of *Halley*, of *Newton*, and placed their portraits in his house near the Busts of their great Masters, the antient Greeks and Romans" (M. Maty, *Authentic Memoirs of the Life of Richard Mead, M.D.*, 1755, pp. 62–3). His collection of books, "numbering at their owner's death some thirty thousand volumes", is described in Austin Dobson's *Eighteenth Century Vignettes*, ser. 3, pp. 29–50. Mead's copy of Pope's *Works*, 9 vols., octavo, large-paper gilt, fetched £2 18s. od. on the twenty-seventh day of the sale of his library (7 May 1755). Sir Hans Sloane (1660–1753) was First Physician to George II and President of the Royal College of Physicians, 1719–35. His collections were bought by the nation after his death and formed the nucleus of the British Museum. Pope knew Sloane slightly and got "two Joints of the Giants Cause way" from him for his grotto (Sherburn, IV 391, 397).

Butterflies] The change from "Rarities" (see textual note) had been suggested by Thomas Cooke in *The Comedian*, no. 2, May 1732, p. 15: "*Rarities*! how could'st thou be so silly as not to be particular in the Raritys of *Sloane* as in those of the other five Persons? What knowledge, what Meaning, is conveyed in the Word *Raritys*! Are not some Drawings, some Statues, some Coins, all monkish Manuscripts, and some Books, *Raritys*? Could'st thou not find a Trisyllable to express some Parts of Nature for a Collection of which that learned and worthy Physician is eminent? Fy, fy; correct and write,

> *Rare Monkish Manuscripts for* HEARNE *alone,*
> *And Books for* MEAD, *and Butterflys for* SLOANE.

Sir Hans Sloane is known to have the finest Collection of Butterflys in *England*, and perhaps in the World." Cooke pointed out, too, that Pope had mis-spelled Sloane's name by omitting the final e, and this correction was also made in the later editions. Cooke was one of the "dunces"; his relations with Pope are discussed in vol. IV, p. 355, and vol. V, p. 435. As it happens, "Butterflies" is interlineated over "Rarities" (which is not crossed out, however) in the autograph draft now in the Pierpont Morgan Library, New York. Perhaps Pope had not been able to discover for certain whether Sloane *was* a serious lepidopterist or not.

For what has Virro painted, built, and planted?
Only to show, how many Tastes he wanted.
What brought Sir Visto's ill got wealth to waste?   15
Some Dæmon whisper'd, "Visto! have a Taste."
Heav'n visits with a Taste the wealthy fool,
And needs no Rod but Ripley with a Rule.

15 Visto's] *Shylock*'s *1731abc.*
16 Visto!] Knights should *1731abc.*
18 Ripley] *S—d 1731abc*; *R–pl–y 1735ab.*

---

13. *Virro*] According to *A Miscellany on Taste* this is "Mr. *S—es* of Hertford-shire". Benjamin Heskin Styles, of Moor Park, Rickmansworth, is probably the *nouveau riche* satirized in ll. 75–6, but it is not clear that there is any allusion to him here.

15. The "Sir Shylock" of the early editions (see textual note) was identified by *A Miscellany on Taste* as "Sir R— W—". Walpole died some £40,000 in debt and in 1731 his fortune had already been impaired by his vast outlay on Hough-ton (completed 1735). The "ill-got wealth" may refer to Walpole's extremely successful speculations in South Sea stock; it may also be an echo of the insinu-ations of *The Craftsman* that the expense of Houghton's "erection and furnishing was fraudulently defrayed out of the public funds" (R. W. Ketton-Cremer, *Horace Walpole*, 1940, p. 46). And Ripley (l. 18) was certainly Walpole's archi-tect. On the other hand, (i) Pope never thought Walpole a "fool", (ii) "Shylock" (used in *To Cobham* and *To Bathurst* for the Earl of Selkirk and perhaps Wortley Montagu) and "Visto" (the view seen at the ends of the avenues of clipped trees that were fashionable in Queen Anne's reign) seem the wrong names for Walpole. Pope probably did not mean anybody in particular. "Sir Shylock" was no doubt intended to suggest a typical City financier. In *The Norfolk Poetical Miscellany* (1744), II 245, the name is used, in a poem that includes a reference to Pope, as "A known Appellation for any Scrivener, or sharping, usurious *Money-lender*." In "A Master Key to Popery" (see Appendix C, p. 182) Pope pretends to identify the character as Sir Gilbert Heathcote (1642–1733), one of the founders of the Bank of England, who was reputed to be the richest commoner in England.

18. *Ripley*] This man was a carpenter, employ'd by a first Minister, who rais'd him to an Architect, without any genius in the art; and after some wretched proofs of his insufficiency in public Buildings, made him Comptroller of the Board of works. [P. *1744–51.*] Thomas Ripley (d. 1758) was a protégé of Sir Robert Walpole, one of whose servants he married. He rebuilt the Customs House, 1718, and carried out (with some happy modifications) Colin Camp-bell's designs for Walpole's seat at Houghton, 1722–35. He was also architect for the Admiralty building, Whitehall, 1724–6, and in 1726 Walpole appointed

See! sportive fate, to punish aukward pride,
Bids Bubo build, and sends him such a Guide: 20

20 Bubo] *Babo 1731abc.*

him Controller of his Majesty's Board of Works over the head of Pope's friend
Kent. Another jeer at Ripley is in *Imit. Hor., Ep.*, II i, 186. Horace Walpole's
comment on Pope's sneers at Ripley is: "The truth is, politics and partiality
concurred to help on these censures. Ripley was employed by the minister, and
had not the countenance of Lord Burlington, the patron of Pope . . . Yet Ripley,
in the mechanic part, and in the disposition of apartments and conveniences,
was unluckily superior to the earl himself. Lord Orford's, at Houghton . . . and
Lord Walpole's at Woolterton, one of the best houses of the size in England, will,
as long as they remain, acquit this artist of the charge of ignorance" (*Anecdotes
of Painting*, ed. R. N. Wornum, 1888, III 49). The charge has, however, been
recently repeated by Sir Reginald Blomfield, who characterizes Ripley as
"unintelligent and ignorant of construction" and dismisses the Admiralty as
"a somewhat clumsy composition, with a very ill-proportioned portico" (*A His-
tory of Renaissance Architecture in England*, II 230). In the early editions (see textual
note) Ripley's place was taken by "*S—d*". This is glossed in *A Miscellany on Taste*
as "One Stafford, a Carpenter". On the other hand *Of Good Nature. An Epistle,
Humbly inscribed to his G–ce the D–ke of C–s* (1732), a violent attack on Pope's
poem (it is attributed to the Rev. John Cowper, the father of the poet Cowper),
which is reprinted in *The Norfolk Poetical Miscellany*, I (1744), has the line
(p. 370),
                No more shall *Sheppard*—dare to draw a Line.
The gloss on this passage in "A Master Key to Popery" (see Appendix C, p. 183)
expands "*S—d*" to "Sh—d" which suggests that Sheppard is the correct identi-
fication, i.e. no doubt Edward Sheppard or Shepherd (d. 1747), the architect of
Lincoln's Inn Fields, Goodmans Fields and Covent Garden Theatres, and the
creator of Shepherd's Market, Mayfair. I can discover nothing about Stafford.

20. *Bubo*] "Mr Doddington" (Walpole, Fraser marginalia, p. 40). George
Bubb, who later took the name Dodington and finally became Baron Melcombe
(1691–1762) had already been satirized by Pope as "Bubo" (Latin for owl)
and "Bufo" (Latin for toad) in *Epistle to Arbuthnot*, 230, 280, and he reappears
as "Bubo" in *Epilogue to Satires I*, 12, 68. Dodington was a clever, cynical Whig
politician, with whom Pope would not seem to have had any personal relations,
though Mr Sherburn identifies him with the "B—" of Pope's letter to Swift,
6 January 1733/4, who was "insupportably insolent in his civility" to him
(Sherburn, III 401). If Dodington is the Dorimant of *A Master Key to Popery* (see
p. 178 below), as seems probable, Pope's animus can perhaps be traced to
Dodington's prominence in the tittle-tattle campaign against *To Burlington*.
Horace Walpole thought Pope "treated him with more severity than he de-
served" (*The Works of Sir Charles Hanbury Williams*, I 23). Dodington spent

A standing sermon, at each year's expense,
That never Coxcomb reach'd Magnificence!
    You show us, Rome was glorious, not profuse,
And pompous buildings once were things of Use.
Yet shall (my Lord) your just, your noble rules   25

23–38 You show . . . of art] *1731abc keep this paragraph to follow l. 180
and continue here with l. 39.*
25 Yet . . . your just, your] Just as they are, yet shall *1731abc.*

£140,000 completing the magnificent mansion that his uncle had begun at
Eastbury, Dorset. The architect was Vanbrugh, for whose abilities Pope shared
Swift's ignorant contempt. "Babo", the reading of the early editions (see
textual note), is identified by *A Miscellany on Taste* as "Lord C–d–n". This
must be Charles, second Baron Cadogan (1685 or 1691–1776), who was a
brother of the general and had married Sir Hans Sloane's daughter. Cadogan had
been elected to the Council of the Royal Society, November 1731, and his estate
at Caversham, Oxfordshire, included "The Great Mansion-House . . . with large
Gardens adorn'd with Statuary, Obalisks, Urns and Vazes, and . . . Great Canals
and Basons in the Garden and Park" (*A Particular of the Manor of Caversham*,
c. 1730). It is more likely, however, that Babo does not represent anybody in
particular; "Dado", an uncancelled variant in the Morgan autograph MS., is
even more impersonal.

23. The Earl of Burlington was then publishing [had publish'd *1735ab*] the
Designs of Inigo Jones, and the Antiquities of Rome by Palladio. [P. *1735a–51.*]
*The Designs of Inigo Jones, consisting of Plans and Elevations for Public and Private
Buildings*, 2 vols., 1727, was published in Kent's name, and only *Fabriche antiche
disegnate da Andrea Palladio Vicentino*, 1730, appeared as by Burlington. No doubt
Burlington was assisted by Kent—who lived at Burlington House—in both
works. For the projected second volume of Palladio see the Introduction, p. xxv
above. The most elaborate recent study of Burlington the architect (Fiske
Kimball, *Journal of the Institute of British Architects*, 15 October, 12 November
1927) ends: "Our study makes us appreciate that there is a packed significance
in Pope's line addressed to Burlington,
          'You taught us Rome was glorious, not profuse.'
Architecture was to be henceforth not baroque, not overladen with academic
details, but Roman in its forms, Roman in simplicity and grandeur."

25. The emendation (see textual note) was perhaps in deference to the criti-
cism in *A Miscellany on Taste* (p. 21): "This, as it stands, is downright Nonsense,
Yet shall your noble Rules, just as they are, fill half the Land, &c. that is, your noble
Rules, such as they are, good or bad, rough as they run, shall fill.—This, I dare
say, is none of your Meaning. The Truth is, your Design was to have been under-
stood in a Sense very different from what the Expressions will bear."

Fill half the land with Imitating Fools;
Who random drawings from your sheets shall take,
And of one beauty many blunders make;
Load some vain Church with old Theatric state,
Turn Arcs of triumph to a Garden-gate;   30
Reverse your Ornaments, and hang them all
On some patch'd dog-hole ek'd with ends of wall,
Then clap four slices of Pilaster on't,
That, lac'd with bits of rustic, makes a Front.
Or call the winds thro' long Arcades to roar,   35
Proud to catch cold at a Venetian door;
Conscious they act a true Palladian part,
And if they starve, they starve by rules of art.
   Oft have you hinted to your brother Peer,
A certain truth, which many buy too dear: 40
Something there is more needful than Expence,
And something previous ev'n to Taste—'tis Sense:
Good Sense, which only is the gift of Heav'n,
And tho' no science, fairly worth the sev'n:

34 That . . . makes] And . . . 'tis *1731a–35b.*
35 Or call] Shall call *1731a–36, 1744–51. The 1739 reading (here
adopted) is much less clumsy.*

28. Cf. Dryden, *To My Honour'd Kinsman, John Driden*, 105–6,
      From Files, a Random-Recipe they take,
      And Many Deaths of One Prescription make.
   30. An allusion perhaps to the entrance to Lord Peterborough's house at
Bevismount, near Southampton. Cf. *Imit. Hor., Ep.,* i i, 7–8. The house itself and
the grounds were greatly admired by Pope.
   32. *dog-hole*] "A vile hole; a mean habitation" (Johnson).
   33. *Pilaster*] "A square column sometimes insulated, but oftner set within a
wall" (Johnson).
   34. *rustic*] "Characterized by a surface artificially roughened or left rough-
hewn" (*OED*).
   36. *Venetian door*] A Door or Window, so called, from being much practised
at Venice, by Palladio and others. [P. *1735c–51.*] Pope's is the first use of the
term recorded in *OED.*
   44. Malone (Bodley MS. Malone 30) compares Henry Peacham, *The Truth*

A Light, which in yourself you must perceive;   45
Jones and Le Nôtre have it not to give.
   To build, to plant, whatever you intend,
   To rear the Column, or the Arch to bend,

---

of our Times: Revealed out of one Mans Experience, 1638, p. 159, ". . . though *Discretion* bee none of the liberall Sciences, it is an Art that gives all other their value and estimation."

46. *Inigo Jones* the celebrated Architect, and M. *Le Nôtre*, the designer of the best Gardens of France. [P. *1731abc–51. 1731abc word differently and add* and plann'd Greenwich and St James's Parks, &c.] André Le Nôtre (1613–1700) laid out the gardens at Versailles and Fontainebleau. He is often said to have designed Greenwich Park and St James's Park, but these are now generally attributed to his pupils. It was the symmetrical style of Le Nôtre and the Dutch that Pope took the lead in challenging.

47–98. Summaries of the evolution of landscape gardening will be found in Sir Reginald Blomfield, *The Formal Garden in England* (3rd edition, 1901), ch. IV (very hostile), Mrs Evelyn Cecil, *A History of Gardening in England* (3rd edition, 1910), chs. XI, XII (mainly practice), and Elizabeth W. Manwaring, *Italian Landscape in Eighteenth Century England* (1925), ch. VI (mainly theory). The movement was initiated by Addison's essays, especially *Spectator*, nos. 412, 414, 477, where Pope's views on "unbounded Views" and "agreeable" surprises and variety are all anticipated. Another important early document was Pope's essay in *Guardian*, no. 173, which ridiculed topiary excesses. According to Walpole ("On Modern Gardening", *Works*, 1798, II 535)—who is now suspected of somewhat overstating the claims of Twickenham, and of Pope, in the propagation of modern landscape gardening—the first professional landscape gardener was Charles Bridgman (d. 1738), a friend of Pope's, who "disdained to make every division tally to its opposite". Bridgman, who laid out the royal gardens at Richmond and Kensington Palace, was succeeded and eclipsed by Burlington's protégé William Kent (1684–1748), another friend of Pope's, who was something of a genius—according to Blomfield, an evil genius. But "Mr Pope undoubtedly contributed to form his taste," and the Prince of Wales's garden at Carlton House certainly—and Rousham, "the most engaging of all Kent's works", probably—derived from Pope's little garden at Twickenham (Walpole, p. 538). Christopher Hussey's introduction to Margaret Jourdain's *The Work of William Kent* (1948) is an admirable assessment both of Kent's significance and of Pope's function in the Palladian movement. Early treatises are *New Principles of Gardening* (1728), by Pope's neighbour Batty Langley, and Stephen Switzer's *Ichnographia Rustica* (1718), the second edition of which (1743) quotes approvingly ll. 117–18. Sherburn (*Early Career*, pp. 277–88) gives details of Pope's part in the gardening projects of Burlington, Bathurst, Cobham, and others as well as of the growth of his own garden. Pope's own theories and preferences are touched on in some of the notes that follow.

> To swell the Terras, or to sink the Grot;
> In all, let Nature never be forgot.   50
> But treat the Goddess like a modest fair,
> Nor over-dress, nor leave her wholly bare;
> Let not each beauty ev'ry where be spy'd,
> Where half the skill is decently to hide.
> He gains all points, who pleasingly confounds,   55
> Surprizes, varies, and conceals the Bounds.
>   Consult the Genius of the Place in all;
> That tells the Waters or to rise, or fall,
> Or helps th' ambitious Hill the heav'n to scale,
> Or scoops in circling theatres the Vale,   60
> Calls in the Country, catches opening glades,
> Joins willing woods, and varies shades from shades,

51–6 But treat . . . the Bounds] *Add. 1735c.*
59 heav'n] heav'ns *1731a–36, 1744–51 (see note).*

55–6. Pope quoted this couplet to Spence about 1742: "All the rules of gardening are reducible to three heads:—the contrasts, the management of surprises, and the concealment of the bounds . . . I have expressed them all, in two verses; (after my manner, in very little compass), which are an imitation of Horace's *Omne tulit punctum, &c.* [*De Arte Poetica*, l. 343]" (Spence, p. 260). The concealment of the bounds was generally affected by hahas which were much used by Bridgman.

57. "In laying out a garden", Pope told Spence about 1729 (p. 12), "the first thing to be considered is the genius of the place: thus at Riskins, for example, Lord Bathurst should have raised two or three mounts; because his situation is all a plain, and nothing can please without variety." "Riskins" is Richings Park near Slough.

59. The *1739* reading, an Overlooked Revision, is clearly preferable. Many of Pope's lines have at least one "s" too many. See Tennyson's comment (*Memoir, By his Son*, 1897, II 286).

62–4. Spence has recorded (pp. 209–10) Pope's views on this subject about 1738: "The lights and shades in gardening are managed by disposing the thick grove work, the thin, and the openings, in a proper manner: of which the eye is generally the properest judge.—Those clumps of trees are like the groups in pictures, (speaking of some in his own garden).—You may distance things by darkening them, and by narrowing the plantation more and more towards the end, in the same manner as they do in painting, and as 'tis executed in the little

Now breaks or now directs, th' intending Lines;
Paints as you plant, and, as you work, designs.
    Still follow Sense, of ev'ry Art the Soul,   65
Parts answ'ring parts shall slide into a whole,
Spontaneous beauties all around advance,
Start ev'n from Difficulty, strike from Chance;
Nature shall join you, Time shall make it grow
A Work to wonder at—perhaps a STOW.   70

---

65 Still follow] Begin with *1731a–43*.

---

cypress walk to that obelisk". Walpole (*Works*, II 536) describes Kent's gardens
in almost identical terms: "The great principles on which he worked were per-
spective, and light and shade. Groups of trees broke too uniform or too exten-
sive a lawn; evergreens and woods were opposed to the glare of the champain;
and where the view was less fortunate, or so much exposed as to be beheld at
once, he blotted out some parts by thick shades, to divide it into variety, or to
make the richest scene more enchanting by reserving it to a farther advance
of the spectator's step. Thus selecting favourite objects, and veiling deformities
by screens of plantation, sometimes allowing the rudest waste to add its foil to
the richest theatre, he realized the compositions of the greatest masters in paint-
ing. Where objects were wanting to animate his horizon, his taste as an archi-
tect could bestow immediate termination."

    63. *th' intending Lines*] Those which lead the eye forward.

    70. STOW] The seat and gardens of the Lord Viscount Cobham in Bucking-
hamshire. [P. *1731abc, 1735c–51*.] An account of Richard Temple, Viscount
Cobham, will be found on p. 15 above. The famous gardens are described by
William Gilpin (*A Dialogue upon the Gardens of Viscount Cobham, at Stow*, 1748) and
by George Bickham (*A Description of the most Noble House and Gardens . . . at Stow,
in Buckinghamshire*, 1756). Engravings by Rigaud and Baron were published in
1739. Austin Dobson has an essay on "Eighteenth-Century Stowe" in *At Prior
Park* (1912), and details about the gardens will be found in Margaret Jourdain's
The Work of William Kent (1948). In Queen Anne's reign the gardens were still
of the formal Dutch type, but under George I Bridgman began the process of
blending the landscape with the garden, and Gibbs, Vanbrugh, and Kent
dotted temples, columns, and arches about. Bridgman was succeeded by Kent,
on whose death the ruralizing of the place continued under "Capability"
Brown. Pope was at Stowe only a few months before *To Burlington* was published.
In a letter to John Knight, 23 August 1731, he wrote: ". . . if any thing under
Paradise could set me beyond all Earthly Cogitations; Stowe might do it. It is
much more beautiful this year than when I saw it before, and much enlarged,
and with variety" (Sherburn, III 217).

    O

Without it, proud Versailles! thy glory falls;
And Nero's Terraces desert their walls:
The vast Parterres a thousand hands shall make,
Lo! COBHAM comes, and floats them with a Lake:
Or cut wide views thro' Mountains to the Plain,   75
You'll wish your hill or shelter'd seat again.
Ev'n in an ornament its place remark,
Nor in an Hermitage set Dr. Clarke.

---

74 COBHAM] *Bridgman 1731abc.*   76 hill or] Hill, and *1731abc.*
77–8 Ev'n in . . . Clarke] *Add. 1744.*

---

71. Until the advent of the landscape gardeners Le Nôtre's gardens at Versailles were considered the best in Europe.

72. Probably referring to the Golden House of Nero. See Suetonius, Life of Nero, cap. XXXI [EC].

74. "This office, in the original plan of the poem, was given to another; who not having the SENSE to see a compliment was intended him, convinced the poet it did not belong to him" [Warburton]. According to Croker (*Suffolk Letters*, I 383) Bridgman's name was omitted in the later editions (see textual note) at his own request. Gilpin's comment on the Stowe lake (*A Dialogue upon the Gardens of Viscount Cobham, at Stowe*, 1748, p. 4) is:

Polypth.   Upon my Word here is a noble Piece of Water!

Calloph.   Not many Years ago I remember it only a Marsh: it surprized me prodigiously when I first saw it floated in this manner with a Lake.

To *float* (= flood, inundate) was the technical agricultural term.

75–6. This was done in Hertfordshire, by a wealthy citizen, at the expence of above 5000 l. by which means (merely to overlook a dead plain) he let in the north-wind upon his house and parterre, which were before adorned and defended by beautiful woods. [P. *1735c–51.*] Walpole (Fraser marginalia, p. 40) annotates: "At Moor Park by Mr. Styles". This is probably correct. Benjamin Heskin Styles, a successful South Sea speculator who became M.P. for Devizes, bought Moor Park, Rickmansworth, from the Duchess of Monmouth in 1720, and Leoni rebuilt the house and laid out the grounds in magnificent style. "The artificial landscape gardening . . . has left many traces to the present day. . . Mr Styles cut a vista through the hill towards Watford, and another towards Uxbridge" (*Victoria County History of Hertfordshire*, II 378). Watford is north-east of Moor Park.

78. Dr S. Clarke's busto placed by the Queen in the Hermitage, while the Dr. duely frequented the Court. [P. *1744–51.*] Although not printed until 1744 the couplet appears in the margin of the Morgan MS. and was probably written many years before. The Hermitage was one of the ornamental features in Rich-

Behold Villario's ten-years toil compleat;
His Quincunx darkens, his Espaliers meet,   80
The Wood supports the Plain, the parts unite,
And strength of Shade contends with strength of Light;
A waving Glow his bloomy beds display,

83 A waving ... beds] His bloomy Beds a waving Glow *1731a–35b*;
A waving Glow the bloomy beds *1735c–36, 1744–51* (*see note*).

mond Park. In 1732, to the amusement of Queen Caroline's enemies, busts of
Boyle, Locke, Newton, and Wollaston by Rysbrack and of Samuel Clarke by
Guelfi were installed in the Hermitage. "Every man, and every boy", Pope
wrote to Gay, 2 October 1732, "is writing verses on the Royal Hermitage." Five
of these epigrams, including one by Swift, are in *The Poems of Swift*, ed. H. Wil-
liams, 1937, II 662–3. The Hermitage was pulled down in the later part of the
century and the busts are now in Kensington Palace. Samuel Clarke (1675–
1729), a Cambridge D.D., was the most distinguished English philosopher be-
tween Locke and Berkeley. According to Warton, "Pope imbibed an aversion to
this excellent man from Bolingbroke, who hated Clarke, not only because he had
written a book which this declamatory philosopher could not confute, but be-
cause he was a favourite of Queen Caroline." An additional grievance was that
Clarke "refused to use his interest with the Queen to get Lord Bolingbroke re-
called from France, with a general pardon" (John Jones, *Literary Anecdotes*, ed.
Nichols, IV 721). One reason why a bust of Clarke was out of place in a hermitage
was Clarke's unorthodox theology, which was suspected of Arianism.

79. According to *A Miscellany on Taste* Villario is "Lord C–le–n". Richard
Child, Earl Tylney of Castlemaine, was the owner of Wanstead House, a magni-
ficent mansion in Essex that he had built in 1715. And Dilke quotes a 1722
Peerage on Wanstead: "very fine and there is said to be some of the finest
gardens in the world". But the gardens were laid out by the firm of London and
Wise (Blomfield, *The Formal Garden in England*, p. 76), who stuck to the formal
French and Dutch style of their founders, and it is clear from ll. 81–2 that
Villario was a landscapist. He is no doubt a synthetic figure. A passage in "A
Master Key to Popery" (see p. 181 below) seems to imply that Hervey believed
Villario to be Lord Bathurst of all people.

80. *Quincunx*] A group of five trees, four planted in a square or rectangle
(one at each corner) and the fifth in the centre. For Pope's own quincunx see
Imit. Hor., Sat., II i, 130.

83. The *1739* reading, an Overlooked Revision, seems preferable ("his"
instead of "the") because it elucidates the syntax. "*The* Wood" and "*the* parts"
in the preceding couplet are in explanatory apposition to "*His* Quincunx" and
"*his* Espaliers"; but with "bloomy beds" the catalogue of items is renewed.

Blushing in bright diversities of day,
With silver-quiv'ring rills mæander'd o'er—   85
Enjoy them, you! Villario can no more;
Tir'd of the scene Parterres and Fountains yield,
He finds at last he better likes a Field.

    Thro' his young Woods how pleas'd Sabinus stray'd,
Or sat delighted in the thick'ning shade,   90
With annual joy the red'ning shoots to greet,
Or see the stretching branches long to meet!
His Son's fine Taste an op'ner Vista loves,
Foe to the Dryads of his Father's groves,
One boundless Green, or flourish'd Carpet views,   95
With all the mournful family of Yews;
The thriving plants ignoble broomsticks made,
Now sweep those Alleys they were born to shade.
    At Timon's Villa let us pass a day,

92 Or see] And see *1735ab*.
98 to shade] *1731abc follow on with ll. 169–76.*

---

84. This line also appears in "The Garden" (Pope's imitation of Cowley),
7–8:   And vary'd *Tulips* show so dazling gay,
             Blushing in bright diversities of day.
See vol. VI of this edition, pp. 47–8.
89. According to *A Miscellany on Taste* Sabinus is "The Son of Virro". Virro
had been previously identified as "Mr S—es of Hertfordshire" and Sabinus
must therefore be a son of Benjamin Styles of Moor Park, Rickmansworth. I
cannot trace any such person and suspect this is a blunder. Sabinus and his son
were probably both imaginary. The point of the name is not clear. A Sabinus
Tyro dedicated a lost book on gardening to Maecenas, but Pope can hardly have
intended to allude to him.
95. The two extremes in parterres, which are equally faulty; a *boundless Green*,
large and naked as a field, or a *flourished Carpet*, where the greatness and noble-
ness of the piece is lessened by being divided into too many parts, with scroll'd
works and beds, of which the examples are frequent. [P. *1735c–51*.]
96. Touches upon the ill taste of those who are so fond of Ever-greens (par-
ticularly Yews, which are the most tonsile) as to destroy the nobler Forest-trees,
to make way for such little ornaments as Pyramids of dark-green, continually
repeated, not unlike a Funeral procession. [P. *1735c–51*.]
99. *At Timon's Villa*] This description is intended to comprize the principles

Where all cry out, "What sums are thrown away!"   100
So proud, so grand, of that stupendous air,
Soft and Agreeable come never there.
Greatness, with Timon, dwells in such a draught
As brings all Brobdignag before your thought.
To compass this, his building is a Town,   105
His pond an Ocean, his parterre a Down:
Who but must laugh, the Master when he sees,

---

103 in] with *1731c* (*a misprint?*).

---

of a false Taste of Magnificence, and to exemplify what was said before, that nothing but Good Sense can attain it. [P. *1735c-51*.] The identification of Timon is one of the most difficult and complicated of the problems connected with Pope. In spite of his protestations to the contrary his eighteenth-century readers persisted in believing that the character was intended to caricature James Brydges, Duke of Chandos (see *To Cobham*, 113*n*). But modern scholarship has vindicated Pope. The principal resemblances and discrepancies between Timon's villa and Chandos's "Cannons", near Edgware, are noted under the separate lines, and a detailed discussion of the Chandos scandal will be found in Appendix B (pp. 170-4 below). See also the Introduction, pp. xxvi*f* above. Timon is almost certainly nobody in particular—a personification of aristocratic pride (not, it will be noted, a vulgar *nouveau riche*, a sort of Trimalchio, as suggested by R. K. Root, *The Poetical Career of Alexander Pope*, 1938, p. 188). But many of the details of the grounds and house derive from actual offences against taste committed by Pope's contemporaries, including Chandos—who wrote to Anthony Hammond, 1 January 1732, "I am not so ignorant of my own weakness, as not to be sensible of it's Justness [i.e. that of the Timon passage] in some particulars." See G. Sherburn, " 'Timon's Villa' and Cannons", *Huntington Library Bulletin*, no. 8, October 1935, and C. H. Collins Baker and Muriel I. Baker, *The Life and Circumstances of James Brydges First Duke of Chandos*, 1949, especially pp. 432-5.

103. *draught*] Sketch or design. The rhyme was a good one, as the usual upper-class pronunciation in Pope's time was *drawt*. Cf. *To a Lady*, 111.

104. It is possible that here and in l. 148 there is an unconscious reminiscence of Milton's "Il Penseroso", l. 166,

And bring all Heav'n before mine eyes.

106. *an Ocean*] Cf. Samuel Humphreys, *Cannons. A Poem*, 1728, p. 7,

In the mid View, a Bason's ample Round
Contains an Ocean in its noble Bound.

107-8. In their *Verses Address'd to the Imitator of the First Satire of the Second Book of Horace*, 1733, ll. 77-8, Lady Mary Wortley Montagu and Lord Hervey rewrote this couplet to describe Pope:

A puny insect, shiv'ring at a breeze!
Lo, what huge heaps of littleness around!
The whole, a labour'd Quarry above ground.   110
Two Cupids squirt before: a Lake behind
Improves the keenness of the Northern wind.
His Gardens next your admiration call,
On ev'ry side you look, behold the Wall!
No pleasing Intricacies intervene,   115
No artful wildness to perplex the scene;

---

116 wildness] Wilderness *1731c, 1735a* (*perhaps a misprint*).

Who but must laugh, this Bully when he sees,
A little Insect shiv'ring at a Breeze?

109–10. One of the houses Pope undoubtedly had in mind in describing Timon's villa was Blenheim, which he had seen (still far from complete) in 1717 (EC, IX 277). In a letter to Martha Blount, 6 August 1718, he calls it "the most proud and extravagant Heap of Towers in the nation" (Sherburn, 1 480). Letter IX of the "Letters to Several Ladies" in *Letters of Mr Pope*, 1735 (Sherburn, 1 432) contains a long satirical account of Blenheim, parts of which Pope utilized in this passage: "I never saw so great a thing with so much littleness in it . . . the Duke of *Shrewsbury* gave a true character of it, when he said, it was a great *Quarry of Stones above ground.*" "A Master Key to Popery" also mentions this "well-known" comment of the Duke of Shrewsbury's on Blenheim (see p. 187 below). As the Duke died in 1718 Blenheim must have been still in process of erection when he saw it.

111–20. According to "A Master Key to Popery" (see pp. 184–8 below) none of the items in this catalogue were to be found at Cannons. "In the Garden, no Walls crossing the eye, no large Parterre at all, no little Cupids, no Lake to the North, no cut Trees, no such Statues. . ."

111–12. The "basin" at Cannons was on the north side of the house (J. R. Robinson, *The Princely Chandos*, 1893, p. 64). The fact that he had such a thing was an indication that Chandos was rather old-fashioned in his tastes. Kent banished basins from his gardens.

114. This was one of the details Pope principally relied on to disprove the charge that Timon was Chandos. "Is his Garden crowded with *Walls*?" (*Daily Journal*, 23 December 1731; Sherburn, III 257). Alexander Blackwell, who laid out the gardens at Cannons, had used iron balustrading instead of walls or hedges (J. R. Robinson, *The Princely Chandos*, p. 68).

115–16. *Intricacies . . . wildness*] The maze and the "wilderness" (see textual note) were both survivals from the seventeenth century. Indeed the wilderness (only wild in that its trees were native) often enclosed a maze.

Grove nods at grove, each Alley has a brother,
And half the platform just reflects the other.
The suff'ring eye inverted Nature sees,
Trees cut to Statues, Statues thick as trees,   120
With here a Fountain, never to be play'd,
And there a Summer-house, that knows no shade;
Here Amphitrite sails thro' myrtle bow'rs;
There Gladiators fight, or die, in flow'rs;
Un-water'd see the drooping sea-horse mourn,   125
And swallows roost in Nilus' dusty Urn.
    My Lord advances with majestic mien,
Smit with the mighty pleasure, to be seen:
But soft—by regular approach—not yet—

---

127 Behold! my Lord advances o'er the Green *1731abc*.

---

120. *Statues thick as trees*] Humphreys celebrated the statues in *Cannons*, p. 8,
      Here Statues breathing from the Artist's Hand
      An awful Troop, majestically stand.

121. This was never true of Cannons. "Do his Basons want *Water*?" (*Daily Journal*, 23 December 1731; Sherburn, III 257). Humphreys boasts (*Cannons*, pp. 7–9) that the water-supplies from the ridge at Stanmore never ran out in the driest weather.

123–6. Here and in l. 120 Pope is repeating the doctrine he had already preached indirectly in *Guardian*, no. 173, 29 September 1713, with its catalogue of "Adam and Eve in yew", "Queen Elizabeth in myrtle", "A lavender pig, with sage growing in his belly," etc. The satire was very necessary. In the late seventeenth and early eighteenth centuries "London and Wise had stocked our gardens with giants, animals, monsters, coats of arms and mottos, in yew, box and holly" (Walpole, *Works*, II 534). Bridgman, perhaps under Pope's influence, banished "verdant sculpture".

124. The two [famous *1731abc*] Statues of the *Gladiator pugnans* and *Gladiator moriens*. [P. *1731–51*.]

126. Sculptured water-pots were common Renaissance garden ornaments. Nilus, the personified god of the Nile, had been enlisted in late classical mythology as the father of the Egyptian Hercules.

127. The reading of the first edition (see textual note) is ridiculed in *A Miscellany on Taste* (p. 16): "Here we find my Lord, first of all, advancing o'er the Green on purpose to expose his Person to view;—And now we are told that our Eyes must not be blest with the Sight, till he appears at the Study-door.—*Quere*, Whereabouts, upon the Green, my Lord's Study-door stands?"

First thro' the length of yon hot Terrace sweat,   130
And when up ten steep slopes you've dragg'd your thighs,
Just at his Study-door he'll bless your eyes.
His Study! with what Authors is it stor'd?
In Books, not Authors, curious is my Lord;
To all their dated Backs he turns you round,   135
These Aldus printed, those Du Suëil has bound.
Lo some are Vellom, and the rest as good
For all his Lordship knows, but they are Wood.
For Locke or Milton 'tis in vain to look,

---

130. The *Approaches* and *Communications* of house with garden, or of one part with another, ill judged and inconvenient. [P. *1735c–51*.]

131. Another detail that was not true of Cannons. "Are there *ten steep Slopes* of his Terrass?" (*Daily Journal*, 23 December 1731; Sherburn, III 257). The monosyllables recall the Poetical Index to Pope's *Iliad*, which lists similar lines "Expressing in the sound the thing describ'd", e.g. "Stiffness and slowness of old age" (*Iliad*, XIII 653):

His tir'd, slow Steps, he drags from off the Field.

132. According to "A Master Key to Popery" (see p. 185 below) Cannons had "no Study opening on a Terras, but up one pair of stairs".

133. The false Taste in Books; a satyr on the vanity in collecting them, more frequent in men of Fortune than the study to understand them. Many delight chiefly in the elegance of the print, or of the binding; some have carried it so far, as to cause the upper shelves to be filled with painted books of wood; others pique themselves so much upon books in a language they do not understand as to exclude the most useful in one they do. [P. *1735c–51*.] Chandos was not a bibliophile. "Is he piqued about *Editions* of *Books*?" (*Daily Journal*, 23 December 1731; Sherburn, III 257). The passage may have been suggested by La Bruyère: "... in vain he encourages me, by telling me they are gilt on the Backs and Leaves, that they are of the best Editions, and by naming some of the best of them, he tells me, his Gallery is full of them, except one place that is painted so like Books, the fallacy is not to be discerned; he adds, that he never reads" (p. 272 of the second edition of the English translation, *The Characters*, 1700).

136. Aldo Manutio, the Renaissance Venetian printer, and the Abbé Du Sueil, a famous Paris binder of the early eighteenth century.

139–40. Chandos was a generous patron of contemporary literature. "Does he exclude all *Moderns* from his *Library*?" (*Daily Journal*, 23 December 1731; Sherburn, III 257). He took twelve sets of Pope's *Iliad*, four sets of Theobald's Shakespeare, and fifty copies of Gay's *Poems* (1720). According to "A Master Key to Popery" (see p. 178 below) Chandos had "no Books dated on the back or painted, and as many Moderns as Ancient ones".

These shelves admit not any modern book.   140
    And now the Chapel's silver bell you hear,
That summons you to all the Pride of Pray'r:
Light quirks of Musick, broken and uneven,
Make the soul dance upon a Jig to Heaven.
On painted Cielings you devoutly stare,   145
Where sprawl the Saints of Verrio or Laguerre,
On gilded clouds in fair expansion lie,
And bring all Paradise before your eye.
To rest, the Cushion and soft Dean invite,

---

141. According to "A Master Key to Popery" (see p. 185 below) there was no silver bell at Cannons. The bell and the Dean (l. 149) reappear in *Epistle to Arbuthnot*, 299–300:

> Who to the *Dean* and *silver Bell* can swear,
> And sees at *Cannons* what was never there.

See also Introduction, p. xxix above.

143. The false Taste in *Music*, improper to the subjects, as of light airs in Churches, often practised by the organists, *&c.* [P. *1735c–51*.] According to Hill (Sherburn, III 262) "the pomp of the chapel, and its musick" was largely responsible for the identification of Timon's villa with Cannons. The chapel at Cannons was famous for the excellence of the sacred music performed there, which Handel superintended for two years. "Is the *Musick* of his Chapel bad, or *whimsical*, or *jiggish*? On the contrary, was it not the best composed in the Nation, and most suited to grave Subjects; witness *Nicol Haym*'s, and Mr. *Hendel*'s Noble *Oratories*?" (*Daily Journal*, 23 December 1731; Sherburn, III 257). The words of Handel's oratorio *Esther*, first produced at Cannons, in its original masque form have been attributed to Pope; see vol. VI of this edition, pp. 423–35.

145. —And in *Painting* [i.e. false taste in] (from which even Italy is not free) of naked figures in Churches, *&c.* which has obliged some Popes to put draperies on some of those of the best masters. [P. *1751*.]

146. *Verrio or Laguerre*] Verrio (Antonio) painted many cielings, &c. at Windsor, Hampton-court, &c. and Laguerre at Blenheim-castle, and other places. [P. *1735c–51*.] As Pope pointed out to Hill, 5 February 1732—and repeated in "A Master Key to Popery" (see p. 185 below)—the paintings in the chapel at Cannons were not by either Antonio Verrio (1639–1707) or Louis Laguerre (1663–1721), but by Antonio Bellucci (1654–1726) and Enoch Zeeman (d. 1744). Laguerre, however, had painted one of the staircases at Cannons as well as the altarpiece in the adjacent church at Whitchurch which Chandos had had built (J. R. Robinson, *The Princely Chandos*, pp. 66, 148).

148. See l. 104*n*.

Who never mentions Hell to ears polite.   150
   But hark! the chiming Clocks to dinner call;
A hundred footsteps scrape the marble Hall:
The rich Buffet well-colour'd Serpents grace,
And gaping Tritons spew to wash your face.
Is this a dinner? this a Genial room?   155
No, 'tis a Temple, and a Hecatomb.
A solemn Sacrifice, perform'd in state,

150. This is a fact; a reverend Dean [of Peterborough *1735cd*] preaching at Court, threatned the sinner with punishment in "a place which he thought it not decent to name in so polite an essembly". [P. *1735c–51*.] This dean is presumably identical with the "eminent divine" mentioned by Steele in *Guardian*, no. 17, 31 March 1713, who "about thirty years ago . . . told his congregation at Whitehall, that if they did not vouchsafe to give their lives a new turn, they must certainly go to a place which he did not think fit to name in that courtly audience". Pope's letter in the *Daily Journal*, 23 December 1731, makes it possible to identify the dean. Speaking of the chapel at Cannons he concludes, "And did ever Dean Ch–w–d preach his Courtly Sermons there?" (Sherburn, III 257). "Dean Ch–w–d" must be Knightly Chetwood (1650–1720), Dean of Gloucester (not Peterborough, as Pope seems at one time to have imagined), who was James II's Anglican chaplain.

152. According to Hill (Sherburn, III 262) "the *hundred foot-steps*, the exact number of his domesticks, for some years, at *Canons*", was one of the reasons why so many readers took Timon for Chandos. Pope replied (Sherburn, III 268), "the Number of Servants never was an Hundred"; and this is repeated in "A Master Key to Popery" (see p. 185 below). A letter from Chandos to Arbuthnot quoted by Sherburn shows that there were eighty-three servants at Cannons in 1718. When Defoe visited Cannons a few years later he found some hundred and twenty servants there (*A Tour Thro' the whole Island of Great Britain*, 1725, II 11). Pope's words, however, clearly apply to the guests as well as to the table-servants (but not presumably the rest of the staff), and a hundred footsteps need only imply fifty people.

153. Taxes the incongruity of *Ornaments* (tho' sometimes practised by the ancients) where an open mouth ejects the water into a fountain, or where the shocking images of serpents, &c. are introduced in Grottos or Buffets. [P. *1735c–51*.]

155. The proud Festivals of some men are here set forth to ridicule, where pride destroys the ease, and formal regularity all the pleasurable enjoyment of the entertainment. [P. *1735c–51*.]

Genial] "Of or pertaining to a feast", *OED*, which cites Pope's *Iliad*, I 772,
    Thus the blest gods the genial day prolong
      In feasts ambrosial.

You drink by measure, and to minutes eat.
So quick retires each flying course, you'd swear
Sancho's dread Doctor and his Wand were there.   160
Between each Act the trembling salvers ring,
From soup to sweet-wine, and God bless the King.
In plenty starving, tantaliz'd in state,
And complaisantly help'd to all I hate,
Treated, caress'd, and tir'd, I take my leave,   165
Sick of his civil Pride from Morn to Eve;
I curse such lavish cost, and little skill,
And swear no Day was ever past so ill.
    Yet hence the Poor are cloath'd, the Hungry fed;
Health to himself, and to his Infants bread   170
The Lab'rer bears: What his hard Heart denies,
His charitable Vanity supplies.

171 his] thy *1731abc*.
172 His] Thy *1731abc*.

160. *Sancho's dread Doctor*] See Don Quixote, chap. xlvii. [P. *1735c–51*.] One
of the few references by Pope to Cervantes. The translation by Pope's painter-
friend, Charles Jervas, was not published until 1742, though it had been begun
many years before.
    162. *God bless the King*] "God save the King"—not printed until *c.* 1743
(in *Thesaurus Musicus*)—seems to have been popular on festal and patriotic occa-
sions from the time of the Restoration.
    169. The *Moral* of the whole, where PROVIDENCE is justified in giving Wealth
to those who squander it in this manner. A bad Taste employs more hands
and diffuses Expence more than a good one. This recurs to what is laid down in
Book i. Epist. II v 230–7 [Essay on Man, Epist. 2, ver. 230, &c. *1736–43*], and
in the Epistle preceding this, v. 161 &c. [P. *1735c–51*.] The passages in *E. on
Man* and *To Bathurst* may have been written first, but they were not published
until later. The earliest statement of Pope's optimistic ethics seems to be a
remark made to Spence (p. 15) about 1729: "As to the general design of Provi-
dence, the two extremes of vice may serve (like two opposite biases) to keep up
the balance of things." Savage told Spence that Bolingbroke had sent Pope "a
long letter on these heads" before May 1730 (see Introduction, p. xxi above),
and presumably the theory must be credited, for what it is worth, to him. It is
also to be found, much more cogently argued, in Mandeville. See *To Bathurst*,
13–14*n*.

Another age shall see the golden Ear
Imbrown the Slope, and nod on the Parterre,
Deep Harvests bury all his pride has plann'd,   175
And laughing Ceres re-assume the land.
    Who then shall grace, or who improve the Soil?
Who plants like BATHURST, or who builds like BOYLE.
'Tis Use alone that sanctifies Expence,
And Splendor borrows all her rays from Sense.   180
    His Father's Acres who enjoys in peace,
Or makes his Neighbours glad, if he encrease;
Whose chearful Tenants bless their yearly toil,
Yet to their Lord owe more than to the soil;
Whose ample Lawns are not asham'd to feed   185

---

174 the Slope . . . the Parterre] thy Slope . . . thy Parterre *1731abc.*
175 his] thy *1731abc.*   177–8 Who . . . Boyle] *Add. 1735a.*
179 'Tis . . . that] In you, my *Lord,* Taste *1731abc.*
180 And] For *1731abc.*   181–90 His . . . Town] *Add. 1735a.*
185 ample Lawns] wide Parterres *1735ab.*

---

173. Warburton's note in *1751*—"Had the Poet lived but three Years longer,
he had seen this prophecy fulfilled"—was modified in 1757 and later editions to
"Had the poet lived but three years longer, he had seen his general prophecy
against all ill-judged magnificence fulfilled in a very particular instance."
Cannons, pronounced unsaleable, was pulled down in 1747—three years after
the deaths of Pope and Chandos. It is therefore clear that Warburton believed
Chandos was Timon. Perhaps the explanation is to be found in the fact that at
the time of the Timon controversy Warburton was on intimate terms with
several of the "dunces", including Concanen, who may have been an editor of
A Miscellany on Taste and was certainly one of the protagonists in the outcry
against Pope. In 1732 Warburton would almost certainly have thought Chandos
was Timon, and he may never have discussed the matter with Pope in later
years.

174. *the Slope*] A technical term for the artificial banks much used by the formal
school of gardening. Pope uses the word in the description of Rendcomb quoted
p. 172 below.

176. *laughing Ceres*] The smiling scene that a cornfield exhibits. Perhaps a con-
flation of Virgil's *omnia nunc vident* (*Ecl.,* VII 55) and *lætas segetes* (*Georg.,* I 1).

178. For Allen, Lord Bathurst see p. 83 above. "Boyle" is Richard Boyle,
Earl of Burlington, the poem's dedicatee.

The milky heifer and deserving steed;
Whose rising Forests, not for pride or show,
But future Buildings, future Navies grow:
Let his plantations stretch from down to down,
First shade a Country, and then raise a Town.   190
    You too proceed! make falling Arts your care,
Erect new wonders, and the old repair,
Jones and Palladio to themselves restore,
And be whate'er Vitruvius was before:
Till Kings call forth th' Idea's of your mind,   195

---

191 You . . . your] Yet thou proceed; be fallen Arts thy *1731abc*.
195 your] thy *1731abc*.

---

190. *a Country*] A tract or district owned by the same lord or proprietor (*OED*).

191. *You too proceed*] A latinism. Cf. Horace, *Odes*, IV ii 49–50,
> teque dum procedis, io Triumpha,
> non semel dicemus.

Pope may have picked up the phrase from Dryden who uses it frequently.

194. M. Vitruvius Pollio (born *c.* 88 B.C.), author of *De Architectura*.

195–204. The poet after having touched upon the proper objects of Magnificence and Expence, in the private works of great men, comes to those great and public works which become a Prince. This Poem was published in the year 1732, [at the time *1736–43*] when some of the new-built Churches [new Churches built *1736–43*], by the act of Queen Anne, were ready to fall, being founded in boggy land (which is satirically alluded to in our author's imitation of Horace Lib. ii. Sat. 2 [l. 119].

> Shall half the new-built Churches round thee fall)

others were vilely executed, thro' fraudulent cabals between undertakers, officers, *&c.* Dagenham-breach had done very great mischiefs; many of the Highways throughout England were hardly passable, and most of those which were repaired by Turnpikes were made jobs for private lucre, and infamously executed, even to the entrances of London itself: The proposal of building a Bridge at Westminster had been petition'd against and rejected; but in two years after the publication of this poem, an Act for building a Bridge past thro' both houses. After many debates in the committee, the execution was left to the carpenter above-mentioned [l. 18], who would have made it a wooden one; to which our author alludes in these lines,

> Who builds a Bridge that never drove a pile?
> Should Ripley venture, all the world would smile.

Proud to accomplish what such hands design'd,
Bid Harbors open, public Ways extend,
Bid Temples, worthier of the God, ascend;
Bid the broad Arch the dang'rous Flood contain,
The Mole projected break the roaring Main;   200
Back to his bounds their subject Sea command,
And roll obedient Rivers thro' the Land;
These Honours, Peace to happy Britain brings,
These are Imperial Works, and worthy Kings.

198 Bid] And *1731abc*.

See the notes on that place [*Imit. Hor., Ep.*, II i, 186]. [P. *1735c–51*.] This "very remarkable" note is quoted in *The Prompter*, no. 135, 24 February 1736, with the comment, "I'll only add, that, I fear, this *Bridge, we expect*, is after all to be only a WOODEN one . . . Oh, Shame! a *wooden Bridge*! . . . no better perhaps than that at *Fulham* [begun March 1729]." There were Acts of 9 and 10 Anne and 1 George I providing for the building of churches in London and Westminster. At least one of these churches, St John's, Smith Square, stands on marshy ground. In the course of building it sank so much that two porticos and four corner towers were added so that each side might sink equally. St Anne's, Limehouse, was finished in 1724, but later the tower, which was built on sand, sank and affected the sides of the church. Further details will be found in the note to *Imit. Hor., Sat.*, II ii, 119, vol. IV, p. 62. Dagenham Breach was the result of a storm in 1707 which broke through a sluice in the bank of the Thames at Dagenham in Essex and flooded some thousand acres of fertile land. The breach cost over £40,000 to repair and was not completed until 1723. See T. Wright, *History of Essex*, 1836, II 488–9. Examples of the corruption and incompetence of the early Turnpike Trusts will be found in S. and B. Webb, *English Local Government*, V ("The King's Highway"), 1913. Of the London turnpikes one of the worst was the Kensington turnpike (H. L. Beales, *Johnson's England*, ed. A. S. Turberville, 1933, I 132, 136). An Act for the construction of Westminster Bridge was passed in 1736, and Burlington was (from 1737) one of the Commissioners appointed to superintend the work. The architect eventually appointed was Charles Labelye. The first stone was laid in 1739 and it was opened in 1750. The bridge was a stone one, not a wooden one. An account of Thomas Ripley will be found in the note to l. 18.
    198. *worthier of the God*] A latinism. Cf. Dryden's trans. of *Aeneid*, VI 898,
                    And Poets worthy their inspiring God.
The whole passage is full of echoes of Dryden's version of this book.
    204. Carruthers notes the reminiscence of Dryden's trans. of *Aeneid*, VI 852,
                    These are Imperial Arts, and worthy thee.

APPENDIXES

APPENDIX A

WHO WAS ATOSSA?

IT is virtually certain that the character of Atossa (*To a Lady*, ll. 115–50) had a living original. Pope's own statement (in a note to l. 199) is that the lines formed part of the original draft of the poem, but were omitted from the early editions as satirizing "Vice too high". This would mean that they were written by the end of 1732, when the poem was apparently complete (Pope to Caryll, January 1732/3; Sherburn, III 340). Pope's statement need not be questioned, and it is confirmed by a passage in his letter to Swift, 16 February 1732/3, "Your Lady friend is *Semper Eadem*, and I have written an *Epistle* to her on that qualification in a female character; which is thought by my chief Critick in your absence to be my *Chef d'Œuvre*: but it cannot be printed perfectly, in an age so sore of satire, and so willing to misapply characters" (Sherburn, III 349). On grounds of style and versification, too, a comparatively early date is probable. The exceptionally low incidence of hiatus per line (5·5 per cent) is particularly significant.[1]

The Atossa lines were certainly in existence in 1735. The eighty-six lines that were omitted at the last moment from the folio edition of the second volume of Pope's *Works* (published in April 1735) must have included this character with the two other scandalous portraits (Philomedé and Queen Caroline).[2] All three appear in a unique set of Pope's writings, now at Harvard, which was once the property of Frederick, Prince of Wales, and had clearly been assembled for him by Pope himself in or about 1738. They occur in a specially printed cancel sheet (of which no other copy has been located), which displaces in the Prince's copy of the quarto *Works*, vol. II, of 1735, the central pages of *To a Lady*. In this version the scandalous passages add up to eighty-eight lines (of which thirty-eight are about Atossa).[3] Thirty-six of the Atossa lines reappear, with signi-

---

1. In the poems written after 1733 there is almost no conscious avoidance of a hiatus. The average is about one hiatus in every four lines (25 per cent). Earlier Pope was still obeying his own injunction in *E. on Criticism* to avoid "the open vowels". A relaxation set in with *E. on Man* and *To Burlington* (14 per cent).

2. See p. 43 above. Their original inclusion would explain the oddities of the line-numbering in this edition.

3. The bibliographical and textual details will be found in an illuminating article by Vinton A. Dearing in the *Harvard Library Bulletin*, 1950, IV 320–38. They demonstrate that the scandalous characters existed in a cruder form some time before 1735 and were overhauled and revised for their projected publication in *The Works*, vol. II.

ficant textual differences, in the "death-bed" edition of 1744. This edition, however, was immediately suppressed in order to prevent their circulation.[1] Its melodramatic suppression, like the printing of the sheet for the Prince of Wales's private eye in 1738, and the last-moment cancellation of the earlier sheet in the 1735 folio *Works*, vol. II, confirms beyond question Atossa's scandalous status.

Who then was the contemporary notability that Pope had dared to satirize so boldly? Only two candidates have ever been proposed—Sarah, Duchess of Marlborough, and Katherine, Duchess of Buckinghamshire. Eighteenth-century gossip was almost unanimous in asserting that Atossa was the Duchess of Marlborough; but later editors have been more hesitant. Dilke, indeed, who examined the problem with great thoroughness and acuteness,[2] came to the conclusion that Pope never intended the character for any one but the Duchess of Buckinghamshire and that the eighteenth-century gossips were all wrong. Courthope, on the other hand, attempted a compromise and suggested that Pope originally intended the lines for the Duchess of Marlborough but later modified them sufficiently to make it *look* as if the Duchess of Buckinghamshire was the butt.[3] Courthope's solution, though it has received some effective pin-pricks recently, still holds the field. Although absolute certainty is not possible, a consideration of the whole body of evidence, including several items that were not available to Courthope, has led me to conclude that Dilke was substantially right and that Atossa, in so far as a living original was intended, was the Duchess of Buckinghamshire and not the Duchess of Marlborough. It is possible, however, that some of the lines derive from a rejected character, which has not survived, of the latter Duchess. Pope, who never wasted a good couplet if he could help it, may therefore have used some of the lines in turn of both Duchesses. The hypothesis would help to explain the general agreement of his contemporaries that his butt *was* the Duchess of Marlborough.

The evidence for identifying Atossa with the Duchess of Buckinghamshire can now be summarized.

(I) INTERNAL EVIDENCE

The principal allusions apparently pointing to the Duchess of Buckinghamshire have already been discussed in the explanatory notes on the passage (pp. 59–62 above). The striking fact here is that not one of the allusions in the final text is altogether inconsistent with what is known of the Duchess of Buckinghamshire. And some of the allusions are so specific that in combination they become applicable to no other contemporary *grande dame*. To whom else could *all* the following be applied—the name Atossa, the exposure of knaves (l. 119), the loveless youth (l. 125), the scandalous age (l. 128), the childlessness with all her children (l. 148), the heirs unknown (l. 149)?

---

1. See p. xiii above.   2. *The Papers of a Critic*, 1875, I 162f, 226f, 269f.
3. EC, III 76f, v 346f.

On the other hand there are no equally specific allusions to the Duchess of Marlborough, and some of the allusions cannot conceivably apply to her. I cannot do better than quote the admirable paragraph on this subject by the Duchess's latest biographer:

"The most exact and detailed lines in it are ridiculous when applied to her, and many others which, though they can be so applied, are so general in character as to be almost equally applicable to any woman of her type. The Duchess can certainly not be said to have been 'scarce once herself' [l. 116]. She was never anything else. She certainly found her life one warfare upon earth [l. 118]. Though she perhaps shone in exposing knaves and painting fools, she cannot be said herself to have been either [ll. 119–20]. Her brain was not 'eddy' [l. 121]. It was clarity itself. In 1744 she was eighty-four, and the world had been her trade for seventy-one years [l. 123]. Her youth was far from loveless and her age certainly not unrespected [l. 125]. Many passions had been gratified beside her rage [l. 126]. No scandal was ever associated with her, and much pleasure had been hers [l. 128]. Her revenge was certainly to be feared [l. 129], but there had been many who had been very well with her [l. 130], and Pope himself had been one. Violent she certainly was [l. 131], but not (except perhaps to Anne) to those to whom she was grateful [l. 132]. Had her love made her hate [l. 134]? No woman ever lived who held so just an estimate of the value of rank [l. 135], or who was so quick to appreciate kindness done to her [l. 138]. She certainly erected both bust and temple to her lord—but were they in the dust [ll. 139–40]? Was Marlborough a knave to her and his will a cheat [l. 142]—to her who idolised him until the day of her death and fought tooth and nail to carry out the instructions in his will? Was she robbed of friends, or of followers [ll. 144–5]—she, who had full measure of both, and still a great deal of power? Was she especially selfish? Or sick of herself [l. 146]? Could she under any circumstances be said to be childless or wanting an heir [l. 148]? And, finally, how is it possible to state either that her wealth was unguarded [l. 149], or that it descended to the poor [l. 150]?"[1]

And the allusions in the printed text are reinforced by some equally specific allusions in the passages from the original MS. cited in Warburton's notes. (The MS. itself has disappeared, but the readings also appear in the Prince of Wales cancel sheet at Harvard.[2]) The first of these passages is a couplet that originally followed l. 122:

> Oppress'd with wealth and wit, abundance sad!
> One makes her poor, the other makes her mad.

These lines point straight to the Duchess of Buckinghamshire who died insane and whose wealth was much reduced by perpetual lawsuits. They could hardly apply to the Duchess of Marlborough who retained all her faculties to the

---

1. Kathleen Campbell, *Sarah Duchess of Marlborough*, 1932, p. 286.
2. See note 2 on p. 159.

end and died enormously wealthy. The second passage had followed l. 148:

> This [i.e. her heir] Death decides, nor lets the blessing fall
> On any one she hates, but on them all.
> Curs'd chance! this only could afflict her more,
> If any part should wander to the poor.

The present ll. 149–50 must have been substituted for these lines when Pope learned, in May 1743, that some distant Irish connections had been found to be the Duke of Buckinghamshire's heirs. The allusion in the second line of the four is to the Duke's illegitimate children, with whom the Duchess had had a series of bitter disputes and who might have been presumed to be coming into the Duke's fortune on her death. Pope's revision would have been pointless if the Duchess of Marlborough had been intended, since she, unlike the Duchess of Buckinghamshire, had an enormous personal estate. The attitudes of the two Duchesses to the poor are indicated by their respective wills. Both left their servants the conventional year's wages, but whereas the Duchess of Buckinghamshire made no bequests to the poor at all, the Duchess of Marlborough left £300 "to the poor of the town of Woodstock". This may not appear a great deal, but in her lifetime the Duchess of Marlborough had been generous to the poor. Thus she gave £1,000 on one occasion for settling poor families in Georgia, and in 1736 she spent £50,000 on almshouses in St Albans. Applied to her Pope's allusion becomes meaningless.

(II) POPE'S OWN STATEMENTS

Pope's extant letters and writings make no direct reference to the Atossa character. Nor do the records of his conversation kept by Spence and others. But a postscript, which has not hitherto been printed, to an undated letter from Pope to Warburton, supplies some important indirect evidence. The letter can be dated, with some certainty, March or April 1744, and the postscript reads as follows: "I have just run over ye Second Epistle frō Bowyer, I wish you c^d add a Note at ye very End of it, to observe ye authors Tenderness in using no *living Examples* or *real Names* of any one of ye softer Sex, tho so free with those of his own in all his other satyrs."[1] In an earlier letter Pope had told Warburton that he had "replaced most of ye omitted lines" in *To a Lady*.[2] The postscript, which only antedates Pope's distribution of the edition to his friends by a few weeks, must therefore refer to a text of the poem virtually identical with the text we now have. The Atossa character *must* have been in it. And yet Pope could calmly instruct Warburton to tell the world what a virtuous poet he was

---

1. B.M. Egerton MS., 1946, f. 96^v and Sherburn, IV 516.

2. *Ibid.*, f. 78^r and Sherburn, IV 495. The letter is dated 27 January, and the year is almost certainly 1743/4. Pope's intention of restoring the suppressed passages had become known by October 1743 (see Hist. MSS. Comm., Denbigh MSS., p. 244, and p. 41 above).

not to employ "living Examples". If he had meant Atossa to be the Duchess of Marlborough, if he had even suspected that any reader could possibly make such an identification, the note would have been unthinkable, because the Duchess was still very much alive in the early months of 1744. As a matter of fact she outlived Pope. If, on the other hand, as seems probable, Pope had intended the Duchess of Buckinghamshire (who had died in March 1742/3) for Atossa, the note becomes natural and intelligible.

It is true that the phrase "living Examples" is not to be found in the note as it was finally printed by Warburton. The significance of the omission is discussed at length on p. 42 above. The probability is that the phrase was omitted, because of the last-minute insertion of the character of Cloe (ll. 157–80), which was based on the Countess of Suffolk, who did not die until many years later. But even if Cloe was already in the text Pope might well have overlooked the fact when suggesting the note to Warburton. For the note was clearly primarily intended to allay suspicions as to the three scandalous characters that he had originally omitted—Philomedé, Atossa, and Queen Caroline. The Cloe character was in a different category. It had not formed part of the original draft of the poem and, as Pope had printed it on its own as early as 1738, it cannot have been considered particularly scandalous. If Atossa was the Duchess of Buckinghamshire, Pope's note would have been an accurate description of the three scandalous characters, since Henrietta, Duchess of Marlborough (the only suggested original of Philomedé), had died in 1733, Queen Caroline had died in 1737, and the Duchess of Buckinghamshire in March 1743. In 1744 they were none of them "living Examples". On the other hand, if Atossa is the Duchess of Marlborough, the note becomes difficult either to explain or justify.

(III) POPE'S RELATIONS WITH THE TWO DUCHESSES

The two central facts in the Atossa problem are, (i) that the character was composed some time, possibly some years, before 1733, (ii) that Pope did not decide to publish it until the autumn of 1743. Do Pope's relations with either of the Duchesses at these two periods assist us to identify Atossa?

The case for the Duchess of Buckinghamshire has already been elaborated in the notes. It can be summed up in a few sentences. We know that the Duchess, after using Pope as a sort of confidential adviser for some ten years, suddenly quarrelled with him in 1729. The quarrel, in Pope's opinion, was over a trifle. At the Duchess's request he had revised a character she had written of herself, and the revision had not satisfied her. We know too that, although the acquaintance had been patched up in 1735 and the succeeding years, Pope had a new grievance against the Duchess in 1743, when he learned, after her death, that his letters to her had been left to her executor to dispose of as he thought fit. For the executor was his old enemy Lord Hervey. These facts are, I submit, amply sufficient to explain why, if Atossa was meant for the Duchess of Buckinghamshire, Pope wrote and decided to publish the satire just when he did.

Are there any comparable facts in the history of Pope's relations with the Duchess of Marlborough? In the years preceding 1733 Pope and the Duchess of Marlborough were not personal enemies. They had never met or had any direct relations with each other. They were, however, if not political enemies, at any rate in opposed political camps. The Duchess had been, in Queen Anne's reign, the bitter opponent of Bolingbroke, Harley, Swift, and other friends of Pope, and she was still a political power. As the widow of the great Whig hero, as the friend and ally of Walpole, and as a vigorous and accomplished election-eer in the Whig interest, she was naturally anathema to Pope's Tory friends. Pope's occasional allusions to her at this period are all unfriendly. She is "the imperious wife" of *E. on Man*, IV 302, and the avaricious "M**o" of *Imit. Hor., Sat.*, II ii, 122. A *political* satire on her by Pope in or around 1730 would not have been surprising. But is the character of Atossa a political satire? Is there a single political allusion in its thirty-six lines? If the character is compared with the suppressed character of Marlborough that Pope wrote in 1733[1] it becomes abundantly clear that Atossa is personal, not political, satire. Pope attacked Marlborough as a public figure and on public grounds, as the traitor to James II, as the plunderer of the French, as the peculator of public money. If Atossa had been Marlborough's wife, it seems inconceivable that some of these charges should not have been repeated.

Again, if Atossa is the Duchess of Marlborough, Pope's motives in 1743 in deciding to publish the character become equally inexplicable. By 1743 Pope and the Duchess were on very friendly terms. She had joined the opposition to Walpole in 1734, if not earlier, and in 1735 she and Pope had met. The acquaintance developed into friendship. Pope's letters to her, all from the years 1741–4, show him *inter alia* sending her fruit, advising and assisting her in the preparation of the *Conduct of the Duchess of Marlborough* for publication, supplying her with an inscription, and proposing to entertain her in his grotto. The Duchess's replies are not extant, but it is clear from Pope's letters that she had made him and Martha Blount generous presents. One sentence from a letter of Pope's of 18 January 1741/2 can bear no other interpretation: "But to use me thus—to have won me with some difficulty, to have bow'd down all my Pride, and reduced me to take That at your hands which I never took at any other; and as soon as you had done this, to slight your Conquest, and cast me away with the common Lumber of Friends in this Town—What a Girl you are?"[2] Is it con-ceivable that in the same year Pope should decide to publish an elaborate satire on this friend and patron? The thing is unthinkable—however low one's opinion of Pope's heart, however high one's estimate of his literary vanity. If nothing else the commonest prudence, a quality with which Pope was admitted-ly well endowed, must have prevented it.

1. It will be found in vol. VI of this edition, pp. 358–9.
2. Sherburn, IV 381. Mr Sherburn does not, however, interpret the passage so prosaically.

(IV) POPE'S SATIRIC METHODS

In and after 1729 Pope had a grudge against the Duchess of Buckinghamshire. She had treated him disgracefully and he resented it. On the other hand he had no personal grievance against the Duchess of Marlborough. He might once have disapproved of her on general and abstract, as well as party, grounds, but it was the moralist in Pope she offended, not the man. Have these facts, which can hardly be disputed, any bearing on the identification of Atossa? Is it possible, on internal evidence, to say this is the writing of a man with a grievance, this is *not* the writing of a moralist with an ethical point to make, or *vice versa*?

Atossa, to me, has all the marks of personal satire. It is the writing of a man who is very angry, and to whom in his anger every quality in his enemy, good or bad, relevant or irrelevant, adds fresh fuel to his satire:

> Peace is my dear Delight—not *Fleury*'s more:
> But touch me, and no Minister so sore.

The Duchess of Buckinghamshire had "touched" Pope, as in their different ways Addison, Lady Mary, and Hervey "touched" him. Atossa is the same kind of satire as Atticus, Sappho, and Sporus. It is in quite a different category from such impersonal satiric portraits as the Wharton of *To Cobham* or the Timon of *To Burlington*, which are both variations round a central theme.

Wharton and Timon are essentially illustrative examples. Each of them exemplifies a single quality that Pope disapproved of, and we hear little or nothing of any other qualities or defects they may have possessed. Wharton is just personified instability and Timon personified bad taste. If Atossa had been intended for the Duchess of Marlborough, it would no doubt have been composed on similar lines. Indeed the structure of *To a Lady* demands something of the sort. The poem consists of a series of, in Pope's own words (in the note to l. 199), "Examples and Illustrations to the maxims laid down". Silia (ll. 29–36) and Papillia (ll. 37–40) exemplify "Contrarieties in the *Soft-natured*" Calypso (ll. 45–52) "Contrarieties in the *Cunning* and *Artful*", Narcissa (ll. 53–68) "In the *Whimsical*", and so on. But what does Atossa exemplify? Contrarieties in the quarrelsome? No doubt that is the *excuse* for the character, but there is much more to Atossa than that. We are presented with many details that have nothing to do with her quarrelsomeness. She has an "Eddy Brain" (l. 121), she is old but still foolish (ll. 123–4), her private life is scandalous (l. 128), she is childless (l. 148), and she has no heir (ll. 149–50). Do these details in any degree illuminate her quarrelsomeness? Are they not simply additional sticks, the most effective sticks that Pope could find, to beat a personal enemy with?

(V) ATOSSA AND THE DUCHESS OF MARLBOROUGH

The evidence summarized in the preceding pages points directly to the Duchess of Buckinghamshire as Atossa's single original. It is disconcerting therefore to find only one of Pope's contemporaries, his editor Warburton, making the identification.[1] What Warburton has to say occurs in the note in his edition of Pope on "The Character of Katherine, late Duchess of Buckingham-shire" (a perhaps spurious piece):

"We find by Letter xix. that the Duchess of Buckinghamshire would have had Mr. Pope to draw her husband's Character. But though he refused this office, yet in his Epistle, *on the Character of Women*, these lines,

> *To heirs unknown descends th'unguarded store,*
> *Or wanders, heav'n directed, to the poor.*

are supposed to mark her out in such a manner as not to be mistaken for another."[2]

The couplet comprises the last two lines of the Atossa passage in its final form, and the note is therefore as unambiguous as it could decently be at the time: Atossa *is* Pope's character of the Duchess. Bolingbroke, however, who might be expected to have been even better informed since he had been the poem's first reader apparently and its then enthusiastic admirer,[3] had no doubt at all that Atossa was the other Duchess. His undated letter to Lord Marchmont, one of the other executors, soon after Pope's death has already been quoted in the Introduction:

"Our friend Pope, it seems, corrected and prepared for the press just before his death an edition of the four Epistles, that follow the Essay on Man. They were then printed off, and are now ready for publication. I am sorry for it, because, if he could be excused for writing the character of Atossa formerly, there is no excuse for his design of publishing it, after he had received the favours you and I know; and the character of Atossa is inserted. I have a copy of the book. Warburton has the propriety of it, as you know. Alter it he cannot, by the terms of the will. Is it worth while to suppress the edition? or should her Grace's friends say, as they may from several strokes of it, that it was not intended to be her character? and should she despise it?"[4]

Bolingbroke's letter is far and away the strongest piece of evidence in exis-tence for identifying Atossa with the Duchess of Marlborough. It is true the latter is not mentioned by name, but it is perfectly clear that she is the Duchess intended. Bolingbroke's words could not apply to any other Duchess. Dilke, who was convinced that Atossa was the Duchess of Buckinghamshire, has

---

1. The Percy MS. annotates Atossa "In some respects the Duchess of Marl-boro' "; the qualification is perhaps significant. Oldys printed the lines from a MS. in the Earl of Oxford's library in *The Harleian Miscellany* (1744–6), VIII 212, as "The Character of a certain great Duchess deceas'd, by a certain great Poet lately deceas'd". The title may be considered to imply that the Poet (Pope) has predeceased the Duchess, i.e. Buckinghamshire rather than Marlborough (who died in 1744, but after Pope).

2. *Works*, 1751, VIII 246. 3. See the letter to Swift quoted on p. xxxvii above.

4. *A Selection from the Papers of the Earls of Marchmont*, 1831, II 334–5.

argued that Bolingbroke, after reading the Atossa lines in *Epistles to Several Persons*, had just jumped to the conclusion, on the internal evidence of some of the allusions, that Pope meant to portray the Duchess of Marlborough. But this explanation hardly fits the facts. Bolingbroke's words certainly imply that both he and Marchmont had seen the Atossa lines before, presumably in manuscript, and already knew that they were a satire on the Duchess of Marlborough. An earlier letter from Bolingbroke to Marchmont (written on the day of Pope's death, 30 May 1744) helps to clear up the situation.

"The arrival of your servant with the message from Lord Stair gives me an opportunity of telling you, that I continue in the resolution, I mentioned to you last night, upon what you said to me from the Duchess of Marlborough. It would be a breach of that trust and confidence, which Pope reposed in me, to give any one such of his papers, as I think no one should see. If there are any, that may be injurious to the late Duke, or to her Grace, even indirectly and covertly, as I hope there are not, they shall be destroyed; and you shall be a witness of their destruction."[1]

In the light of these letters the situation immediately after Pope's death can be reconstructed with some certainty. By Pope's will his MS. remains were to go to Bolingbroke, "either to be preserved or destroyed". Some of the MS. pieces were already known to Pope's circle, and one of these pieces, the character of Marlborough (which Pope discussed with Spence about 1735[2]), the Duchess of Marlborough may well have heard of. In 1744 Bolingbroke was her friend and it was natural for her to ask him to look through Pope's remains and hand over anything of this kind.[3] But, when approached, Bolingbroke decided that he could not surrender anything of Pope's, though he agreed to destroy anything satirizing the Duke or Duchess. And it was with this object, anxiously alert to detect any direct or indirect references to the Marlboroughs, that he and Marchmont must have gone through Pope's papers. What did they find? Apparently they did not find the character of Marlborough, as Warburton had that.[4] But almost certainly they did find a MS. of the character of Atossa, and in the circumstances, knowing that Pope had satirized the Marlboroughs, suspecting everything, they can hardly be blamed for having thought Atossa was intended for the Duchess. The MS. was presumably destroyed. When a few days later Bolingbroke also found the character in print in *Epistles to Several Persons*, a new problem was raised. Were they to destroy that too? Bolingbroke wrote to Marchmont to ask his opinion. Marchmont's reply has not survived,

1. *A Selection from the Papers of the Earls of Marchmont*, 1831, II 332–3.

2. Spence, p. 143.

3. Bolingbroke's and Marchmont's anxiety to help the Duchess may have been stimulated by financial expectations. A codicil added to her will in August 1744 appointed Marchmont one of the two executors and left two manors to him. Bolingbroke was not a beneficiary.

4. Spence, p. 366.

but no doubt he recommended that the edition should be suppressed. And apparently this was done.[1]

The next step in the growth of the Atossa legend was the publication of the character early in February 1746 under the title *Verses Upon the Late D—ss of M — — —. By Mr. P — — — —.* This six-page leaflet has a final note:

"These Verses are Part of a Poem, entitled *Characters of Women.* It is generally said, the D—ss gave Mr. *P.* 1000 l. to suppress them: He took the Money, yet the World sees the Verses; but this is not the first Instance where Mr. *P's* practical Virtue has fallen very short of those pompous Professions of it he makes in his Writings."

It is now generally agreed that the author or inspirer of this publication was Bolingbroke. In 1746 Bolingbroke was busy reviling Pope's reputation as a result of his discovery that Pope had secretly printed a whole edition of his *Patriot King.* Bolingbroke, in Courthope's words, "was one of a very few persons who knew at this date that Pope had intended to publish the character of Atossa; and he was the only one of them who had any grudge against Pope; so that the concoction of the footnote to the anonymous folio sheet looks like a deliberate conspiracy, on his part, against the poet's reputation."[2]

At about the same time that *Verses Upon the Late D—ss of M — — —* was published, a more elaborate version of the identical scandal was being circulated in society. William Cole heard the story from Horace Walpole and entered it, and the Atossa lines, into a blank page of his edition of Pope:

"The following Verses, made by M[r]. Pope upon Sarah late Duchess of Marlborow, & shown to her by one who was employed by him for that purpose, had such an Effect upon her y[t] she sent him a Present of a thousand pounds, upon w[ch]. he never printed them: but they were found in his Study after his Death: it is moreover said that he shewed y[m]. alternately to y[e] Duchesses of Buckingham & Marlborow, & pretended y[t]. they were design'd for y[e] different Character to whom he at that time showed them. They are authentic & I had them fr. y[e] Hon: Horatio Walpole Esq[r]. 3[d]. Son to y[e] late Earl of Orford 1745."[3] By 1745 Cole may have meant 1745/6. In that case Walpole's story may simply have been an embellished version of the leaflet's, though Cole's version of the lines unquestionably derives from *Epistles to Several Persons* rather than from *Verses Upon the Late D—ss of M — — —.*

The legend, with minor variations of detail, turns up again and again in the eighteenth century. Walpole entered it into his copy of *Additions to Pope* (Huntington marginalia, p. 484), and it is also to be found in his *Works.*[4]

---

1. See Introduction, p. xiii above.

2. EC, III 79.

3. Cole's copy (*The Works of Alexander Pope. Vol. II,* 1736) was presented to the Bodleian Library by the late B. H. Newdigate.

4. Cole's little comedy of the lines being passed off to each Duchess in turn as a portrait of the other receives some confirmation in what Warburton told

Warton has it in his edition of Pope (*Works*, III). The Duchess of Portland, Warton's immediate source, put it into her note-books (see EC, III 79). And it may be recorded elsewhere. It was natural that so spicy a piece of gossip should continue to be repeated. In all its various shapes and forms, however, the story is substantially the same, and in none of its stages are any confirmatory details introduced.

The possibility that Pope did indeed write a character of the Duchess of Marlborough, which contributed some lines to Atossa, may now be considered. The phrase "others are still wanting" in Pope's note on the restoration of the missing characters suggests that at an early stage of the poem such a character may well have existed. More positive evidence, however, is provided by a statement made to Spence in August 1744 by Anne Arbuthnot, the daughter of Pope's old friend, who became an old friend herself: "In the Satire on Women there was a character of the old Duchess of Marlborough, under the name of Orsini, written before Mr. Pope was so familiar with her, and very severe."[1] The anecdote carries conviction because of the aptness of the name Orsini as a satiric label for the Duchess Sarah. Marie Anne de la Trémoille (1642–1722) was the widow of Flavio Orsini, Duke of Bracciano, and later assumed the title Princess de Orsini. The Princess dominated the court of Philip V of Spain for many years, much as the Duchess of Marlborough had dominated the English court, and like her she was eventually expelled by a queen of her own making (on Philip's remarriage). The exactness of the parallel would seem to guarantee the character's authenticity, and if Anne Arbuthnot knew of it Bolingbroke and others, including perhaps the Duchess herself, must also have known of its existence. If so, the situation at Pope's death becomes comprehensible. By then Pope would have presumably destroyed the Orsini lines. If they were indeed "very severe" they could clearly never be made public *after* his "being so familiar with her".

In these circumstances the Duchess's anxiety and Bolingbroke's confusion of the Orsini lines and the Atossa lines would both be natural. But Bolingbroke's mistake becomes even more understandable if the Atossa actually included lines that he had read some fifteen years or so earlier in the Orsini. There is one crucial couplet that Bolingbroke would have met in the Atossa MS. (which may be assumed to have been more or less the same in 1735, if not earlier, as the Prince of Wales text) that is not in the "death-bed" or later editions:

Spence (p. 364) in 1755: "Read his character of the Duchess of Marlborough to her, as that of the Duchess of Buckingham; but she spoke of it afterwards, and said she knew very well whom he meant." Spence was in the habit of recording whatever he was told in his own words and the phrase "his character of the Duchess of Marlborough" may be Spence's interpolation. (But the interpolation would nevertheless be evidence of Bolingbroke's success in persuading Pope's world that Atossa was that Duchess.)

1. Spence, p. 364. See Sherburn, II 461.

> Thus, while her Palace rises like a Town,
> Atossa cheats the Lab'rer of a crown.

The Duchess of Marlborough's battles, in and out of the law-courts, over the costs of the erection of Blenheim Palace were common knowledge, and the character of Orsini would not have been complete without some reference to them. On the other hand, Buckingham House had been finished before Katherine Darnley became Duchess of Buckinghamshire.[1] It is perhaps significant that Warburton did not print the couplet among the "Variations" in his edition (1751), although the other discarded lines from the Prince of Wales text of Atossa appear there.

But if the character of Atossa at one time included two lines that had originally been meant for that of Orsini, may it not have included others? For example, "Full sixty years the World has been her Trade" (l. 123)? The Duchess of Marlborough first came to court in 1673 and, if this was originally an Orsini line written about 1733-4 (the suppressed character of Marlborough *was* written in 1734[2]), the "sixty years" would make excellent sense. Applied to the Duchess of Buckinghamshire, who was only sixty-one when she died in 1743, they are nonsense. Bolingbroke's mistake in confusing such Orsini parts with the Atossa whole is intelligible, if not pardonable. That so many of his contemporaries shared the illusion was no doubt due to the general similarity between the two Duchesses. Horace Walpole, a representative opinion, considered "old Sarah" just as mad and proud as "Princess Buckingham".[3]

APPENDIX B

TIMON AND THE DUKE OF CHANDOS

The character of Timon (*To Burlington*, ll. 99–168) raises almost as many problems as that of Atossa. The verdict of Pope's contemporaries was summarized by Johnson:

> By Timon he was universally supposed, and by the Earl of Burlington, to whom the poem is addressed, was privately said, to mean the Duke of Chandos; a man perhaps too much delighted with pomp and show, but of a temper kind and beneficent, and who had consequently the voice of the publick in his favour.

> A violent outcry was therefore raised against the ingratitude and treachery of Pope, who was said to have been indebted to the patronage of Chandos for a present of a thousand pounds, and who gained the opportunity of insulting him by the kindness of his invitation.

---

1. See Vinton A. Dearing, *Harvard Library Bulletin*, 1950, IV 331.
2. See vol. VI of this edition, p. 359.   3. *Letters*, ed. Toynbee, I 331.

The receipt of the thousand pounds Pope publickly denied; but from the reproach which the attack on a character so amiable brought upon him, he tried all means of escaping. The name of Cleland was again employed in an apology, by which no man was satisfied; and he was at last reduced to shelter his temerity behind dissimulation, and endeavour to make that disbelieved which he never had confidence openly to deny. He wrote an exculpatory letter to the Duke, which was answered with great magnanimity, as by a man who accepted his excuse without believing his professions. He said, that to have ridiculed his taste or his buildings had been an indifferent action in another man, but that in Pope, after the reciprocal kindness that had been exchanged between them, it had been less easily excused.[1]

How his editors and biographers have hated Pope! Johnson, the Christian moralist, who professed to be an admirer, is just as delighted to believe the worst of Pope as the Rev. William Lisle Bowles and the Rev. Whitwell Elwin. In fact, as Professor George Sherburn has shown in a remarkable article,[2] Johnson's charges are a pack of lies. (i) Burlington did *not* say that Timon was the Duke of Chandos. (ii) The Duke was *not* a popular favourite but rather the reverse. (iii) The Duke hardly knew Pope and never made him any present. (iv) Pope's "apology" in the newspapers was *not* made in the name of Cleland (though one of the letters when reprinted some years later in *some* editions of Pope's correspondence was headed "Mr. Cleland to Mr. Gay"). (v) Chandos's letter (reprinted in the Introduction, p. xxviii above) was really couched in the friendliest terms and bears no resemblance whatever to Johnson's alleged summary. On the other hand, Pope's own statements about the poem have been substantiated in almost every detail by recent research. An example is the account of the episode he gave Spence about 1734:

When there was so much talk about the Duke of Chandos being meant under the character of Timon, Mr. Pope wrote a letter to that nobleman: (I suppose to point out some particulars which were incompatible with his character.) The Duke in his answer, said, "he took the application that had been made of it, as a sign of the malice of the town against himself;" and seemed very well satisfied that it was not meant for him.[3]

The discovery of Chandos's Letter Books, now in the Huntington Library, California, has provided a remarkable confirmation of the accuracy of this précis of the Duke's letter. There is really no reason to think that Pope had anybody in particular in mind when he created Timon.[4] Timon is a composite

---

1. *Lives of the Poets*, III 152–3.
2. " 'Timon's Villa' and Cannons'', *Huntington Library Bulletin*, no. 8, October 1935.
3. Spence, p. 145.
4. The alternative form "Vatia" (instead of "Timon"), which Pope was contemplating at one time (see p. xxvii above) may—or may not—confirm the appar-

portrait, and if, as is possible, Chandos's "Cannons" provided Pope with one or two details, so did Blenheim and a dozen other of the "stately piles" in which the Augustan oligarchs were accomplishing their ritual of conspicuous waste.[1]

Pope's poem was published on 13 December 1731 and the first printed attack on him for his alleged ingratitude to Chandos did not come until 21 December. (It was by one of the dunces, John Henley, in his *Hyp-Doctor*.) Oral gossip, however, must have been busy before this, and on 23 December *The Daily Journal* printed two unsigned letters "To J. G. Esq." (dated 16 and 19 December) which represent Pope's defence.[2] Pope also wrote privately to Burlington on 21 December, and to Aaron Hill on 22 December 1731 and 5 February 1731/2. And on 27 January 1731/2 he prefixed an open letter to Burlington to the third edition of the poem. The anonymous "A Master Key to Popery or A True and Perfect Key to Pope's Epistle to the Earl of Burlington" can also be confidently ascribed to Pope. This ironical attack, dating from about February 1731/2 or a little later, was apparently never printed, but a MS. copy in Lady Burlington's hand is preserved at Chatsworth. It is given in Appendix C below. Pope's last words on the matter are in the note to the *Epistle to Arbuthnot*, l. 375. The case against Pope was (i) that he should not have ridiculed so deserving a person as Chandos, (ii) that his conduct was especially disgraceful as Chandos was his friend and had given him a large sum of money.[3] The second charge is quite without foundation. Chandos figures in Gay's "Mr.

---

ent impersonality of the character. The historical Vatia had retired to his villa to be out of harm's way in a manner vaguely paralleling Chandos's behaviour. The fact that none of the surviving autograph drafts of the poem include the Timon passage may—or may not—also be significant. If the draft had contained any libellous, or quasi-libellous, lines, their destruction would have been an elementary precaution once the dimensions of the Chandos row were realized by Pope.

1. Rendcomb, Gloucestershire, "a large handsome new-built house with pleasant beautiful gardens, and a large park adjoining" (Sir Robert Atkyns, *The Ancient and Present State of Glostershire*, 1712, *s.v.*), can probably be included in the list. Rendcomb was the seat of Sir John Guise (d. 1732), who had deeply resented his sister's marriage to Pope's friend Edward Blount (*Memoirs of the Family of Guise*, ed. G. Davies, Camden Soc., 3rd ser., XXVIII 142–3), and is ridiculed by Pope in "Duke upon Duke" (see vol. VI, pp. 217–24). In a letter to Blount, 3 October 1721 (Sherburn, II 86), Pope describes "the Mansion, Walls, and Terraces; the Plantations, and Slopes" of Rendcomb, which he has just seen. An engraving by Kip in *Britannia Illustrata* (vol. II, 1716) confirms Rendcomb's symmetrical formality at the time; it was "landscaped" later in the century (engraving in Samuel Rudder, *A New History of Gloucestershire*, 1779).

2. They had been "incorrectly printed" as a single undated letter in *The Daily Post-Boy*, 22 December 1731. See Sherburn, III 254–7.

3. £500 was the figure mentioned by Welsted (see *Epistle to Arbuthnot*, 375*n*), not £1,000, as reported by Johnson.

Pope's Welcome from Greece", but he knew Pope only slightly and the story of the present is probably a distortion of the fact that Chandos had taken twelve sets of the *Iliad* (seventy-two guineas). The main charge is more difficult to disprove *in toto*. Pope's portrait of Timon is clearly, as Pope claimed, a synthesis of a large number of wealthy offenders against taste—a category that certainly included Chandos. But that Pope intended Timon as a portrait of Chandos is most unlikely. For one thing Chandos, though only an acquaintance of Pope's, was an intimate friend of many of Pope's best friends, including Burlington, Bathurst, Bolingbroke, and Arbuthnot. Moreover the resemblances between Timon's villa and Cannons have been greatly exaggerated; details are discussed in the notes under the separate lines. Professor Sherburn prints letters of Chandos to Pope and others which make it clear that Chandos did not doubt Pope's innocence, though the third Duke told Warton that his grandfather was thought to be not "perfectly satisfied" with Pope's asseverations. The Burlingtons too never suspected Pope. Indeed, judging from such letters as have survived, many of the fashionable world would seem to have accepted Pope's version of the affair. Orrery's letter to Lady Kaye, 27 December 1731, is typical: "The censures on Mr. P are universal and severe; none to take his part, and all out of envy or, you may suppose, judgment, running him down. He has wrote too many things that have afforded me much pleasure, for me to join in this clamorous throng, nor dare I speak my opinion of so powerful a man, but under your Ladyship's roof in Bond Street. I see he has vindicated himself (or endeavoured at it) in the Daily Journal, I think of last Friday. I hope he'll not be so intimidated as never to write again, for tho' his enemies are powerful in their tongues, they are not so in their pens."[1]

Pope seems to have intended the name Timon to connote ostentatious magnificence rather than misanthropy. Both qualities were equally prominent in Shakespeare's Timon. The plausibility of the application of the name to Chandos was, as Hill pointed out to Pope, 23 December 1731, "a present reverse, (as is reported) to the splendor of that great man's fortune". Hill was referring to Chandos's losses in the Royal African Company, which are also mentioned in Swift's "The Dean and Duke" (1734):

> Since all he got by Fraud, is lost by Stocks,
> His wings are clipp't; he tryes no more in vain
> With Bands of Fidlers to extend his Treyn.[2]

Pope has another Timon in *Imit. Hor., Ep.*, ɪ vi, 85–8,

> His Wealth brave Timon gloriously confounds;
> Ask'd for a groat, he gives a hundred pounds;
> Or if three Ladies like a luckless Play,
> Takes the whole House upon the Poet's day.

1. Hist. MSS. Comm., xi, App. V, pp. 327–8.
2. *Poems*, ed. H. Williams, ɪɪ 678.

This later Timon has so far not been identified; Croker's suggestion of the Duke of Wharton, improbable enough in itself, depended upon the report that Wharton had given Young £2,000,[1] but this is now known to have been denied by Young.[2] It is clear that this Timon is a real person, and it seems probable that the allusion was intended to divert the old suspicions about Chandos to somebody else whom Pope did not mind offending. A clue that has so far been overlooked is Mottley's statement that the younger Thomas Killigrew's comedy *Chit-Chat* (1719) owed its success to "the Duke of Argyll, a great Friend to the Author, whose Interest was so powerfully supported, that it was said the Profits of his Play amounted to above a Thousand Pounds".[3] Did Pope intend John Campbell, second Duke of Argyll (1678–1743) to be taken for Timon? Argyll, who was one of the most distinguished soldiers of the day, was eminently "brave", was immensely wealthy, had recently built a showy mansion at Sudbrook, near Richmond, and, though an acquaintance, as a keen Whig (until 1738) would have been politically obnoxious to Pope. Moreover the "three Ladies" are almost certainly that famous trio the Misses Bellenden, Lepell, and Griffin who were celebrated by Pope in "The Court Ballad" (1716–17) and who had already sent Gay a purse of gold in token of the pleasure his comedy, *Three Hours after Marriage* (January 1716/17), in which Pope and Arbuthnot had helped Gay, had given them. They were then Maids of Honour to the Princess of Wales and Killigrew was one of the Prince's Gentlemen of the Bedchamber. Argyll is known to have been on the friendliest terms with the three Maids, and his cousin (later the fourth Duke) married Miss Bellenden in 1720. The identification of the later Timon with Argyll would also explain a puzzling item of gossip recorded by Warton on *Epilogue to Satires II*, 86–7: "The two lines on *Argyle* are said to have been added, on the duke's declaring in the House of Lords, on occasion of some of Pope's satires, that if any man dared to use his name in an invective, he would run him through the body, and throw himself on the mercy of his peers, who, he trusted, would weigh the provocation."[4] Warton's anecdote seems to imply that Pope had been satirizing Argyll, but not by name. But where? No allusion has hitherto been detected. Argyll's bluster would, however, be understandable if he had recognized himself—or thought that he had—in Timon. Unfortunately little or nothing seems to be known about the early history of Sudbrook and its gardens.[5] Horace Walpole was often there and it was generally thought "charming".[6] Norman Ault has an informative chapter on "Pope and Argyle" in his *New Light on Pope* (1949).

---

1. Spence, p. 255.   2. Sherburn, *Early Career*, p. 6.

3. *A Compleat List of all the English Dramatic Poets*, p. 255, appended to Whincop's *Scanderbeg*, 1747.

4. *Essay*, II 357.   5. *Victoria County History of Surrey*, III 529.

6. *The Works of Sir Charles Hanbury Williams* (1822), I 31.

APPENDIX C

"A MASTER KEY TO POPERY"

THIS amusing "irony" was discovered by the General Editor at Chatsworth and was published by him in *Pope and his Contemporaries: Essays presented to George Sherburn* (1949).[1] Although unsigned there can be no doubt that it is by Pope. Lady Burlington, in whose hand the MS. is, seems to have acted more than once in the early 1730's as Pope's unpaid copyist, and the internal evidence points directly to Pope. Some of the more important items of evidence have already been discussed in the Introduction, pp. xxx–xxxii above. Two additional points may be made here:

(i) The anonymous author does not confine his attacks to people already satirized by Pope, such as Mrs Haywood, Breval, Moore Smythe, Concanen, Welsted, Theobald, Cibber, and Goode. He also attacks a number of people whom Pope had not yet satirized in print, but who were shortly to appear in one or more of Pope's satires. Examples of this are Bubb Dodington, Henry Kelsall, Sir Gilbert Heathcote, Peter Walter (these identifications are certain), and *probably* Lord Hervey, Sir William Yonge, and Lord Cadogan.

(ii) The discrepancies between "Timon's Villa" and the Duke of Chandos's "Cannons", as pointed out in the third paragraph of p. 185, bear a striking resemblance to the following passage in the second letter "To J. G. Esq." which was printed (unsigned) in *The Daily Journal* for 23 December 1731 and is now generally accepted as Pope's (Sherburn, III 257):

> Is his Garden crowded with *Walls*? Are his Trees cut into *Figures of Men*? Do his Basons want *Water*? Are there *ten steep Slopes* of his Terrass? Is he piqued about *Editions* of *Books*? Does he exclude all *Moderns* from his *Library*? Is the *Musick* of his Chapel bad, or *whimsical*, or *jiggish*?

And an even closer parallel is provided by a passage in Pope's letter to Aaron Hill of 5 February 1731/2 (Sherburn, III 268):

> I'll only just tell you, that many Circumstances you have heard, as Resemblances to the Picture of *Timon*, are utterly Inventions of Lyars; the Number of Servants never was an Hundred, the Paintings not of *Verrio* or *La Guerre*, but *Bellucci* and *Zaman*; no such Buffet, Manner of Reception at the Study, Terras, &c. all which, and many more, they have not scrupled to forge, to gain some Credit to the Application.

The MS. is undated, but it is possible to determine the date of composition of *A Master Key* within fairly narrow limits. It can hardly have been written before January 1731/2, and if the discussion of Babo on p. 182 derives, as it

---

1. It is printed here by permission of the Chatsworth Estates Company. The notes signed JB incorporate new material derived from Professor Butt's article.

Q

seems to, from *A Miscellany On Taste*, which was only published on 15 January 1731/2, it cannot have been written before the second half of the month. The reference to "Faux-hall" on p. 183 provides a *terminus ad quem*. After June 1732 when Jonathan Tyers opened the new Gardens with a *Ridotto al' fresco*, at which the Prince of Wales was present, Vauxhall could not possibly be called a "Scene of Lewdness". The reference must be to its earlier and more unsavoury reputation when it was still the Spring Garden. On the whole, February 1731/2 seems to me the best guess. I base it largely on the coincidence between *A Master Key* and the letter to Aaron Hill. Both make the points that there were not a hundred servants at Cannons and that the paintings in the chapel were by Bellucci and Zeeman instead of Verrio and Laguerre. In none of his previous pronouncements on the subject, public or private, had Pope made these points (which were clearly good ones)—presumably because he had only just acquired the information (perhaps through Arbuthnot, who was an old friend of Chandos's). On the other hand, Pope is still angry in *A Master Key*. The sore is still open and running. It must have been written fairly soon after he had discovered one acquaintance after another engaging in the whispering campaign against him. The controlled icy contempt that he displays in the first *Imitation of Horace* (*Sat.*, ii i), written in January 1732/3, was still a mood of distant achievement.[1]

A Master Key to Popery
or
A True and Perfect Key to Pope's Epistle to the Earl of Burlington

I have undertaken at the Request of Several Persons of Quality, the Explanation of a piece very loudly and justly complain'd of; or more properly a Dissection of the Bad Heart of the Author. It cannot be displeasing to any Man of Honour, to see the same Fair Opinions and good Reasons in *Print* which he has vented & propagated in all Conversations: It must be pleasing, to see here the *Proofs* of many Charges against him, which have hitherto been advanc'd without full demonstration: And it must be an additional Satisfaction to find him guilty of many *others*, which I shall prove, upon the *Same Principles*.

The Poet's Design is two-fold, to *affront* all the *Nobility & Gentry*, and to *Starve*

---

1. Professor Butt (*Pope and his Contemporaries*, 1949, pp. 43–4) had reached the same conclusion independently. He points out that the ascription to Welsted of "the most *considerable writings*" on the topic (p. 172) implies Pope's knowledge of *both* Welsted's poems attacking him for his ingratitude to Chandos—*Of Dullness and Scandal* (published 3 January 1731/2) and *Of False Fame* (published 10 February 1731/2). The latter was advertised on 3 February 1731/2, which is therefore the *terminus a quo* for the date of composition of this passage. Butt regards the passage in the letter to Aaron Hill of 5 February as a "summary of the arguments used" in it.

all the *Artisans* & *Workmen* of this Kingdom. Under pretence of destroying the *Vanity* of the former, he aims to ruin the *Support* of the latter; and by rend'ring the Patrons discontented with all such works, put a Stop to the Arts, & obstruct the Circulation of Money, in this Nation, to Send a begging the Industrious Mechanicks we have at home, & introduce Italians, Frenchmen, Papists & Foreigners, in their Stead.

I appeal to all my Superiors, if any thing can be more insolent than thus to Break (as I may say) into their Houses & Gardens, Not, as the Noble Owners might expect, to *Admire*, but to *laugh* at them? or if any thing can be more Grating and vexatious, to a Great Peer or an Opulent Citizen, than to see a Work, of the expence of twenty or thirty thousand pounds, which he thought an Ornament to the Nation, appear only a Monument of his own Folly? Insolent Scribler! that being unable to tax Men of their Rank & Worth with any Vice or Fault beside, is reduced to fall upon their *Taste* in those polite Expences & elegant Structures which are the Envy of all other Nations, and the Delight of our own![1] God forbid, it should hinder any of those Magnificent Persons, from enjoying their Noble Fancies, & delighting in their own Works! May every Man *Sit peaceably Under his own Vine*,[2] in his own Garden; May every *Man's House be his Castle*,[3] not only against Thieves, but against *Ill Eyes* & Envious Observers; and may those who have succeeded the worst, meet with a better fate than to be at once *Ill-lodg'd* & Ridiculed.

To avoid the imputation of any Envy against this Poet, I shall first confess that I think he has some Genius, and that it is *Only his Morals* that I attack.

But what seems very unaccountable is, that A Man of any *Genius* (which one wou'd think has its foundation in *Comon Sense*) shou'd be the *Greatest Fool* in his age, & constantly choose for the Objects of his Satire, the Best Friends he has? All the Noblemen whom we shall prove him to abuse in this Epistle are such, whose Esteem and Distinction he seem'd most to Court, & to possess; or whose Power and Influence cou'd best protect or credit him: Nay all the Criticks who have been most provok'd at it, are such, as either had been his Friends or call'd themselves so, or had made some pretence to his Acquaintance or Correspondence.

---

1. Burlington's short preface in Italian to Palladio's *Fabriche Antiche* (1730) includes the claim, advanced in all seriousness, that no other period in history had exhibited "maggiore disposizione a dispendiose Fabriche". But no other period had "più ignoranti Pretenditori che guidano altrui fuor delle vere Traccie di tanto bell' Arte".

2. Cf. *Henry VIII*, v v 34–5:

> every man shall eat in safety
> Under his own vine . . .

The original source is *Micah*, iv 4.

3. The proverb appears in this form in John Ray's *English Proverbs* (1670), p. 106.

It it [*sic*] to *some of these* that I am beholden for many In-lets into his *Meaning & Thoughts*: For a man's meanings & Thoughts lye too remote from any such, as cou'd make the discovery from *Private Conversation*, or some degree of *Confidence*, or *Familiarity*. The Honour & Veracity of such I will not doubt; especially of so honourable Persons as Lord Fanny,[1] Mr Dorimant,[2] the Lady De-la-Wit,[3] the Countess of Methusalem, & others.

I confess further, that I am in many instances, but the Collector of the dispers'd Remarks of his Majesty's Poet Laureat,[4] his Illustrious Associate Sr William Sweet-Lips,[5] the Lady Knaves-acre[6] & Mrs Haywood[7] (those ornaments of their Sex) and Capt. Breval,[8] and James Moore[9] Esqr: and Mr Con-

---

1. Probably Lord Hervey, though Pope's first use of the soubriquet in print, in *Imit. Hor.*, *Sat.*, II i, 6 (February 1732/3), is later than the probable date of composition of *A Master Key* (February 1731/2). Pope's relations with Lord Hervey are discussed in vol. IV of this edition, pp. xv–xxii, and by Robert W. Rogers, *The Major Satires of Alexander Pope* (1955), Appendix D.

2. Probably George Bubb Dodington (see *To Burlington*, 20n). Dorimant is the witty hero of Etherege's *The Man of Mode*, and Dodington was celebrated both for his wit and his magnificent clothes. Pope has a Dorimant again in *Imit. Hor.*, *Ep.*, I i, 88, who may also be Dodington. Cf. Atticus and Addison, Worldly and Wortley, etc.

3. Perhaps Mary Howard, Countess of Delorain (1700–44), a mistress of George II whom Pope was to attack in *Imit. Hor.*, *Sat.*, II i, 81 (February 1733). See vol. IV, p. 365. It is more likely that Lady Mary Wortley Montagu was intended. Butt quotes the MS. variant of *Epistle to Arbuthnot*, 369, "that dang'rous thing, a female wit".

4. Colley Cibber (1671–1757), appointed Poet Laureate December 1730 and an old enemy of Pope's (see vol. V, pp. 433–4).

5. Probably Sir William Yonge (d. 1755), the Whig politician, who was often satirized in Pope's later poems. The association with Cibber may allude to Yonge's contributing the songs to *The Jovial Crew*, a successful ballad opera produced by Cibber at Drury Lane in February 1730/1. Hervey's description of Yonge as "good-natured and good-humoured, never offensive in company" (*Memoirs*, p. 36), suggests that "Sweet-Lips" was an appropriate name to give him. See also *E. on Man*, IV 278n and vol. IV, p. 394.

6. I do not know who Pope intended Lady Knaves-Acre to represent. Her association with Eliza Haywood suggests that she may have been somebody with literary pretensions.

7. Eliza Haywood (1693?–1756), novelist, dramatist, and writer of scandalous memoirs. See vol. V, p. 443.

8. John Durant Breval (1680?–1738), one of the "dunces". See vol. V, pp. 430–1.

9. James Moore Smythe. See *To a Lady*, 243–8n and vol. V, p. 455.

canen,[1] & Mr Welsted,[2] and Henry K—y Esqr[3] of the two last of whom I ought in Justice to say, we owe to the one the most *considerable writings*, & to the other the *Longest Discourses* on this Subject.

My First Position is, that this Poet is a man of so *Bad* a *Heart*, as to stand an Exception to the Rule of Macchiavel, who says 'No Man, in any Nation, was ever Absolutely Wicked, *for nothing*.' Now this Poet being so, it is fair to Suppose, that of *two* or *more* persons whom he may be thought to abuse, we are always to understand it of the Man he is *most oblig'd to*: but in such cases where his obligations seem *equal*, we impartially suppose the Reflection on *both*. Secondly, when so malevolent a man draws any character consisting of *many Circumstances*, it must be apply'd, not to the person with whom *most* but with whom *fewest* of those Circumstances agree: And this for a plain reason, because it is a stronger mark of that Artifice & Cowardice on the one hand, and of that Injustice & Malice on the other, with which such a Writer abounds.

I am nevertheless so reasonable as not to insist as some Criticks on this occasion have done, that when a Circumstance will not suit with a Father, it shou'd be apply'd to a Son or Grandson, but I must insist on my two former Positions, upon which depends all which others have said, & which I shall say on this subject.

To begin with his Title, It was first, of *Taste*, Now 'tis of *false Taste*, to the Earl of Burlington.[4] Is this alteration made to impute False Taste to that Earl? or out of unwillingness to allow that there is any True Taste in the Kingdom?

Nothing is more certain, than that the Person first & principally abus'd is the said Earl of Burlington. He cou'd not well abuse him for *Want* of *Taste*, since the allowing it to him was the only Channel to convey his Malignity to others: But he abuses him for a *worse want*, the want of *Charity* (one from which his Lordship is as free as any man alive). This he tells him directly, without disguise, and in the second person,

---

1. Matthew Concanen (1701–49), a "dunce" who was suspected of a hand in the retaliatory *A Miscellany on Taste* (1732), ridiculing *To Burlington*. See p. 128 above and vol. v, pp. 434–5.

2. Leonard Welsted (1688–1747), a "dunce", who had published on 3 January 1731/2 a poem attacking Pope entitled *Of Dulness and Scandal. Occasion'd by the Character of Lord Timon*, and had followed this up on 10 February with the more offensive *Of False Fame*. See vol. v, p. 166.

3. Probably the "Kelsey" whose talkativeness is satirized in the later editions of *Dunciad* A, II 382. The MS. of that passage gives "Kelsall". Henry Kelsall (d. 1762) was one of the four Chief Clerks to the Treasury. Nothing is known about Kelsall's relations with Pope. He was clearly a staunch Whig, and the fact that he is always referred to as "Esquire" indicates that he was of gentle birth.

4. For the changes of title in Pope's poem see p. 128 above.

—What thy hard heart denies,
Thy charitable Vanity supplies.

So much for Malice; now for ill-nature,

Another age shall see the golden Ear
Imbrown *thy* Slope, and nod on *thy* Parterre,
Deep Harvest bury all *thy Pride* has plann'd,
And laughing Ceres re-assume the Land.

That is, 'My Lord, your Gardens shall soon be Plow'd up, & turned into Corn-fields.'

How he indulges himself in drawing this picture? and with what joy does he afterwards expatiate upon the mortifying Consideration, how all his Lordships labours in Architecture shall be lost, and his Models misapply'd by imitating Fools?

—Reverse your Ornaments & hang them all
On some patch'd Dog-hole &c

This is his Element! this his Pleasure! when he comes at last, with much ado, to com̄end the Noble Lord, how spareing, how short, is he! The whole is but two lines,

In you, my Lord, Taste Sanctifies Expence,
For Splendour borrows all her rays from *Sense*.

which amounts just to this, 'My Lord, you are no Fool.' but this we shall see by what follows, he thinks a great distinction for a Lord in these days.

Oft' have you hinted to your Brother Peer—
Something there is—'Tis Sense.—Good Sense.

A Hint does he call it? 'tis a very broad one, that there is a Want of Sense in his Brother Peers, that is to say, in the whole House of Lords. Mr Concanen[1] & Mr Theobald[2] (both Lawyers) are of opinion, this may be prosecuted as Scandalum Magnatum on the whole Collective Body. From what we have observ'd of his Prophecy of the Destruction of Chiswick Gardens,[3] it shou'd seem as if this wretch alluded to his Lordship's want of a *Male Heir*. If he had

---

1. Matthew Concanen was appointed Attorney-General of Jamaica 30 June 1732.

2. Lewis Theobald (1688–1744), the king of the "dunces", started life as an attorney but soon abandoned the law for literature.

3. Burlington's country house was at Chiswick. Gay's *Epistle to Burlington* (before 1720) begins

While you, my Lord, bid stately piles ascend,
Or in your *Chiswick* bow'rs enjoy your friend;
Where *Pope* unloads the boughs within his reach,
Of purple vine, blue plumb, and blushing peach.

one, he had been probably treated like another of his *Friends*, the Lord Bathurst[1]: whose noble Plantations at Cirencester he prophecy's with like Malignity shall be destroy'd & lay'd levell by his Lordships *Son*; for which no doubt, that ingenious and sober young Gentleman is much oblig'd to him.

> Thro' his young Woods how pleas'd Sabinus stray'd,
> Or sate delighted in the thick'ning Shade,
> With annual joy the red'ning shoots to greet,
> And see the stretching branches long to meet.
> His Son's fine Taste an op'ner Vista loves,
> Foe to the Dryads of his Fathers Groves;
> The thriving Plants ignoble Broomsticks made
> Now sweep those Allyes they were born to shade.

I wonder this piece of Malice has escap'd all the Criticks; and I suspect it was to screen this Author, that his gentle Friend Lord Fanny[2] apply'd to this Nobleman the Character of Villario

> His bloomy Beds a waving Glow display,
> Blushing in bright Diversities of Day,
> With silver-quiv'ring Rills mæander'd o'er,
> —Enjoy them you! Villario can no more:
> Tir'd with the Scene Parterre & Fountains yield,
> He finds at last he better likes a Field.

For first, my Lord Bathurst is known to be of the most constant temper in the world in all his Pleasures: Secondly, he never was a *Florist*, is so much an Enemy to *nice Parterres*, that he never mows, but grazes them, & thirdly, has no water at Cirencester to squander away in Mæanders. I should rather think we are still at Chiswick, abusing all my Ld Burlington's Friends & Neighbours. I know such a Garden, which has an Out-let too into the *Fields*, where this Nobleman sometimes takes the Air,[3] the name of Villario shews him to live near the Town; where Flowers & Parterres are most in Vogue; & (which is more with me than all other circumstances) where this very Author has been often receiv'd in a manner far superiour to his deserts.

The Houses of these two Lords have escaped Abuse, for a plain reason;

---

1. For Allen, Lord Bathurst, see p. 81 above. His eldest son Benjamin (1710?–67) was to marry in November 1732.

2. Lord Hervey.

3. Possibly the estate adjoining the Burlington estate at Chiswick. It was bought by Sir Stephen Fox in 1682, who built a house there on the site of the present great conservatory of Chiswick House. Pope's acquaintance, Spencer Compton, Earl of Wilmington (1673?–1743), the politician, lived there from 1728 until his death [JB].

neither of them wou'd be hurt by it—and the latter has by good fortune some
Works at present under the direction of the Earl of Burlington.[1]

We have now done with Chiswick, a Soyl so fruitfull of Satyr for the Poet,
that I tremble for the *Reverend Vicar* of the *Parish*! not only as he is his *Friend*,
but as his eminent Learning, & particularly in the *Greek*, must have made him
sorely obnoxious to him.[2]

Being arrived in Town, where should he begin but with the *Best*, *Good Man*
of the City, even the Father of the City, Sir Gilbert![3]

What brought Sr Shylocks ill-got wealth to waste!

There could not be invented a falser Slander, or one that would *more hurt* this
eminent Citizen, than to insinuate that he had *wasted his wealth*. 'Tis true, I
think as well as Sir Gilbert, that *every Expence is Some Waste*: yet surely so small
a sum, as ten pounds eleven shillings, for Iron Rails to secure his Court-yard,
ought never to have been thus pointed out & insulted? But what means he by
wealth ill-got? neither Sir G nor I know of any such thing. This is as errant
nonsense as what follows—*A Wealthy Fool*. How can that be? Wealth is the
proof of Wisdom, & to say that Sir G—'s wealth is wasted, is to say that his
Parts are decay'd.

See Sportive Fate—Bids Babo build—

Here the Cricks differ. Some read, for Babo, Bubo.[4] Others fix this on a Peer

---

1. F. Kimball, "Burlington Architectus", *Journal Royal Institute of British
Architects*, 15 October, 12 November 1927, does not record that Burlington ever
acted as Bathurst's architect, but it is *a priori* probable. Most of his friends con-
sulted Burlington when they had any building on hand.

2. The Vicar of Chiswick at this time was Thomas Wood (1681–1732). *Gent.
Mag.*, 1735, V 253, prints an epigram said to have been written by Pope on
Wood's presenting Kent, the architect and landscape-gardener protégé of Bur-
lington, with a copy of Evelyn's *Numismata*. (It is reprinted in vol. VI of this
edition, pp. 340–1.) Although Wood had been educated at Wadham College,
Oxford, I can find no contemporary confirmation of the depth of his Greek
scholarship. The shallowness of Pope's, for a translator of Homer, was an old jibe,
of course.

3. Sir Gilbert Heathcote (1652–1733), one of the founders of the Bank of
England and reputed to be the richest commoner in England. "Father of the
City" is the traditional soubriquet for the Senior Alderman of the City of Lon-
don. For Heathcote's reputation for parsimony see *To Bathurst*, 101*n*.

4. Until 1735 the printed editions of Pope's poem read "Babo" in l. 20.
"Bubo" is the reading of the Burlington MS. (an early draft of the poem) and
all the later editions. According to *A Miscellany on Taste* (1732), Babo was "Lord
C–d–n", i.e., presumably, Charles, second Baron Cadogan (1691–1776). By
Bubo Pope undoubtedly meant Bubb Dodington.

who I confess is noble enough for our Authors abuse; but (what I always take for a cause to doubt it) one to whom he has no sort of Obligation. Tis certain Sh—d is this Nobleman's Builder, but why should he satyrize Sh—d? Sh—d is none of his *Friends*. I am persuaded that by Sh—d he means *Gibs* with whom he is acquainted.[1]

The next we shall take notice of is the only Person he seems willing to praise, & perhaps loves (if he loves anybody) the Lord Cobham. Yet when he speaks of his Gardens or some other of his L^{d}ships personal performances (for I am not clear of which) what a filthy stroke of smut has he bestowed upon him?

> Parts answ'ring Parts, shall slide into a *whole*

As if his L^{d}sps fine Gardens were to be just such another Scene of Lewdness as Cupids Gardens or Faux-hall.[2]—I ought not to suppress, that I owe this Remark to a Right Honourable Lady.

Here we have a fling at honest Bridgeman. I don't wonder to see his name at length, for he is his particular Acquaintance. What a Malicious Representation of one who lives by his profession, as taking pleasure to destroy and overflow Gentlemens fine Gardens!

> The vast Parterres a thous^d hands shall make
> Lo Bridgeman comes, & floats them with a Lake.

As if he should have the Impudence, when a Gentleman has done a wrong thing at a great Expence, to come & pretend to make it a right one? Is it not his business to please Gentlemen? to execute Gentlemen's will and Pleasure, not his own? is he to set up his own Conceits & Inventions against Gentlemen's fine Taste & Superiour Genius? Yet is this what the Poet suggests, with intent (doubtless) to take the Bread out of his mouth, & ruin his Wife & Family.

We come now to the Character (or rather Description) of Timon: and it is in this I shall principally labour, as it has chiefly employ'd the pains of all the Criticks. I shall enumerate the several opinions of all others, & shew the Malice & Personal Reflection to extend much farther than has hitherto been imagin'd

---

1. James Gibbs (1682–1754), a distinguished architect; he was probably to have been the architect of the town house that Pope was thinking of building in 1718. "Sh—d" is Edward Sheppard or Shepherd (d. 1747) who had recently designed Covent Garden Theatre (opened 3 December 1733) and was probably the architect of Cadogan's country seat at Caversham, Oxfordshire, which was built in 1718.

2. "Faux-hall" is, of course, Vauxhall. Pope's allusion, however, is not to the famous Gardens of Jonathan Tyers, which were only opened in June 1732, but to their less fashionable precursor on the same site, the old Spring Garden described in *Spectator*, no. 383. "Cupid's Gardens", *recte* "Cuper's Gardens" (from Boydell Cuper, who opened them *c.* 1680), were at Lambeth, exactly opposite Somerset House.

by any. It is shewing the Author great & undeserv'd Indulgence to confine it
to any One, tho' that one were the Best Man in the world: There are so many
By-peeps & squinting Glances, besides the main View, that instead of twenty
things being aim'd at one, every one Circumstance is aim'd at twenty.

I must first take notice of the greatest Authorities which seem against me,
and great ones they are indeed, Sir William Sweet-lips and Mr Dorimant.[1]
Equal Genius's! Equal Judges! every way equal Ornaments to their Country!
the Mecænas, & the Phoebus of our Age! and to both of whom our Poet has
been indebted for as great Commendation & Praise as was consistent with their
own Superiority. In order to give due Weight to their several arguments, I
must take a View of Timon's character in all its Circumstances.

A Proud, haughty Man, with no other Idea of Greatness but Bulk and Size,
but himself a little contemptible Creature. His House consists of Unequal
Parts, heap'd one upon another like a Quarry of Stones. His Gardens are
choak'd up with Walls, every where in sight, which destroy all Appearance of
Natural Beauty. The Form of his Plantation is stiffly regular, & the same
repeated. A vast Lake-fall to the North: an immense Parterre with two Small
Cupids in it: Trees cut into human figures, & statues as close as Trees: his
Fountains without Water: a Terras of Steep Slopes with a Study opening upon
it, where he receives his guests with the utmost Affectation: his Books chosen
for their Printers or Binders, no good Modern Books, & (to make them perfectly
a Show) the upper Shelves only Wooden and painted ones. He has a Chappel,
with Musick & Painting in it, but the Musick consists of Jigs and loose Airs, and
the painting of indecent or naked figures. He gives Entertainments attended by
an hundred Servants, in a Hall paved with Marble; his Bufet is ornamented
with Serpents & Tritons; his Dinner is a solemn, formal, troublesome thing,
with perpetual rounds of Salvers & Sweet wine, & upon the whole with so
much Pride & affected State, as to make every man Sick both of his Dinner
& of Him.

This is the Character, which Mr Dorimant, M^r K—y,[2] the Lord Fanny, have
imputed to the D. of C.[3] This is what has been affirmed with Oaths by M^r
C—r[4] and very publickly by Mr Theobalds, Mr Goode,[5] Mr James Moore, the
whole Herd of Criticks, & all the honourable Gentlemen of the Dunciad.

---

1. Possibly Sir William Yonge and Bubb Dodington (see p. 178, notes 2, 5).
Dodington, the patron of Young, Thomson, Fielding, Glover, and Whitehead,
was certainly a "Mecænas"; Yonge's claim to being a "Phoebus" rested on the
songs contributed to *The Jovial Crew* and such trifles as "A Ballad Occasioned
by the enlarging of the House of Office at the D. of D—'s Seat in Sussex, for the
Accommodation of three Ladies at once" (*Gent. Mag.*, 1736, p. 103).

2. Henry Kelsall (see p. 179, note 3).

3. Duke of Chandos.   4. Colley Cibber.

5. Barnham Goode (1674–1739), another "dunce". See vol. v of this edition,
p. 441.

I have the greatest temptation imaginable to wish this could be proved. Nothing would be so high an instance of this Man's Wickedness as to fix the worst-natured Satire on the best-natured Man; to tax with Pride the most Affable, with Vanity the most Charitable, with the worst Choice of Books one of the most Learned of our Nobility, with the Pride of Prayer one of the sincerest Worshippers of God, and with ill-judged Extravagance one of the most hospitable and hearty Lovers of his Neighbour.[1]

This would have been such a Pleasure to me, that I thought no pains too great to procure it; and therefore (out of my great Love to Truth, & for the same reason that Pythagoras and Plato travel'd into Ægypt) I took a Journey to C–n–ns.[2] I may venture to say, few Criticks have been at the trouble: & yet it is impossible to judge exactly of this Authors Spite & Malice, without being at the pains, both of knowing the place, & of reading the Poem.

I went first to the Chappel: I ask'd after the *Musick*; they told me there had been none for several years. I ask'd for the *Dean*, there was no such Man. I enquir'd for the *hundred servants*, there had been no such number. There was no *Silver Bell*; no Paintings of Verrio or La guerre, but of Bellucci or Zeman[3]; no Study opening on a Terras, but up one pair of stairs; no Books dated on the back or painted, and as many Modern as Ancient ones. In the Garden, no Walls crossing the eye, no large Parterre at all, no little Cupids, no Lake to the North, no cut Trees, no such Statues, no such Terras; in a word, no one Particular resembling: only what is common to all great Men, there was a large House, a Garden, a Chappel, a Hall, and a Dinner.

I must declare Not One of these Circumstances to be True, which *so many Gentlemen have affirm'd upon their own Knowledge*. I am sensible of the Consequence of giving *Gentlemen* the LYE, but it is ever held fair among *Criticks*, practis'd by the *most Learned* and both given & taken reputably by the best Authors.

Yet far be it from me to say, but in spite of the disagreement of All the Particulars, there may yet be Excellent Reasons for fixing the whole on the Duke. However it is but fair to report the Arguments on all sides. Timon (says one) was a Man-Hater, ergo it is not the Duke. But Mr Moore replys very wittily, Timon lov'd Mankind *before* he hated them, he did not hate men till they had *abus'd* him, and the Duke may now with some cause, for he has been *very much abused*. Timon was famous for Extravagancies, the Duke for well-judg'd Bounties; but Peter W—rs Esq.[4] argues thus. 'He that is bountifull: is 'not so rich as if he had never been bountifull: whatever a man parts with, he 'is so much the poorer for; & he that has but a hundred pounds less than he

---

1. All that is known of Chandos goes to show that he was indeed, as Johnson has said, "of a temper kind and beneficent" (*Lives of the Poets*, III 152).

2. Cannons, Chandos's mansion near Edgware.

3. See *To Burlington*, 145n.

4. Peter Walters or Walter (1664?–1746), the notorious moneylender, who was continually satirized by Pope. See *To Bathurst*, 20n.

'had, is in some decline of Fortune.' This he thinks a plain reason for any body to disesteem, or abuse a Man. And Mr Dorimant also thinks nothing so natural, as to *Desert* or *fall upon* a *Great Man* on the *first suspicion* of his *Decline* of *Fortune*. But certainly every Man of Honour who is what another-guess Author than this, in another-guess Epistle than this, describes himself,

In Power a Servant, out of Power a Friend,[1]

must feel the highest Indignation at such a practise. Indeed our Poets Enemies (and to such only I give Credit) have often severely lash'd him in sharp Satyrs & lively Ballads for the Contrary practise: for his adhering to some Folks in their Exile, to some in their disgrace, & others in their Imprisonment.[2] And I do think there is one good reason why he should rather attack a Man in Power, because it were a greater Object of his Envy, and a greater Proof of his Impudence.

Let us then hear Sir William (who thinks in this against the Majority, as he never sides with it, but on cogent reasons.) Why (says he) for God's sake may not this be Sir Robert?[3] are not his works as great as any man's? Who has more Groves nodding at Groves of his own plantation? I cannot say much as to his Chappel; but who has rival'd his Dinners? especially at the Time this Poem was publish'd, when he was splendidly entertaining the Duke of Lorain?[4] Has he not a Large Bufet? Has he not a hundred, nay near five hundred, Servants? (In power, your Servants) and who oftener drinks the King's Health? How convincing are all these circumstances! I defy the Partizans of the other opinion to match them. And yet there is one which convinces me more than all; the Author never Saw Houghton[5]: and how marvellously does it suit with his Impudence, to abuse the Things he never Saw?

But what principally inclines Sir William to this opinion is, that unless Sir Robert be abus'd here, he is not abus'd in the whole Poem, a thing which he thinks altogether Incredible. And I may add another reason which persuaded Mr Welsted (and doubtless will many others) that the Duke does not take this to himself, therefore it can do the Poet no hurt; unless we can fix it on another.

---

1. Pope is quoting from Bubb Dodington's *Epistle to The Right Honourable Sir Robert Walpole* (1726), p. 9. The line is also quoted in *To Cobham*, 161n., *Epilogue to Satires*, Dia. II 161, and an undated letter to Fortescue (Sherburn, II 294, V 2).

2. Atterbury, Harley, and Bolingbroke among others.

3. Sir William Yonge was one of Walpole's principal lieutenants in the House of Commons.

4. The Duke of Lorraine's visit to England, which aroused much public interest, had been from 13 October to 8 December 1731. The Duke later became the Emperor Francis I, the husband of Maria Theresa. On Monday, 15 November, the *Daily Journal* reported that his Serene Highness had returned to London from Sir Robert Walpole's seat in Norfolk [JB].

5. Walpole's magnificent country house in Norfolk. See *To Burlington*, 18n.

Furthermore, if (as some have suggested) this Malevolent Writer hates any man for Munificence to his Brethren, certainly Sir Robert of all Mankind must be the Man he hates. Tis true he never endeavour'd to obstruct that Munificence to any of them, but that is to be imputed to his Malice, as he thought those Distinctions would be no Credit to that great Minister.

Be it as it will, this Poet is equally happy when he can abuse either side. To shew his wicked Impartiality, at the same time he is squinting at Sir R. he has not spared his old Friend the Lord Bolingbroke.

> A gaping Triton spews to wash y^r face,

is the exact Description of the bufet at Dawley.[1] Nothing sure can equal the Impudence of such a Guest, except the Indifference of that stupid Lord, who they say is not provok'd at it. I doubt not the Honourable Mr Pulteney wou'd have had his share, but that he, poor Gentleman! has no Villa to abuse.[2]

I return to my first Position. The Extent of this mans malice is beyond being confin'd to any One. Every Thrust of his Satyr, like the Sword of a Giant tranfixes four or five, and serves up spitted Lords and Gentlemen with less ceremony than Skew'r'd Larks at their own Tables.

I am very sure that all he says of the Chappel, its Painting & its Musick, is to be apply'd to his Grace the Duke of R–tl–d's at Be—ir-Castle. Why not to several other Lords who have Musick in their Chappels, unless Organs be no Musick?

I am as certain that what follows was to ridicule the Dignity & the Dinners, the Solemnity and the Salvers, the numerous attendants & gaudy Sideboard, of a Nobleman (who to inhance the Ill-nature of the Satyr) has lay'd all his Vanities in the Grave. I mean the Companion in arms & Friend of the great Duke of Marleborough.[3]

I know that the Building describ'd to be so huge, so like a Quarry, such a Heap, &c. is the Immortal Castle of Blenheim (to which the Spite of a Papist may well be imagin'd) and I know my Lord F—th will be of my opinion. And possibly had not the Duke of Shrewsbury been once a Papist, he wou'd never have call'd it a *Quarry of Stone above-ground*: That well known saying of his fixes this to Blenheim.[4]

---

1. Pope had often stayed with Bolingbroke at Dawley Farm near Uxbridge. He was drinking asses' milk there in May 1731.

2. William Pulteney, later Earl of Bath (1684–1764), was notoriously parsimonious. Burlington's design for a "House with an Arcade" in Kent's *Designs of Inigo Jones* (1727) was for Pulteney, but apparently was not proceeded with.

3. Probably William, Earl Cadogan (1675–1726), a favourite *bête noire* of Pope's, who was Marlborough's quartermaster-general in the War of the Spanish Succession. See *To Bathurst*, 91, and Spence, pp. 154, 156, 163, 164.

4. See *To Burlington*, 109–10n. Charles Talbot, only Duke of Shrewsbury (1660–1718), was brought up as a Roman Catholic but became a Protestant in

Were it to be apply'd to a House and not a Castle, I should fancy it must be to one in Dorsetshire of the same Architect; It would be like this Poets Injustice, to reflect on a Gentleman's Taste for a thing which he was oblig'd to build on another Man's scheme—But this Gentleman's Taste is since fully vindicated, by what has been built on his own Directions, that most Genteel Pile in Pall-Mall, which is the Admiration of all Beholders.[1]

No, the Greater the Object, the Stronger is his malice. Greatness itself is his Aversion; nay he hates Pride for being only the Shadow of Greatness. From National Works he would proceed to Royal, if he durst. Who but must have observ'd in this light that monstrous Couplet?

—Proud Versailles! thy Glory falls,
And Nero's Terrasses desert their walls.

What an Impudent Reflection on the memory of Lewis the Fourteenth of France, and another Great Prince!

I hope the Zeal which has been shewn hitherto only in general against this Poet, may soon operate farther when the Three Estates are assembled, and Proper Pains and Penalties be found to repress such Insolence.

After all, it would seem unfair not to own, there is something at the end of his Epistle which looks like a Complement to the King: But sure 'tis a very strange one! just to single out the Only Good & great things which his Majesty has *Not* done for his Subjects. His Majesty may do them yet; but so much as I wish the Publick Good, I can hardly desire it should be just at the Time, when an Impertinent Poet prescribes it. No—may those Usefull and popular Works be first advised by such whose Office and Dignity it better agrees with, by Men less warp'd by Interest than he, less led by Party than he, less affected by Passion than he; in whom, the same suggestions, wch in him are doubtless Dis-affection & Malice, may be look'd upon as Affection & Loyalty: And who (tho' the Things propos'd be the same) may yet be better heard, & therefore may better deserve the Thanks of the Publick.

FINIS

1679. "Lord F—th" is Hugh Boscawen, Viscount Falmouth (1680?–1734), who had married Marlborough's niece [JB].

1. Vanbrugh, the architect of Blenheim, was also responsible for Bubb Dodington's mansion at Eastbury, Dorset. This was begun by Dodington's uncle and was only half finished when Dodington inherited it. See *To Burlington*, 20n. Dodington's town house, in Pall Mall, was an undistinguished affair opposite Carlton House.

INDEX

Acton (Middlesex), 25*n*

Addison, Joseph, on gardening, 141*n*; writings cited, 72*n*, 121*n*, 123*n*

Admiralty Building, Whitehall, 137*n*

Adonis, 91

Aldus Manutius, 150

Allen, R. J., *Clubs of Augustan London*, 31*n*, 91*n*

Allen, Ralph, see Pope, correspondence

Allen, Mrs Ralph, 47*n*

Allestree, Richard, *Decay of Christian Piety*, 101*n*

Ames, Joseph, antiquary, 112*n*

Anjou, Duke of, 93*n*

Anna Ivanovna, Czarina, 28*n*

Arbuthnot, Anne, daughter of P.'s friend, xi*n*, 169

Arbuthnot, John, xxxix*f*, 85*n*, 87*n*, 173, 176; and see Pope, correspondence

Arcadia's Countess, 48*f*

Argyll, John Campbell, Duke of, 174

Athenaeus, 35*n*

Atkyns, Sir Robert, historian, 172*n*

Atossa, xi*f*, 59*ff*, 159*ff*

Atterbury, Francis, Bishop of Rochester, 97*n*; letter quoted, xx*n*; Pope's epitaph on, 38*n*

Audra, E., *L'Influence française dans l'Œuvre de Pope*, 16*n*, 20*n*, 27*n*, 35*n*, 106*n*

Augustus II, King of Poland, 103*n*

Ault, Norman, 56*n*; *New Light on Pope*, 49*n*, 63*n*, 174; *Poems on Several Occasions*, 68*n*

Ayre, William, *Memoirs of the Life of Pope*, 46*n*, 67*n*

Babo, 139*n*, 182

Bacon, echoed, 34*n*, 111*n*

Baker, C. H. Collins, *Life of Chandos*, 23*n*, 147*n*

Balaam, xxi, 121

'Balance of Things', xxi, xxiii*f*, xxvi, 106*f*, 153*n*

Bateman, Sir William, 37*n*

Bathurst, Allen, Earl, x*n*, xlii, 111, 120*n*, 154, 173; on Warburton's text, 79; career summarized, 83*n*

Bathurst, Benjamin, 181*n*

Beales, H. L., *Johnson's England*, 156*n*

Beattie, L. M., *John Arbuthnot*, 87*n*

Beauclerc, Lord Sidney, collector, 134*n*

Bedford, Wriothesley Russell, Duke of, 91*n*

Bellucci, Antonio, 151*n*

Benedict XIII, Pope, 28*n*

Bennet, William, Bishop of Cloyne, 104*n*, 116*n*

Berkeley, George, *Alciphron*, 23*n*

Bertie, James, M.P., 25*n*

Betty, 36

Bevismount (Hants), 140*n*

Bible, cited, 107*n*, 177*n*

Bickham, George, on Stowe, 143*n*

Blackburne, Lancelot, Archbishop of York, 34*n*

Blackwell, Alexander, gardener, 148*n*

Blenheim Palace (Oxon.), 19*n*, 148*n*, 151*n*, 170, 187

Blomfield, Sir Reginald, *Renaissance Architecture in England*, 138*n*; *Formal Garden in England*, 141*n*, 145*n*

Blount, Edward, P.'s friend, 172*n*

Blount, Martha, P.'s mistress(?), xiii*n*, 63*n*, 70*ff*, 131*n*, 148*n*; biographical summary, 46*n*

Blount, Teresa, Martha's sister, 47*n*, 71*n*

Blunt, Sir John, financier, 85*n*, 99, 104

Boileau, echoed, 25*n*

Bolingbroke, Henry St John, Viscount, 173, 187*n*; suppresses *Epistles to Several Persons*, xi*f*, 166*f*; *E. on Man*,

R

R*